Why Love Matters

Why Love Matters explains why loving relationships are essential to brain development in the early years, and how these early inter-actions can have lasting consequences for future emotional and physical health. This second edition follows on from the success of the first, updating the scientific research, covering recent findings in genetics and the mind/body connection, and including a new chapter highlighting our growing understanding of the part also played by pregnancy in shaping a baby's future emotional and physical well-being.

Sue Gerhardt focuses in particular on the wide-ranging effects of early stress on a baby's or toddler's developing nervous system. When things go wrong with relationships in early life, the dependent child has to adapt; what we now know is that his or her brain adapts too. The brain's emotion and immune systems are particu-larly affected by early stress and can become less effective. This makes the child more vulnerable to a range of later difficulties such as depression, anti-social behaviour, addictions or anorexia, as well as physical illness.

Why Love Matters is an accessible, lively account of the latest findings in neuroscience, developmental psychology and neurobi-ology – research that matters to us all. It is an invaluable and hugely popular guide for parents and professionals alike.

Sue Gerhardt has been a psychoanalytic psychotherapist in private practice since 1997. She co-founded the Oxford Parent Infant Project (OXPIP), a pioneering charity that today provides psychothe~~~~~~~~ ~~~~ ~~ ~~~~~~~~ ~~ ~~~~~~ ~~~ babies in Oxfordshi   ' around the count   2010).

For my children, Jessica and Laurence

Contents

Foreword by Steve Biddulph   ix
Acknowledgements   xii

Introduction to the second edition   1

PART 1
The foundations: babies and their brains   13

1 Before we meet them   15
2 Back to the beginning   28
3 Building a brain   48
4 Corrosive cortisol   74
  Conclusion to Part 1   104

PART 2
Shaky foundations and their consequences   107

5 Trying not to feel: the links between
  early emotional regulation and the immune
  system   113
6 Melancholy baby: how early experience can
  alter brain chemistry, leading to adult
  depression   134
7 Active harm: the links between trauma in
  babyhood and trauma in adult life   157
8 Torment: the links between personality
  disorders and early experience   174
9 Original sin: how babies who are treated
  harshly may not develop empathy for others   193

PART 3
**Too much information, not enough
solutions: where do we go from here?**   **219**

10 'If all else fails, hug your teddybear':
    repairing the damage   221
11 Birth of the future   238

Bibliography   251
Index   298

Foreword

When our children were little, we once, when they were finally asleep in bed, settled down to relax by watching a movie called *Parenthood*. In this film, Steve Martin's character, a harassed but caring dad, had two fantasies in rapid succession, triggered by moments with his little boy. In the first fantasy, his now grown-up son is giving the graduation address as the star student, and thanking his wonderful father for all his help. He points to his dad in the auditorium, and the audience applauds! Then, the dad is jerked back to reality, his little boy is misbehaving. And suddenly he finds himself imagining a very different scene – chaos on a campus as students ran from a crazed shooter in a high tower.

'It's the "Martin" kid!' they are screaming. 'His father was no good!'

We all do this, I think – hope for our kids, and fear for them. But in the last few decades the fearing side of this has reached a kind of fever pitch. It's as if parents have never felt quite so lost, while at the same time so plagued by so-called experts. It all seems to get more and more complex, and we doubt ourselves more and more.

Part of the problem, though it's almost never admitted, is that the experts themselves have been confused. That happens in science sometimes, when the old models no longer match the data, and a new way of looking is needed. A period of confusion precedes a sudden leap to a new understanding, and everyone breathes a sigh of relief. Luckily, we have just arrived at one of those times. In the last ten years, helped hugely by the technology that allows us to look inside the working human brain, neuroscience has transformed what we know about how little children grow.

You may be thinking – well, if there's a revolution in child development, why haven't I heard about it?

And the reason is this: first, it's made up of thousands of research papers on tiny fragments of the problem, and second, it's really hard to understand. For example, the very best book in the field is Allan Schore's *Affect Regulation and the Origin of the Self*. You can tell from the catchy title that this is a doorstopper of a book. I am a professor of psychology, but I still only made it half way through, before collapsing like Frodo on the slopes of Mount Doom. But Sue Gerhardt is made of sterner stuff. Alongside her work as a psychotherapist and specialist in mother and baby relationships, Sue set herself the task of reading and absorbing pretty much the whole field of developmental neuroscience, speaking to the researchers, synthesising it all with a view to discovering 'How does this help real mums and dads, as well as teachers and policy makers and so on?'. She did this because she recognised that this knowledge would change everything. And she was right.

In short, our problems with kids' lives and with our own lives have arisen because we have completely missed the importance of affection. We thought it was just something nice that parents did. But in fact, it's the key to all mental health, intelligence and functioning as a human being. If someone is a great human being, it can only mean one thing. They were loved.

Those moments of soothing, playfulness, touching and tickling, hugging and holding that happen between mother and baby, husband and wife, old people walking hand in hand, stimulate the brain and build connections that are the foundations of intelligence, people skills and being a decent and wonderful human being. All the enrichment, education, money and resources, courses and expensive schools won't make up for having parents who were rushed, tense and had trouble settling with their baby or toddler and having a loving and fun time.

There are astonishing new findings in this book . . .

That stress on a pregnant mother can already begin to shape her baby's brain – affecting the volume of its hippocampus (a brain structure involved in memory) or amygdala (another brain structure central to emotional reactions).

That a gene called MAOA-L makes some children twice as likely to have trouble holding back emotional impulses. (Yet this gene is in forty per cent of the population, so most of us have learned to get it under control).

That money worries, or long working hours during pregnancy, can affect an enzyme in the placenta, which normally blocks cortisol from the mum going to the baby, allowing stress hormones to flood into the baby. The result is a baby who is born already stressed out, who may be much harder to care for.

There are clear remedies, too – for society, and for our own parenting. If in early parenthood we can slow down, minimise stress, value kindness and time, fun and playfulness, and if governments make this possible so that young mums and dads see their work of parenthood as valuable and precious, then the benefits in resilient, empathic, good humoured and interpersonally effective adults will be enormous. With the knowledge summed up in this superb book, we can ensure that our child and every child gets close to the very limits of human potential.

As a populariser myself, an explainer who realises it's no good what the researchers discover if we can't get the message out to everyone, I greatly admire what Sue has done. She has taken one of the most complicated fields in the world today and made it useful.

Love matters. And we have the science to prove it.

Steve Biddulph
Psychologist and author of *The Secret of Happy Children*

Acknowledgements

Many people have participated in the making of this book, some perhaps without knowing it. I would particularly like to thank all my patients over the years who have taught me so much.

I would like to thank those friends who gave their time to read the whole manuscript and gave me invaluable feedback: Jane Henriques, Paul Gerhardt, Diana Goodman, Paul Harris, Mollie Kenyon-Jones, John Miller, John Phibbs, Pascale Torracinta and Andrew West.

I would also like to thank Carmine Pariante, Fiona Duxbury, John Edginton, Morten Kringelbach and Allan Schore, for helpful comments on particular chapters, and especially Vivette Glover for her guidance on pre-natal matters.

In my professional work, I would like to acknowledge Daphne Briggs for her inspiring introduction to baby observation, which started it all off. I would also like to thank Penny Jaques for her steady support as I struggled to develop work with parents and babies, and all my colleagues at the Oxford Parent Infant Project who helped me sustain a commitment to it – particularly Joanna Tucker. Both Jean Knox and Graham Music have been immensely supportive colleagues and have helped to enrich my thinking about attachment issues.

Behind the scenes, I would like to thank all my friends for their encouragement, but particularly Jane Henriques, Angie Kaye and Nigel Barlow for brainstorming and spurring me on, my children for putting up with it all and John Phibbs for his support in the last stages of the book.

My greatest debt is to Paul Gerhardt, who was behind me every step of the way and without whom I could not have written this book.

Permissions acknowledgments

Text

'Late Fragment' from *A New Path to the Waterfall* © 1989 by the Estate of Raymond Carver. Used by permission of Grove/Atlantic, Inc. Any third party use of this material outside of this publication, is prohibited.

A description of *Dennis Potter: A Biography*, by Humphrey Carpenter. Courtesy of Faber and Faber Ltd.

Excerpts from *Anne Sexton: A Biography* by Diane Wood Middlebrook. Copyright © 1991 by Diane Wood Middlebrook. Reprinted by permission of Houghton Mifflin Company. All rights reserved.

Approximately 53 words from *The Blank Slate: The Modern Denial of Human Nature*, by Steven Pinker (Viking Penguin, a member of Penguin Putnam Inc., 2002). Copyright © Steven Pinker, 2002. Reproduced by permission of Penguin Books Ltd.

Approximately 194 words from *Of Women Born: Motherhood as Experience and Institution*, by Adrienne Rich. Copyright © 1977 Adrienne Rich. Reprinted by permission of Time Warner Books UK.

Excerpt from 'Anger and Tenderness', from *Of Women Born: Motherhood as Experience and Institution*, by Adrienne Rich. Copyright © 1986, 1976 by W.W. Norton & Company, Inc. Used by permission of W.W. Norton & Company, Inc.

Approximately 200 words from *Billy*, by Pamela Stephenson. Copyright © 2002 Pamela Stephenson. Reprinted by permission of HarperCollins Publishers Ltd .

Approximately 300 words from *A Life's Work*, 2001, 2008; by Rachel Cusk. Copyright © 2001/2008 Rachel Cusk. Reprinted by permission of HarperCollins Publishers.

'O Tell Me the Truth About Love' copyright © 1940 and renewed 1968 by W.H. Auden; from *W.H. Auden Collected Poems* by W.H. Auden. Used by permission of Random House, an imprint and division of Random House LLC. All rights reserved.

53 word excerpt from *The Analyst* by John Katzenbach by permission of Penguin Random House.

Figures

Figure 4.1 from *Does Stress Damage the Brain? Understanding Trauma-Related Disorders from a Mind-Body Perspective*, by J. Douglas Bremner. Copyright © 2002 J. Douglas Bremner. Used by permission of W.W. Norton & Company, Inc.

Figure 6.1 Depression and Bipolar Support Alliance advert. Used with permission of the DBSA.

All reasonable efforts have been made to contact copyright holders, but in some cases this was not possible. Any omissions brought to the attention of Routledge will be remedied in future editions.

Introduction to the second edition

A new way of understanding

This book is the outcome of many years of casual observations, followed by training and practising as a psychotherapist, particularly working with the disturbed or malfunctioning relationships between babies and their mothers. Following my hunches about the impact of the early relationship on later psychological functioning, I began to explore the growing body of research on the development of the brain in babies and small children. I then found myself linking these data with the data on psychologically disturbed adults – people suffering from a range of problems, from mild depression to mental and physical psychopathology.

In the process, I discovered that something new and exciting is happening, and that my own exploration was a timely one. We have in fact arrived at a moment in which different disciplines are converging to produce a new understanding of emotional life. I want to offer you a guide to these developments, and what they might mean to you as a parent, as a clinician, as a partner. The often dense and technically written medical, scientific and academic sources on which I draw contain vital information, yet they have not reached public awareness to the extent that they deserve. Certainly, this information has changed my understanding of emotional life dramatically. By bringing these sources together and 'translating' them, I offer you a chance to experience this for yourself.

The new perspective is not due to any single breakthrough but to the remarkable impact of many things happening at once, in neuroscience, psychology, psycho-analysis, biochemistry. As these disciplines begin to com-municate and to influence each other, they are offering a deeper understanding of how human beings become fully human and how they learn to relate emotionally to others. For the first time, a full biological explanation of our social behaviour is becoming available – by understanding human infancy and the development of our 'social brain' and the biological systems involved in emotional regulation. The challenge now is to put this scientific knowledge of human infancy at the centre of our understanding of emotional life.

For me this has been an exhilarating but at times painful journey. On the one hand, my discoveries led me to the conclusion that parental misinformation or lack of ability to cope with caring for an infant could set up lifelong handi-caps in their offspring that could potentially harm others too. On the other hand, behavioural traits, illness and crimi-nality that are usually taken to be 'in the genes', predestined and inevitable, may be seen as avoidable. Most of all, my research leads me to believe that, if the will and resources were available, the harm done to one generation need not be transmitted to the next: a damaged child need not inevitably become a damaged and damaging parent.

Well-intentioned governments have recognised the need to support family life. They have put measures in place to do so – from tax credits to parenting classes. Politicians and policy makers are only too aware of the cost to society of dysfunctional families, with their links to crime, violence and drug abuse. Although such supports are vital to those who receive them, they are like occasional food parcels for the starving, or to use another analogy, it is most like pouring money into the maintenance of a badly built house. The persistent damp problems, poor heat or sound insulation, subsidence due to poor foundations, may be temporarily alle-viated – but nothing can change the fact that the house is not well built and will continue to be high maintenance. Likewise with human beings whose foundations have not been well built. Although expensive repairs may be under-taken later in life, the building stage – when adjustments can be made – is largely over. For prevention to be effective, it needs to be targeted at the point when it can make the most difference.

These foundations are laid during pregnancy and in the first two years of life. This is when the 'social brain' is shaped and when an individual's emotional style and emotional resources are established. In Part 1 of this book I describe the development of the social brain, the part of the brain which learns how to manage feelings in line with other people, as well as the development of a person's stress response, immune response and neurotransmitter systems, which all affect future emotional life. This second edition of the book adds new information about the importance to emotional life of the earliest development in the womb, when the foetus begins the process of adapting to the human environment. Starting inside the mother's body, brain systems designed to maintain stability already start to take shape, influenced not only by the mother's diet but also by the biochemicals of emotion circulating in her body. These systems face new challenges once the baby is born, when he or she embarks on the lifelong process of adapting to external reality. Early parenting guides this process, but emotion systems are also shaped by wider social and cultural expectations.

When these influences are less than benign, the groundwork is laid for a variety of later social and emotional difficulties. Part 2 of the book looks at the specific early pathways that may lead to particular conditions such as anorexia, psychosomatic illness, addiction, antisocial behaviour, personality disorder, or depression.

What can science offer?

The scientific community has provided all sorts of cures for our ills – a pill to help addicts overcome addiction, antidepressants for the depressed, and so on. But until relatively recently it has not had a great deal to offer in understanding emotional life. The scientific enterprise, begun in the period of the Enlightenment, was founded on a particular approach to knowledge which could not be applied to emotions. It had to be linear and predictable: cause was followed by effect, stimulus by response. Feelings could only muddy the waters because they were neither predictable nor measurable. They seemed to have little to do with the technological advances that science could contribute.

This logical approach was the perfect antidote to the superstitious medieval worldview. The project that came to dominate the seventeenth century and beyond was the drive to find a way out of hunger, discomfort and early death, through improving the material conditions of life. Scientists and inventors were remarkably successful in this project. But we have come to take these transformations for granted. Now, at least in the affluent societies, we can mostly assume that we will have enough to eat and that we will survive into old age. With these achievements behind us, we have different opportunities.

Ironically, the current public fascination with emotion is being fuelled by our own recent technological progress. Science has finally reached a point where it can measure and quantify emotion – up to a point. In the 1990s, exciting new scanning techniques such as fMRI took off. These enabled scientists to make a visual map of the brain's activity when emotions are being experienced – making it possible for the first time to have some sort of technical measurement that corresponds to emotion. In the same decade, neuroscientists such as Antonio Damasio and Jaak Panksepp were leading thinkers within a lively current of researchers exploring what became known as 'affective neuroscience'. About the same time, in the biochemistry field, the immunologist Candace Pert started to identify receptors for some of the important biochemicals of emotion such as endorphins, while 'psychobiologists' such as Megan Gunnar deepened our understanding of the biochemistry of stress. So after 300 years of stand-off, hard science was finally renewing its interest in emotion.

Developmental psychology has also used technology to increase our understanding of early emotional life. In the early 1970s, a psychiatrist called Daniel Stern began to explore the world of mother and infant using video. He filmed the interactions of mothers and babies and then began to analyse them, frame by frame – building up a more complete understanding of early development than had been available before. His work was informed by the framework of 'attachment theory', first established by the psychoanalyst John Bowlby and the psychologist Mary Ainsworth in the 1960s. They had led the way in attempting to integrate scientific developments with psychoanalytic thinking – to understand emotional life in its biological context. Mary Ainsworth herself devised an experimental procedure called the Strange Situation Test to measure secure and insecure emotional attachments between toddlers and their parents (Ainsworth et al. 1978). It sets up a situation in which the toddler is briefly separated from his parent under controlled conditions that test his reactions to his parent's departure and subsequent reunion, as well as to the arrival and depar- ture of a stranger in the room. This proved to be such a reli- able measure of the quality of parent–infant relationships that it has been used with confidence as the springboard for further research ever since.

Since Stern's major contribution, another pioneer, Allan Schore, has laboured to synthesise a huge quantity of infor- mation from all these different disciplines, and it is his dense and technical synthesis that is the backbone of this book. His work opens up the possibility of understanding emotional life in both its biological and its social aspects.

Reintegrating emotions

What is striking about all this work is the way that it has begun to integrate disciplines that have for far too long been kept in rigid compartments. I experienced this as a teenager when I wanted to study both literature and biology, but was told that I could not mix art and science and would have to choose between them. I chose literature and later became a psychotherapist, but the enforced split always struck me as something that diminished each discipline. This recent possibility of integrating them seems to breathe new life into them both.

Ironically, what has now been discovered by these scientific processes is that 'feelings come first', as the poet e.e. cummings put it, and that our rationality, which science from its inception prized so highly, is built on emotion and cannot exist without it. It is increasingly being recognised that cognitions depend on emotions, as Damasio has argued. As he points out, the rational part of the brain does not work on its own, but only at the same time as the basic regulatory and emotional parts of the brain: 'Nature appears to have built the apparatus of rationality not just on top of the apparatus of biological regulation, but also *from* it and *with* it' (Damasio 1994: 128). The higher parts of the cortex cannot operate independently of the more primitive gut responses. Cognitive processes elaborate emotional processes, but could not exist without them. The brain constructs representations of internal bodily states, links them to other stored representations, and then signals back to the body in a process of internal feedback, which may then trigger off further bodily feelings in a cyclical process.

This would no doubt come as a shock to the Enlightenment philosophers and scientists whose attempts to assert the power of rationality involved splitting emotion off as a thing apart – not because they were uninterested, but largely because there was no way of understanding it scientifically at that time. There were pragmatic reasons to split mind and body as well. By establishing them as separate territories, the powerful religious authorities could be persuaded to tolerate the scientific dissection of bodies, in what Candace Pert called a 'turf deal with the Pope' (Pert 1998: 18). Desacralising the body was an important turning point for both medicine and religion. This deal made it possible for a more rational, free-thinking culture to emerge. As a result of this pact, science and technology were freed to blast into the machine age of the eighteenth and nineteenth centuries with technical fixes for many aspects of human life. But emotional life could not be 'fixed' by technology, and so it became a sideline – something to be explored in fiction not fact.

To some extent, emotions were also a hindrance to the practical drive to produce more and more, which resulted in such dramatic improvements in the material quality of life in industrialised countries. Without doubt, the industrial way of life has been enormously successful in terms of achieving unprecedented levels of comfort, literacy, entertainment, mass communication and longevity. But so much human feeling was also swept aside in the relentless expansion of capitalism. The most glaring damage was done to the least powerful, but these changes affected emotional life in all classes and genders. In particular, the drive to maximise production encouraged factory owners to treat their workers as extensions of their machines, not as people with feelings. Standing for long hours at their looms, they were not even allowed to speak to each other. We have moved away from these extremes, but perhaps not as far as we might think. The sweatshop conditions of early capitalism have now been exported to the Third World, where goods are manufactured for consumption by Westerners, while those in the developed world are often required to put their emotional selves on hold for the largest part of the day, even if they no longer work in factories.

By the early twentieth century, Sigmund Freud had realised that we were paying a heavy price for this new 'civilisation', with the repression of many of our strongest emotions. However, as a man of his time, he thought this a price worth paying and devoted his energies to managing these powerful feelings in a more rational way. His aim was to provide an alternative to the blanket repression of forbidden sexual or aggressive feelings. His 'talking cure' offered a more sophisticated and conscious recognition of these feelings and the ability to talk oneself out of them. Early psychoanalysts believed this would cure 'neurosis' and strange, hysterical behaviour.

However, by the time such psychoanalytical procedures were in vogue, and people were becoming ever more willing to talk about their sexual feelings, the economic system was already beginning to move on. With new techniques of mass production, it became increasingly important to create markets and willing consumers. The balance shifted from a tightly controlled workforce whose values centred around self-control and saving for the future towards a mass consumer society whose desires were to be indulged. The marketing of new products was inspired by psychoanalytic insight into the ubiquity and power of unconscious feelings and desires. In particular, the advertisers appealed not only to people's sexual urges but also to their wish to be loved, admired and accepted by others, which advertisements suggested could be achieved by wearing the right clothes, driving the right car, eating the right foods, or purchasing the right furniture. Clearly, it would be important that such people did not control their impulses too tightly if they were going to spend money in pursuit of their desires.

Constraints on sexual behaviour were incrementally lifted decade by decade. Formal behaviour and tight controls on desire were increasingly replaced by a greater recognition of sexual feelings. It might appear that feelings were being reintegrated into culture. Yet the divide between 'mind' and 'body' remained within science. The exclusion of emotion from medical science with its origins in the analysis of component parts of the body such as the circulation of the blood or the process of infection, largely continues today, as doctors and pharmaceutical companies still persist in looking for quick fixes for symptoms of malfunction rather than seeking understanding of how the human organism works as a whole.

The new paradigm

Yet a new perspective, a new paradigm, has been waiting in the wings for some time and may be taking its first steps under the spotlight. This paradigm has been described variously as 'ecological', 'systemic', 'cybernetic' and 'holistic'. It has gained ground in various disciplines, but not yet become the dominant way of viewing the world. To some extent, the struggle to establish this systemic paradigm has been a struggle between 'new science' and 'old science'. Its origins lay in the same period of the 1920s and 1930s that had seen a relaxation in the control of feelings. During this time, there were also revolutionary discoveries in physics which challenged our taken-for-granted sense of human perception. Max Planck's quantum theory revealed that matter was not as solid and static as we perceive it to be, but could better be described as a kind of relationship operating at a certain rhythm for a certain period of time. Albert Einstein's theory of relativity showed that space and time were a continuum which curved and enfolded around itself. Such radical notions revealed the limitations of human sensory equipment: 'The world we see is a function of our size', as Bryan Appleyard put it (1992).

Given the limitations of human perception, it became clear that the assumptions of the old science could no longer hold. Some scientists, such as Werner Heisenberg, began to claim that 'the conception of objective reality has thus evaporated'. The reality you see depends on where you are standing. The electron is a wave or a particle depending on your point of view. Even when we are observing reality, we are involved in bringing about the situation we are observing. So the linear explanations of old science that X causes Y cannot be the whole truth.

Instead, a new, more interactive perspective was developed, initially in computer science. A mathematician called Norbert Wiener first identified the importance of feedback in maintaining systems. Although his theory was developed in work on rockets and missiles, the theory was soon taken up more widely, by the maverick anthropologist Gregory Bateson among others, to help to explain human systems such as the family or even the workings of the human organism itself. What they discovered was that systems managed to stay stable only by constantly adapting to changing conditions. And the way that they managed to do this was through using feedback about what worked and what didn't. This meant that if you looked at the system as a whole, you would realise that it was circular, not linear. Instead of breaking a system into identifiable parts, and treating these parts as if they functioned in isolation, you had to understand that every system is connected to other systems and they are reciprocally determined. How one person behaves affects how another behaves and his or her behaviour then influences the original person in a circular process. Cause and effect depend on your vantage point, on where you start in the loop, and how much information you include or exclude. There is not one truth, but several possible truths.

This systemic approach percolated into many disciplines. In biology, there was ecology and ethology. In psychology, there was John Bowlby, who recognised that to understand people you had to understand their environment, just as the plant nurseryman had to make a scientific study of soil and atmosphere. Over time, his insights have gradually contributed to a more interactive approach within psychotherapy, and a greater recognition that patient and analyst are in a mutual field of activity, a system in which each influences the other, rather than assuming that the influence is one way.

My view of emotional life is also a systemic one. My understanding is that human beings are open systems, permeated by other people as well as by plants and air and water. We are shaped not only by what we breathe and eat but also by our interactions with other people. We live in a social world, in which we depend on complex chains of social interaction to bring food to our table, put clothes on our bodies and a roof over our heads as well as to bind us together in a culture that provides a shared sense of meaning. We cannot survive alone. But more than that, both our physiological systems and our mental systems are developed in relationship with other people.

Parents are the people who matter most in our early lives. They create us and give us our unique genetic identity. But even with the 'best' genes in the world, this does not determine how we will live our lives or even what our strengths and weaknesses will be. Each human cell has around 30,000 genes, but only a fraction are active at any one time. Moreover, they don't turn themselves on and off, but are stimulated into action by the environment, as and when they are useful. So one set of genes has many potential futures. Which one emerges depends on what happens. In particular, genes respond to and are guided by the body's biochemical activity. Plenty of nourishing food activates one set of genetic processes, while lack of food will trigger different genes. Perhaps less obviously, our emotional and social experiences also release biochemicals such as cytokines, hormones and neurotransmitters – which play a major part in activating genes and in determining who we become.

One reason why our relationship with our parents is like no other relationship is because the influence of other people is at its most powerful in early life. The period from conception through the first two years – roughly speaking, the first 1000 days – is uniquely significant, because this is when the nervous system itself is being established and shaped by experience. During this period, how parents *behave* has as much influence on their child's emotional make-up as his or her genetic inheritance. Their responses to their baby teach him what his own emotions are and how to manage them. This means that our earliest experiences as babies (and even as foetuses) have much more relevance to our adult selves than many of us realise. It is as babies that we first feel and learn what to do with our feelings, when we start to organise our experience in a way that will affect our later behaviour and thinking capacities.

PART 1

The foundations: babies and their brains

1

Before we meet them

When it comes, will it come without warning
Just as I'm picking my nose?
Will it knock on my door in the morning,
Or tread in the bus on my toes?
Will it come like a change in the weather?
Will its greeting be courteous or rough?
Will it alter my life altogether?
O tell me the truth about love.

W.H. Auden (1938)

The very first weeks

New life can take us by surprise. It doesn't always follow a predictable story line of boy meets girl; they settle down, create a home and start a family. Some pregnancies happen unexpectedly after a drunken night out with a passing stranger, or with a partner you don't even like any more. Like love, it can happen when you least expect it – or when you have been trying to have a baby for so long the thought of pregnancy has become a constant painful disappointment. Although pregnancy is easier to achieve (and sustain) in a situation of abundant nutrition and emotional well-being, in practice the scenarios are as various as people themselves.

However it does start, a biological event is triggered. Egg and sperm connect and suddenly everything is changed. The fertilised cell beds down in the nourishing wall of a woman's womb. It rapidly grows into clusters of cells which then start to negotiate their place in the structure of the new body that is being made. Will this new tissue become a hand or a kidney or an area of the brain? It depends on where it finds itself in relation to other cell tissue. An extraordinary process begins of assembling the makings of a new human being.

Within a few weeks, the developing embryo is collaborating with the mother on a mutual construction project. Beween them, they create the placenta – which works both as an exchange hub for nutrients, oxygen and biochemical secretions (such as hormones) and as a protective barrier designed to filter out anything toxic in the mother's system and stop it from reaching the embryo. (The placenta itself releases a substance called HCG which can make the mother more sensitive to toxins and even nauseous.) This protective system works well if the mother has a reasonably healthy lifestyle, but the placenta can find it challenging to protect the foetus if the mother is using drugs such as alcohol or nicotine.

Heavy alcohol use can cause damage at any time throughout pregnancy, but unfortunately, it has a very strong impact on the vulnerable, developing embryo during those first few weeks before it has officially become a 'foetus' with organs that have started to function. In these first weeks, physical structures are forming such as the shape of the face. This is when drinking 'binges' (defined as drinking more than six units or three or four glasses of wine at a time) especially on a regular basis can have the strongest impact, potentially leading to the distinctive facial features such as small eyes and flattened upper lip associated with Foetal Alcohol Syndrome (FAS). In an ideal world, any woman who is even half considering or risking getting pregnant would be careful not to drink too much alcohol so that this early damage can be avoided. Yet the risk continues throughout pregnancy. Even in later pregnancy, alcohol can still have serious effects on the foetal brain (RCOG 2006; Cockburn 2013). It has many different negative impacts, but it is particularly associated with smaller brains and less ability to connect right and left brain, leading to significant difficulties in learning and paying attention, as well as in empathising with and communicating well with other people (Maier and West 2001; Cockburn 2013).

The world according to mother

No foetus can flourish when it is on the receiving end of toxic chemicals. However, the foetus is also responding to a whole range of other biochemical signals from the mother. He (or she) is already actively adapting to what those signals tell him about 'world according to mother'. Hormones, neurotransmitters and nutrients all have particular stories to tell.

What his mother eats has the biggest impact on the foetus in the first three months of pregnancy (Gluckman and Hanson 2004; Roseboom et al. 2006). The foetus needs various ingredients to develop well; in particular, sufficient protein as well as various vitamins and minerals. But he is not just relying on her nutrients for his own immediate growth. The foetus is also building up assumptions about the life ahead – as in 'weather forecasting', he needs to prepare for future conditions. Is it going to be a life with plentiful nutrition or one where you have to store as many calories as possible in order to survive? If the mother is undernourished or is eating junk food during early pregnancy, the foetus may reach the conclusion that there won't be much on offer, so he develops what has been named a 'thrifty phenotype' designed to make the best of the resources available (Barker 1992).

Stress also has surprisingly wide-reaching effects on the developing nutritional systems of the foetus. High levels of stress hormones tend to increase the secretion of leptin, the hormone that manages appetite and food intake. They also affect the propensity of the foetus to store fat around the tummy, in the part of the body between the intestines and the abdominal wall – increasing his chances of middle-aged spread or a 'pot belly', which has been compared to a camel's hump, also an effective fat storage system (Gillman et al. 2006; Entringer et al. 2012; Paternain et al. 2013). The critical window for programming this tendency to store belly fat is during mid-pregnancy, between 14 and 23 weeks (Pilgaard 2011).

Reading this research, I have been surprised at how little public discussion there has been of its implications. Poor nutrition in pregnancy may even be a major contributor to the explosion of obesity in our time. The problem arises at least in part because of the mismatch between the expectations of an undernourished foetus programmed with a predisposition to store fat, who becomes a baby and toddler unprepared for a world awash with cheap sugary and fatty fast foods and Macdonalds outlets, and rapidly puts on weight, especially round the middle (Maiorana 2007; Entringer et al. 2012). Increasingly, this is becoming a problem in developing countries such as India where 30% of babies start life underweight – but where obesity rates are dramatically increasing (Yajnik 2004; Paul 2010).

Thoughts create reality and reality creates thoughts

The mother's quality of life is shared by her foetus. But this is not just about her physical state. The foetus also shares in her state of mind.

Once pregnant, women are prey to huge anxiety as well as huge excitement. A new role in life awaits and as in any new challenge, there may be optimism about the opportunity to develop as a person, or there may be many doubts about this transition. Hopes and fears jostle in the mind of the new mother. Will her partner cope with the baby? Will the baby's birth be dangerous? Will she be able to meet her baby's needs? She may feel alienated from her body as her breasts expand and her belly swells, feeling the baby is a parasite. She may feel her negative experiences are 'wrong'.

Alternatively, there can be a strong pull to idealise the baby and herself. She hopes this is going to be the most perfect baby and she is going to be a glowing mother throughout pregnancy and beyond, who keeps her figure like the celebrities in magazines. When she finds herself groaning with nausea or compulsively eating puddings (or, in my case, egg and chips), she is disappointed with herself. Yet all these thoughts, positive and negative, are part of the mental adjustment and preparation for the new relationship that has already begun.

These extremes of idealisation or rejection can be a rollercoaster. For some women, it's hard to strike a balance and to have confidence in the pregnancy. This is particularly true for women who are dealing with other stresses in their lives, such as a demanding job, conflicts in their relationship, or a lack of resources.

Good and bad stress

Women who are under stress may pass on their stress to their child. However, there is no easy definition of 'stress' in this context. Many women who do a demanding job find this a source of stimulation rather than stress; even challenging or intense relationships can be fundamentally secure and a source of strength. In any case, moderate levels of stress can be a good thing for the foetus, according to one study by Janet Di Pietro (2006). She and her colleagues in Baltimore found that mild stress or anxiety in an otherwise stable and healthy pregnancy could prompt the nervous system to mature more quickly, and could stimulate motor and cognitive development of the foetus – effects that were followed through up to the age of 2.

However, there is stress that is not helpful to the foetus. In particular, even relatively ordinary low-level stress can affect the development of emotional systems.

It is difficult to quantify this, particularly as women don't always have an accurate perception of how stressed they are, according to Di Pietro. Some report feeling stressed yet have few biological markers of stress, while others are so used to their stressful lives (such as living in poverty or having a demanding working life) they think they are fine even when their bodies tell a different story. For most women, a job with long working hours does create a sense of strain, and during the first vulnerable months of a pregnancy, this can adversely affect the developing nervous system of the foetus, and can impair foetal growth, resulting in lower birthweights (Vrijkotte et al. 2009). This is highly undesirable, as when babies are born significantly underweight – under 5.5 pounds (2.5kg) – they face some serious health risks in later life, particularly of various diseases such as diabetes, high blood pressure or heart disease.

So while a little stress may be fine, or even beneficial in some ways, more intense or chronic forms of stress can have consequences for the baby. In particular, any situation which makes the mother feel out of control, such as domestic violence, financial anxieties or being *compelled* to work long hours, can over time lead to a decreased activity of the special enzyme in the placenta which normally is able to block the stress hormone cortisol from reaching the foetus (Di Pietro 2006). When this enzyme is disabled, cortisol can cross the placenta and reach the foetus, potentially affecting its developing stress response (a system I explore in more detail in future chapters). These babies exposed to their mother's stress hormones are born more irritable and prone to crying (van der Wal et al. 2007) and are more likely to be born with more fussy 'behavioural stress responses' (Davis and Sandman 2007). The stress response itself can end up being reprogrammed and altered (Glover et al. 2010; Glover 2011; Oberlander et al. 2008a; Garcia Segura 2009; Sandman et al. 2011).

This may be in part due to the effects of stress hormones on the infant amygdala. The amygdala is at the epicentre of the brain's emotional reactions and is involved in triggering the stress response itself. It is the operatic primadonna of the brain, reacting intensely to experiences of basic pain and pleasure, fear and anger, grief and joy. It is strongly connected to other important brain structures such as the hypothalamus, hippocampus and frontal cortex. In fact, it is such a core element of human life that all major amygdala structure is formed by 15 weeks of pregnancy (Buss et al. 2012).

When the developing amygdala is exposed to high levels of the stress hormone cortisol, particularly in early pregnancy, it can respond by becoming more active and growing extra connections. In fact, in some babies exposed to prenatal stress, it can increase by as much as 6 per cent in volume (Viltart and Vanbesien-Maillot 2007; Sandman and Davis 2012; Buss et al. 2012). (Strangely, this only seems to affect girl babies.)

Prenatal stress can also affect the brain in other ways. It can reduce the volume of the hippocampus (a brain structure involved in memory) and alter the size of the corpus callosum, an area in the centre of the brain connecting the right and left hemispheres of the brain (Glover 2011). Research in rats has found it also reduces connections in the prefrontal cortex (Braun et al. 2006; Murmu et al. 2006 Garcia-Segura 2009; Murgatroyd and Spengler 2011).

Late pregnancy and the brain

The last few months of pregnancy can also have a particularly strong effect on the baby's rapidly growing brain. During this final stage of preparation for birth, the foetus is sleeping and dreaming a lot, while the neurons connect up and start to establish pathways. These pathways also start to become 'myelinated', coated with a slippery, fatty sheath which speeds up the nerve signalling, enabling messages to whiz along more quickly. In late pregnancy, the back of the brain is myelinated first, gradually moving across the cortex towards the frontal areas.

When a mother is very stressed during this last stage of pregnancy, her baby's own stress response can become more reactive (Oberlander et al. 2008a). A mother who has high levels of anxiety or depression at this time is in turn more likely to have the kind of baby who finds it hard to cope with stress or new stimuli and who takes longer to get over stress (Sandman and Davis 2012). Even as a newborn, her baby may be more fearful, and is more likely to have higher than average cortisol levels at the age of 4 months (Kaplan et al. 2008). At worst, babies whose mothers are in the top 15 per cent of most anxious mothers are more likely to grow up with behavioural and emotional problems or ADHD symptoms (O'Connor et al. 2002, 2003).

Although the mother's diet is less important in late pregnancy than it was at the start of pregnancy, there are exceptions to this. The mother's intake of omega-3 fatty acids – found in oily fish – has an important protective effect. It seems to reduce the impact of stress and anxiety on the foetus (Hennebelle et al. 2012; Buydens-Branchey et al.

2008). The amount of omega-3 fatty acids in the mother's blood at the time of delivery also predicts the baby's attention span well into his or her second year (Colombo et al. 2004). Recent research suggests that choline (found in egg yolks, cauliflower and nuts, including peanut butter) may also be essential for optimum brain development at this time, particularly for the development of the hippocampus, which is also involved in managing stress as well as being responsible for some kinds of memory (Yan et al. 2013; Mehedint et al. 2010).

The unsupportive culture

In a modern, egalitarian culture where women have established their right to work on equal terms to men, attitudes to pregnancy have shifted. The gallantry of men opening doors for more fragile women is long gone. Yet pregnancy does deserve special consideration. A pregnant woman is not a woman with a medical condition but she is a new mother facing a big emotional transition as well as the demanding physiological challenge of nurturing a new human existence within her own body. She needs extra rest and she needs to know she is emotionally and financially supported. This is easy to say but hard to square with the reality of most women's lives. Women of childbearing age are normally working full time and they and their partners may be subject to the stresses of a long working hours culture, or low pay and status.

These apparently irreconcilable realities can give rise to cynical responses like that of the journalist Catherine Bennett, who mocks the extensive precautionary advice given to pregnant women by the Royal College of Obstetricians and Gynaecologists. She believes such advice 'infantilises' women. As she puts it, the advice implicitly treats pregnant mothers as 'mutinous half-wits' because they 'continue to work when earlier studies have proved the foetal welfare dictates maternal rest and calm. How, if not by cognitive failure, can this be explained?' (Bennett 2013).

Obviously life is about adapting to reality. This is mostly a bumpy and uneven process of taking steps forward and steps back, of gains and losses. In our recent past, there have been major adjustments in the place of women in society. This has had huge benefits. Women have been able to create a more equal life with men, by taking advantage of the decline in heavy industry and the rise in service industries. But these positive gains have also brought unanticipated negative effects. One example is the way the fast food industry expanded as more women started to work full time. At the end of a long working day, it can be a great relief to use a ready-made meal that doesn't demand any further effort; yet this has had an unforeseen impact on our consumption of fresh food, under-mining nutritious eating habits. Similarly, having two incomes enabled many better-off families to fulfil their dream to buy their own house. However, the increased demand on a fairly static stock of housing eventually led to inflated house prices and huge mortgage debt; as a result, many women got locked in to paid employment just so they could fund their housing costs (while less well-off families got completely priced out of the market). In turn, this new economic reality contributed to the current assumption that it is a good thing for mothers to work, even during their baby's earliest months and years when he is still dependent on his parents for continuous emotional regulation and bodily care. As a result, many parents now turn to substitute care at an ever earlier age, despite the fact that the need to keep costs down means that its quality rarely matches that of parental care. These unfolding processes affect the lives of millions of small children. Yet we keep stumbling from one unintended consequence to the next.

Although the market can and does respond to social change, when it opens up profitable commercial opportunities it is reactive and rarely promotes human needs for good care and quality nourishment unless there is strong social pressure to do so. Currently, employers have little incentive to provide more support for pregnant women as public health messages are not being aggressively championed by women themselves – and indeed, may even be mocked by female journalists.

But there is a big difference between patronising or infantilising women and giving them the support they need to fulfil their mothering task. Support, however, seems to be ruled out as an option in the harsh commercial world. The rhythms of working life cannot apparently be challenged to include the opportunity for a pregnant woman to take a nap in the middle of the day, to be protected from extra demands at work, or to have time off for morning sickness or in the uncomfortable last couple of months of pregnancy when it is so important to reduce emotional stress.

Different civilisations at times have taken a different view. In the eighteenth century, the poet Byron's grandfather was captain of a ship that sailed to unknown territory in South America. There he encountered a tall, well-built people he called the Patagonians. He was amazed at their robust health and well-being compared to the 'excess and debauchery' he had left behind in London. In particular, he was struck by their attitude to pregnancy:

> While a female Patagonian is with child, all disagreeable objects are kept from her; she is awakened by musick; they study to divert her with amusements most suitable to her taste; her mind is brightened with joy, without allowing her to grow slothful for want of action, she has exercise, such as walking, or such husbandry work as is most agreeable to her. The Patagonians do not doubt the mother's influence over both the physical and moral constitution of the child, as a sound tree produces large fruit. (*Journal of a Voyage Round the World* 1767)

What a delight it would be to learn from such cultures and their ability to cherish pregnant women, recognising the long-term benefits to all society.

Passing on unhappiness

This vision of a cosseted pregnancy is a far cry from the reality of many pregnant women. For many, pregnancy is a stressful and destablising experience, particularly for those who lacked strong emotional foundations in their own early lives, and who don't have an inner feeling of being 'cushioned'. After all, pregnancy doesn't change the personality or make previous problems vanish. The state of things before pregnancy is still the state of things during pregnancy.

Parents can't help being who they are and having the emotional histories they have.

But this also affects their babies, who share in their mother's emotional life both before and after birth. Without realising it, her state of mind and her way of relating will tend to get passed on to her baby. One study found that an assessment of a mother's own attachment status during pregnancy could predict the attachment style of her as yet unborn baby (Steele et al. 1996). This is fine for the majority of parents who were securely attached to their own parents and are reasonably confident of being able to create a good relationship with their own offspring. But when parents have had more negative early experiences, they are likely to need extra help to create a secure bond. For example, women who have suffered from an early separation from their own parents or other negative early experiences tend to have lower levels of oxytocin, the bonding biochemical, and this can affect their own mothering (Mileva-Seitz et al. 2013).

Women who had an unhappy childhood or who had been depressed earlier in their lives are also much more likely to become depressed when they become pregnant. Basically, the rates of depression during pregnancy are much the same as for post-natal depression – around 13 per cent of all mothers. These are also not much different from depression rates in general.

Depression in pregnancy is particularly likely when women have experienced some kind of emotional rejection in their own early life, leaving them with a depleted sense of self-worth. Because they didn't get enough emotional support in childhood, they learnt not to express their thoughts and feelings or to turn to others for help in managing their emotions. One intriguing fact unearthed by researchers is that a depressive reaction to the prospect of becoming a mother is also more common when there are family secrets (Plant et al. 2013; Dayan et al. 2010).

Inheriting depression

Unfortunately a mother's depression during pregnancy can predict the unborn baby's own future tendencies to depression.

Two prospective studies have found that when those babies become teenagers, their own risk of depression is much greater – as much as four times greater according to one small study (Pawlby et al. 2009) with a much smaller but still significant effect in a very large recent study focusing more narrowly on 'major depression' (Pearson et al. 2013).

How could this be? One route is through the depressive mother's cortisol and its impact on the amygdala. In a very recent research, Anne Rifkin-Graboi and her colleagues have found that prenatal depression affected the way the newborn baby's right amygdala was wired up: it was less well connected (Rifkin-Graboi et al. 2013).

Another route is through the effects of the mother's stress on the foetal serotonin system. Serotonin is an important biochemical which circulates in the brain and around the body from very early in gestation. It plays an important role in regulating emotions, particularly in modulating impulsivity and aggression. Low levels are also associated with anxiety and depression.

When the mother is stressed, it can affect not only her serotonin system but also her ability to make serotonin available to the foetus via the placenta. This has an impact on connections in the areas of the brain which rely on serotonin, such as the cortex and hippocampus. It can reduce the level of serotonin in these key areas of the brain, even into adulthood (Field et al. 2006; Goeden et al. 2013).

In fact, a whole cluster of important emotional regulators are beginning to be established before the baby is even born. Neurotransmitter systems such as serotonin and dopamine systems have already started to be programmed, in a way that may or may not be reversible. In turn, they influence other systems such as the development of the amygdala and the stress response, which, as we have already seen, are also developing rapidly during pregnancy (Viltart and Vanbesien-Maillot 2007; Ansorge et al. 2008). All these early developments can have far-reaching impacts, not only because all these systems are connected, but also because the brain is an 'iterative system': each step is built on the previous step, from the bottom up. This makes it hard to undo the impact of even small differences in early experience which set the organism off in a particular direction. As the nursery rhyme goes: 'For want of a nail, the shoe was lost. For want of a shoe, the horse was lost. For want of a horse, the rider was lost. For want of a rider, the battle was lost. For want of a battle, the kingdom was lost.'

Does love matter?

It may seem extraordinary that this hidden period of development in the womb should have such significance in our lives. But the foetus is already preparing for its future life, and adjusting to the information it gets about the conditions that lie ahead. This includes the cultural conditions: will it be a loving culture which enables mothers to feed themselves well, to rest and enjoy their lives? Or does the foetus need to brace itself for threatening and stressful times, for a culture in which nourishment and love are scarce resources? The foetus needs an accurate picture so that it can adapt to its circumstances.

However, if things have not gone well during pregnancy, all is not lost by any means. These questions are still open to further interpretation by the baby in the post-natal period. Because human babies are born with a brain that is only a quarter of its final adult size – a much more incomplete brain even than other mammals – human care in early childhood (and beyond) plays a much bigger role in shaping the brain. Many regulatory systems are still in development, and further adjustments to reality are being made. There are still good chances for some of these early developing systems to recover, particularly in the immediate post-natal period (Bergman et al. 2008). For example, positive bonding and secure attachment during the first year can enable a small hippocampus affected by stress to be restored to normal volume (Buss et al. 2012). New growth also takes place in the pre-frontal cortex in response to positive social experiences. This can offer different ways of managing and regulating emotion. In other words, if love can be found, it still has the power to shape a new reality.

2

Back to the beginning

A male and female Tiger is neither more or less whether you suppose them only existing in their appropriate wilderness, or whether you suppose a thousand Pairs.

But man is truly altered by the co-existence of other men; his faculties cannot be developed in himself alone, and only himself. Therefore the human race not by a bold metaphor, but in sublime reality, approach to, and might become, one body.

S.T. Coleridge, *Letters*, 1806

One dark winter's night, I was woken by the telephone ringing to let me know that the home birth I was planning to film had begun. I had met the mother before but did not know her well. I arrived at her home and was directed up three flights of stairs to a room at the top of the house – lugging my sound equipment and a light with me. I found the mother and father sitting on the edge of a single bed in a rather bare, poorly lit room with newspaper spread over the floor. There was an atmosphere of quiet practicality, focused on the mother's body. The midwife moved around, while I kept to one corner of the room. Things moved fast, and soon the mother was squatting over the newspaper, supported by her partner, while I recorded the amazing range of sounds she made, sounds that gathered urgency and soon became deep groans as the baby was starting to be born. My camerawoman did not arrive in time to film the birth, but I was past caring, caught up in witnessing this primal event. When the baby finally emerged from the mother's body, we all had tears in our eyes, overwhelmed with emotion, awed by the start of this new life and enthralled by the mystery of life itself.

That baby would now be about to leave home and embark on his adult life, the part of life that obituaries describe – four marriages or one, a public life or a more private one, tragedies along the way, the story of an individual's contribution to the social whole. But these stories leave so much out. They leave out all that went into making that baby into the young man he is today, and especially they don't acknowledge the powerful impact of other people on how that new baby was able to manifest his temperamental and genetic potential.

It is difficult to get to grips with this level of reality. Even biographies tell us only that a baby was born on a particular date, in a particular place, to parents whose lives were unfolding in a particular way at the time, but it is virtually impossible to recreate the dynamics of the relationship between them and their baby. So we can never find out what happened in our own individual infancy by direct enquiry, although sometimes anecdotal evidence throws us some clues. My mother's reports that I was a difficult baby who cried with colic every evening for months, and walked and talked very early, offered me themes of pride and rejection which have in fact been a significant part of my own story. But there are other ways to excavate our own infant story because we carry it inside and we live it in our close relationships.

In essence, our early experiences form characteristic ways of relating to other people and of coping with the ebb and flow of emotions which are not only psychological predelictions but also physiological patterns. They are the bones of emotional life, hidden and outside awareness – the invisible history of each individual. Like Freud, who saw himself as a kind of archaeologist of the person, I too find myself looking at people with an eye that scans for hidden structures. But unlike Freud, who searched beneath the surface of personality for the primal drives, the sexual and aggressive urges that he felt were the unseen motors of human life, I look instead for the unseen patterns of relationship that are woven into our body and brain in babyhood. These patterns orient our lives in a particular direction. Freud's own early relationship with his mother forged a sense of being special which he took into later relationships – along with a feeling of guilt that he had stolen this specialness by killing off his rival, a baby brother whom he had wished dead. Rivalries later played a big part in Freud's professional life. There is something powerful about the earliest themes of our lives, which chaos theory may help to explain. It suggests that small differences at the beginning of a process can lead to hugely different outcomes. But this time of our lives is what neuroscientist Doug Watt has referred to as 'unrememberable and unforgettable' (2001: 18). We cannot consciously recall any of it, yet it is not forgotten because it is built into our organism and informs our expectations and behaviour.

There *is* something underneath the surface, there *are* forces which propel us, but they are not quite as Freud described. Freud saw them as bodily urges within the human biological animal. He thought that these urges came into conflict with the social rules or pressures of civilisation which the individual took on board mentally as an inner 'superego', creating a tension or conflict between mind and body which only a strong controlling 'ego' could deal with. This account has been very influential and so nearly makes sense. But although it may have fitted Freud's own personal history, it is not a satisfactory account for the modern sensibility which is less tightly constrained by social pressures. Certainly it does not satisfy my own sense of the way that mind and body develop, because it proposes a much more self-generated and self-made individual than I believe to be the case. I will argue, and later describe in detail, that many aspects of bodily function and emotional behaviour are shaped by social interaction. For example, the poorly handled baby develops a more reactive stress response and different biochemical patterns from a well-handled baby. The brain itself is a 'social organ', as Peter Fonagy, a distinguished researcher into early attachment, has put it. Our minds emerge and our emotions become organised through engagement with other minds, not in isolation. This means that the unseen forces which shape our emotional responses through life, are not primarily our biological urges, but the patterns of emotional experience with other people, most powerfully set up in infancy. These patterns are not immutable but, like all habits, once established they are hard to break.

Women's realm

In order to understand each person's unique pattern of reactivity, we need to go back to the beginning, back to the wordless days of infancy when we were held in our mother's arms, and even as far back as the womb. This time of our lives has been so difficult to talk about not only because we have no language or conscious memory during babyhood, but also because historically babyhood has been lived out through a relationship between a woman and a baby. It takes place out of public view, in an inarticulate territory of bodies and feelings, of milk and poo and dribble, driven by overpowering hormonal tides which make mothers want to constantly touch and look at their baby – feelings that seem irrational when put into words, as difficult to describe as having sex or falling in love. And because this has largely been the private experience of women, not men, it has been hidden from view and unrepresented culturally, except on rare occasions by feminist writers such as Adrienne Rich:

> The bad and the good moments are inseparable for me. I recall the times when, suckling each of my children, I saw his eyes open full to mine, and realised each of us was fastened to the other, not only by mouth and breast, but through our mutual gaze: the depth, calm, passion, of that dark blue, maturely focused look. I recall the physical pleasure of having my full breast suckled at a time when I had no other physical pleasure in the world except the guilt-ridden pleasure of addictive eating . . . I remember moments of peace when for some reason it was possible to go to the bathroom alone. I remember being uprooted from already meagre sleep to answer a childish nightmare, pull up a blanket, warm a consoling bottle, lead a half-asleep child to the toilet. I remember going back to bed starkly awake, brittle with anger, knowing that my broken sleep

would make next day a hell, that there would be more
nightmares, more need for consolation, because out of my
weariness I would rage at those children for no reason
they could understand. I remember thinking I would
never dream again. (Rich 1977: 31)

It was the women's movement of the 1960s and 1970s which
opened up the possibility of speaking about the private experiences of domesticity, and which contributed to breaking
down the boundaries between public and private worlds. We
now publicly discuss sexual practices, we no longer require
emotions to be repressed with a stiff-upper-lip demeanour in
public, and we are openly curious about the emotional lives
of the rich or famous. We have given up being shocked to find
that public figures are just as human as the rest of us and
frequently fail to live up to their own standards of morality.
We are able to recognise that sexual abuse happens to children. Emotion is no longer the 'unspeakable' in the public
sphere. By a sort of parallel process, the split between mind
and body, rational and irrational, is increasingly called into
question. As I have suggested, this has contributed to the
increased scientific interest in emotion, breaking through
one last frontier in science – the exploration of our emotional
selves.

But measuring the brain activity or chemical levels
involved in adult emotional behaviour can only be an aid to
our understanding of emotional life. It cannot provide the
answers to why we behave the way we do. It is like dissecting
a fully grown animal expecting to find the source of its
behaviour. Adults are the result of complex histories
inscribed in organisms whose systems have already evolved
in time. They are too specific and unique. Instead, we need to
go back to the origins of emotional life, to the early processes
which determine our emotional trajectories – to the baby
and his or her emotional environment.

The unfinished baby

Babies are like the raw material for a self. Each one comes
with a genetic blueprint and a unique range of possibilities.

There is a body programmed to develop in certain ways, but by no means on automatic programme. The baby is an inter-active project not a self-powered one. The baby human organism has various systems ready to go, but many more that are incomplete and will only develop in response to other human input. Some writers have called the baby an 'external foetus' and there is a sense in which the human baby is incomplete, needing to be programmed by adult humans. This makes evolutionary sense as it enables human culture to be passed on more effectively to the next genera-tion. Each baby can be 'customised' or tailored to the circum-stances and surroundings in which he or she finds him or herself. A baby born into an ancient hill tribe in Nepal will have different cultural needs from a baby born in urban Manhattan.

Each little human organism is born a vibrating, pulsating symphony of different body rhythms and func-tions, which co-ordinate themselves through chemical and electrical messages. Within the organism there are many loosely connected systems, often overlapping with each other. These systems communicate through their chemical and electrical signals to try to keep things going within a comfortable range of arousal, by adapting to constantly changing circumstances, both internally and externally. In the early months of life, the organism is establishing just what the normal range of arousal is, establishing the set point which its systems will attempt to maintain. When things drop below or rise above the normal range of arousal, the systems go into action to recover the set point or normal state.

But first the norm has to be established, and this is a social process. A baby doesn't do this by himself, but coordi-nates his systems with those of the people around him. Babies of depressed mothers adjust to low stimulation and get used to a lack of positive feelings. Babies of agitated mothers may stay over-aroused and have a sense that feel-ings just explode out of you and there is not much you or anyone can do about it (or they may try to switch off their feelings altogether to cope). Well-managed babies come to expect a world that is responsive to feelings and helps to bring intense states back to a comfortable level; through the experience of having it done for them, they learn how to do it for themselves.

Early experience has a great impact on the baby's physiological systems, because they are so unformed and delicate. In particular, there are certain biochemical systems which can be set in an unhelpful way if early experience is problematic: both the stress response, as well as other aspects of emotional processing can be adversely affected. Even the growth of the brain itself, which is growing at its most rapid rate in the first year and a half, may not progress adequately if the baby doesn't have the right conditions to develop. Like a plant seedling, strong roots and good growth depend on environmental conditions, and this is most evident in the human infant's emotional capacities which are the least hard-wired in the animal kingdom, and the most influenced by experience.

The baby is also like a seedling in his psychological simplicity. Feelings start at a very basic level. A baby experiences global feelings of distress or contentment, of discomfort or comfort, but there is little nuance or complexity involved in his processing of these feelings. He doesn't yet have the mental capacity to do complex information processing. But while he relies on adults to manage these states – to reduce discomfort and distress and increase comfort and contentment – he is gradually grasping more and more of the world. As people come and go around him, smells and sounds and sights constantly changing through the day and night, patterns begin to emerge. Slowly, the baby begins to recognise the most regular features and to store them as images. These might typically be a soothing image of a smiling mother coming through the door when he cries in his cot, or it might be a disturbing image of a hostile face grimacing as she approaches. Meaning emerges as the baby begins to recognise whether the mother coming through the door will bring pleasure or pain. Early emotion is very much about pushing people away or drawing them closer, and these images will become expectations about the emotional world in which he is living that help the baby to predict what will happen next and how best to respond.

Although the baby is a simple creature in many ways, he also contains the blueprints for a complex life within his cells. Each baby has a unique personal store of genes which can be activated by experience. Already, in the first weeks, a temperamental bias may be apparent. Some babies may be born more reactive and sensitive to stimulation than others. Different babies have different thresholds and their typical ways of responding may already be distinctive. This may be due to their experiences in the womb or due to their genetic make-up – or a combination of the two. Recent research has identified variations of the serotonin gene which has been linked with greater sensitivity to the social world. Babies who have these genes are colloquially referred to as 'orchids' while the majority of babies are 'dandelions'. Orchid children are more susceptible to harsh parenting or neglectful nurseries; in difficult circumstances, they may end up prone to depression or antisocial behaviour. On the other hand, if they are well cared for, they have the least depression and poor behaviour and are often successful and socially skilled individuals (Belsky and Pluess 2009; Pluess and Belsky 2013; Ellis and Boyce 2008).

The baby's temperament or genetic make-up inevitably has an impact on the caregiver who has his or her own personality style too. A sensitive mother who gives birth to a robust, energetic, less sensitive baby might feel out of tune with him and think of him as aggressive; or, alternatively, she might be relieved that he is so easy to settle and to take anywhere. Some sort of dynamic interaction between personalities has already begun.

The point is, however, that the outcome depends far more on the mother and father than on the baby. Researchers have found that even the most difficult and irritable babies do fine with responsive parents who adapt to their needs. Some have even failed to identify any such thing as a 'difficult' baby in the early weeks of life, suggesting that this is largely the perception of the parent (Wolke and St James-Robert 1987) and that reactive style is established over the course of the first year (Sroufe 1995). Difficult babies may be difficult in response to their parents' emotional unavailability to them (Egeland and Sroufe 1981). In any case, difficult temperaments do not predict poor outcomes (Belsky et al. 1998), although the more sensitive type of baby may be at greater risk of developing poorly if his parents fail to adapt to his particular needs.

From the point of view of the baby, there may indeed be 'difficult' parents. These parents tend to fall into two types: neglectful or intrusive. At the neglectful end of the scale, there are depressed mothers who find it very hard to respond to their babies, who tend to be apathetic and withdrawn and don't make eye contact with their babies or pick them up much except to clean them or feed them. Their babies respond by developing a depressed way of interacting with people themselves (Field et al. 1988). They show less positive feelings (and their left brains are less active). In toddlerhood, they perform less well on cognitive tasks and they are found to be insecurely attached. Later in childhood, their emotional problems tend to persist (Murray 1992; Cooper and Murray 1998; Dawson et al. 1992).

At the intrusive end of the scale, there is another type of mother who may also be depressed, but is much more angry, even if only covertly. This is a more expressive kind of mother who at some level resents the baby's demands and feels hostile to him. She may convey this to the baby by picking him up abruptly or holding him stiffly. However, she is usually very actively involved with him in an insensitive way, often interfering with the baby's initiatives and failing to read his signals. Abusive mothers tend to be at this end of the spectrum (Lyons-Ruth et al. 1991), and their children also tend to develop less well and to be insecurely attached in an emotionally avoidant or disorganised kind of way.

Fortunately, most parents instinctively provide enough attention and sensitivity to their babies to ensure their emotional security. But what seems to be most crucial for the baby is the extent to which the parent or caregiver is emotionally available and present for him (Emde 1988), to notice his signals and to regulate his states; something which the baby cannot yet do for himself except in the most rudimentary ways (like sucking his own fingers when hungry, or turning his head away from distressing stimulation).

Early regulation

It is not popular these days to spell out just how great the responsibilities of parenthood are, since women have struggled desperately to establish themselves as men's equals in the workplace and do not want to feel guilty about keeping their careers or pay cheques going while someone else takes care of their babies. When I teach, I have found that students inevitably raise the question of whether mothers should be blamed for not being perfect mothers. The guilt and anxiety often fuel intense hostility to researchers like Jay Belsky of the University of London who pioneered some of the most important research in this area in identifying the impact of inadequate caregiving on babies, both at home and in daycare.

Certainly, there is little to be gained by criticising parents. Criticism doesn't improve their capacity to respond positively to their children. However, positive support for parents may help to reduce some of the defensive behaviour that harms their children and continues vicious cycles of insecurity and inability to regulate feelings well down the generations.

At a wider social level, I believe that the real source of many parenting difficulties is the separation of work and home, of public and private, which has had the result of isolating caregivers in the home, without strong networks of adult support and without variety in their daily routines. These conditions – equally applicable to fathers who stay at home – themselves create much of the depression and resentment that are so problematic for babies' development. Parents face the artificial choice of devoting themselves to their working life or to their babies, when the evidence is that they want both. Research has inevitably focused on mothers in the past and has found that, in fact, most mothers working full time would like to work fewer hours (Hakim et al. 2008; Newell 1992). One study, drawing on extensive data from the major American NICHD Study of Early Child Care, corroborated this desire: they found that mothers of babies and pre-schoolers who are employed part time enjoy better health, are less likely to be depressed, are less conflicted about their work–life balance and are also more sensitive to their children than mothers who make other choices (Buehler and O'Brien 2011). Nevertheless, no matter what practical circumstances or preferences shape parents' choices, it is surely vital that their decisions should also be based on an accurate understanding of just what they might mean for their baby.

Physiologically, the human baby is still very much part of the mother's body. He depends on her milk to feed him, to regulate his heart rate and blood pressure, and to provide immune protection. His muscular activity is regulated by her touch, as is his growth hormone level. Her body keeps him warm and she disperses his stress hormones for him by her touch and her feeding. This basic physiological regulation keeps the baby alive. Rachel Cusk, a novelist who has written about her experience of motherhood, describes these basic regulatory processes:

> My daughter's pure and pearly being requires considerable maintenance. At first my relation to it is that of a kidney. I process its waste. Every three hours I pour milk into her mouth. It goes around a series of tubes and then comes out again. I dispose of it. Every twenty-four hours I immerse her in water and clean her. I change her clothes. When she has been inside for a period of time I take her outside. When she has been outside for a period of time I bring her in. When she goes to sleep I put her down. When she awakes I pick her up. When she cries I walk around with her until she stops. I add and subtract clothes. I water her with love, worrying that I am giving her too much or too little. Caring for her is like being responsible for the weather, or for the grass growing. (Cusk 2001: 134)

The difficult thing about babies is that they need this care almost continuously for many months. As Cusk puts it, these tasks 'constitute a sort of serfdom, a slavery, in that I am not free to go'. Babies need a caregiver who identifies with them so strongly that the baby's needs feel like hers; he is still physiologically and psychologically an extension of her. If she feels bad when the baby feels bad, she will then want to do something about it immediately, to relieve the baby's discomfort – and this is the essence of regulation. In theory, anyone can do it, especially now we have bottled milk substitutes, but the baby's mother is primed to do these things for her baby by her own hormones, and is more likely to have the intense identification with the baby's feelings that is needed, provided she has the inner emotional resources to do so.

Early regulation is also about responding to the baby's feelings in a non-verbal way. The mother does this mainly with her face, her tone of voice and her touch. She soothes her baby's loud crying and over-arousal by entering the baby's state with him, engaging him with a loud mirroring voice, gradually leading the way towards calm by toning her voice down and taking him with her to a calmer state. Or she soothes a tense baby by holding him and rocking him. Or she stimulates a lacklustre baby back into a happier state with her smiling face and dilated sparkly eyes. By all sorts of non-verbal means, she gets the baby back to his set points where he feels comfortable again.

Caregivers who can't feel with their baby, because of their own difficulties in noticing and regulating their own feelings, tend to perpetuate this regulatory problem, passing it on to their own baby. Such a baby can't learn to monitor his own states and adjust them effectively, if mum or dad doesn't do this for him in the first place. He may be left without any clear sense of how to keep on an even keel. He may even grow up to believe he shouldn't really have feelings since his parents didn't seem to notice them or be interested in them. Babies are very sensitive to these kinds of implicit messages, and they initially respond to what parents do rather than what they say or think they are doing. But if parents do track the baby's states well and respond quickly to them, restoring the feeling of being OK, then feelings can flow and be noticed. They can come into awareness. Particularly if caregivers respond in a predictable way, patterns will start to emerge. The baby may be noticing that 'when I cry, mum always picks me up gently', or 'when she gets her coat down, I will soon smell the fresh air'. These unconsciously acquired, non-verbal patterns and expectations have been described by various writers in different ways. Daniel Stern (1985) called them representations of interactions that have been generalised (RIGs). John Bowlby called them 'internal working models' (1969). Wilma Bucci calls them 'emotion schemas' (1997). Robert Clyman calls them 'procedural memory' (1991). Whatever particular theory is subscribed to, all agree that expectations of other people and how they will behave are inscribed in the brain outside conscious awareness, in the period of infancy, and that they underpin our behaviour in relationships through life. We are not aware of our own assumptions, but they are there, based on these earliest experiences. And the most crucial assumption of them all is that others will be emotionally available to help notice and process feelings, to provide comfort when it is needed – in other words, to help regulate feelings and help the child get back to feeling OK. Those children who grow up without this expectation are regarded as 'insecurely attached' by attachment researchers.

Parents are really needed to be a sort of emotion coach. They need to be there and to be tuned in to the baby's constantly changing states, but they also need to help the baby to the next level. To become fully human, the baby's basic responses need to be elaborated and developed into more specific and complex feelings. With parental guidance, the basic state of 'feeling bad' can get differentiated into a range of feelings such as irritation, disappointment, anger, annoyance, hurt. Again, the baby or toddler can't make these distinctions without help from those in the know. The parent must also help the baby to become aware of his own feelings and this is done by holding up a virtual mirror to the baby, talking in babytalk and emphasising and exaggerating words and gestures so that the baby can realise that this is not mum or dad just expressing themselves, this is them 'showing' me my feelings (Gergely and Watson 1996). It is a kind of 'psychofeedback' which provides the introduction to a human culture in which we can interpret both our own and others' feelings and thoughts (Fonagy 2003). Parents bring the baby into this more sophisticated emotional world by identifying feelings and labelling them clearly. Usually this teaching happens quite unselfconsciously.

Insecure attachments and the nervous system

But if the caregiver doesn't have a comfortable relationship to her own feelings, she may not be able to do this very effectively. If her own awareness of her own states is blocked, or if she is overly preoccupied with them, she could find it hard to notice her baby's feelings, to regulate them by some means, or to label them. Good relationships depend on finding a reasonable balance between being able to track your own feelings at the same time as you track other people's.

They also depend on being able to tolerate uncomfortable feelings while they are being processed with another person. Perhaps one of the most common difficulties in relationships, which is particularly acute in the parent–child relationship, is a problem with regulating the more 'negative' states such as anger and hostility. If the caregiver hasn't learnt how to manage such feelings comfortably, then she will find them very hard to bear in her children; she might feel very distressed and uncomfortable and urgently want to push such feelings away. How many people have heard the mother or father who yells at their baby 'Shut up! Don't try it on with me!' or at their toddler 'You little devil. Don't you dare look at me like that!' Their children will be learning to hold back their feelings – either to deny they exist, or to avoid expressing them as they are going to upset or anger mother. She certainly won't be able to help regulate them or think about them with the child. In effect, the child has to regulate the parent by protecting her from his feelings. But the child's feelings don't go away. Attachment researchers have found that children in such families learn to appear calm and unconcerned, but when measured, their heart rate and autonomic arousal is rocketing. The organism is dys-regulated. Rather than getting help with returning to the comfort zone, the child is learning there is no regulatory help with such feelings. He tries to suppress them and switch them off altogether, but is rarely successful. This is known as an 'avoidant' attachment pattern.

Other children, living with parents who are more incon-sistent in the way that they respond to their child's feelings – sometimes concerned, sometimes switched off – are forced to focus closely on the parent's state of mind to optimise their chance of getting a response. They tend to keep their feelings close to the surface, bubbling away, until they can make a bid for parental attention when they think there is a chance of getting it. They too learn that help with regulating their feelings is not reliably available – but rather than choose the strategy of suppressing their feelings, they may learn to exaggerate them; to be overly aware of their fears and needs in a way that can undermine their independence. Indeed, this may be what their parent unconsciously wants, as very often these are adults who deal with their own inse-curities through being needed by others. Their unpredict-able behaviour ensures that the child's attention is always available for them. Or they may simply be so preoccupied with their own dysregulated feelings that they cannot reli-ably notice those of other people. Children with this pattern have what is called a 'resistant' or 'ambivalent' attachment.

A child caught up in either of these patterns of attach-ment will have a weaker sense of self than a securely attached child, because he or she will have lacked optimum 'social biofeedback'. The parent will not have provided enough information about the child's own feelings to equip the child to enter the domain of psychological interpretation of self and others with confidence. Instead, the child may try to protect a shaky sense of self by withdrawing from others when he feels uncertain (the avoidant pattern), or alterna-tively clinging on to others to try to elicit more feedback (the resistant pattern) (Fonagy 2003).

A third pattern has been identified in recent years, known as the 'disorganised' attachment. This has the strongest links with serious future emotional difficulties. In these families, the child struggles to find a coherent defen-sive strategy. Very often, the parents themselves have been overwhelmed by traumatic experiences in their own lives that have not been processed effectively, such as a bereave-ment or some kind of important loss, or some form of abuse. As a result of these preoccupations, the parent can behave strangely. He or she might 'blank out' or dissociate from reality, perhaps failing to respond to his child's needs or signals. The parent may make sudden unpredictable and frightening movements towards the child or might himself look afraid or act submissively towards the child. (Out et al. 2009). Parents in this state of mind are unable to provide the most basic parental functions of protecting the child and creating a safe base from which to explore the world. Their children not only lack 'psychofeedback', but are also left feeling afraid and uncertain of how to manage their feelings when under pressure.

All these kinds of dysfunctional parental responses actually disturb the body's natural rhythms. Normally, being aroused physiologically by some intense emotional state will lead to action of some kind, and then once the feeling has been expressed, the organism will wind down and come back to a resting state. This is the normal cycle of the sympathetic and parasympathetic nervous systems. But if arousal isn't soothed, this rhythm can be disrupted. As in the avoidant pattern, the body's braking system may be applied over the top of its 'let's go' system – or vice versa, a withdrawn, inhibited (parasympathetic) state such as sadness or depression may be overridden by the sympathetic system demanding 'let's get on with it'. These 'incompleted cycles' as Roz Carroll (unpublished) calls them, can lead to organismic disturbances such as muscle tension, shallow breathing, immune or hormonal disturbances. The cardiovascular system, in particular, will remain activated even if feelings are suppressed (Gross and Levenson 1997). There is then turbulence within the system rather than straightforward processing of emotional states.

Emotional flow

The sympathetic and parasympathetic nervous systems are only one internal system. But the human organism has many others which are constantly oscillating according to their own particular rhythms and timings – blood pressure, sleep patterns, breathing and excreting all follow different patterns simultaneously, while influencing each other and signalling to each other and to the brain (Wiener 1989). The internal symphony of fluctuating inhibitory and excitatory activity is self-organising through a process of feedback loops, so that influences are mutual and constantly adjusting to each other. Cells and organs regulate themselves and each other; they have their own functions but are part of the whole system. This is much the same as the wider picture of the human organism within the social system. We learn to regulate ourselves to some extent, but we also depend on other people to regulate our states of body and mind so that we can fit into the wider systems of which we are a part.

This works because there is a free flow of information round all the systems, both internally within the body and externally with other people, making it possible to adapt to current circumstances. Our most intimate relationships throughout life are comfortable precisely because of this rapid exchange of emotional information – something that Tiffany Field has called their 'psychobiological attunement' (Field 1985). This capacity to pick up on the other person's states enables individuals to adjust quickly to each other's needs. More formal (or disturbed) relationships lack this quick responsiveness and, as a result, adjustments are more laborious and awkward. But individuals may also be more or less attuned to their own internal states. Both emotional and physiological pathology may arise when information does not flow freely through the electrical and chemical channels of the body through the brain and other systems. We need the emotional information provided by our bodies to judge how best to act.

Children who have developed insecure strategies for dealing with their emotions cannot tolerate feelings and so cannot reflect on them. Their emotional habits for managing feelings kick in too quickly. Avoidantly attached children are likely to automatically slam on their emotional brakes when strong feelings start to arise, so that they don't have to be aware of feelings they don't know what to do with. Resistantly attached children are more likely to plunge headlong into expressing strong feelings without restraint, without regard for others' feelings. (More damaged children may swing between the strategies.) Either way, they are denied access to emotional information about their own state or that of other people, and without it have much less choice about how to act. They are really hampered in their ability to co-ordinate their own (biological) needs with their (social) environment and to exchange emotional information with others in a useful way.

These emotional habits are learnt in infancy with our earliest partners, usually our parents, and can already be measured by the age of 1 year old. However, parents are also part of wider systems and these broader social forces can also play a part in distorting patterns of emotional regulation. When a society is focused on building up its productive capacities, as in the nineteenth century, then some of its babies might be socialised to become highly controlled personalities through strict control and denial of feelings. The Freudian project perhaps was an attempt to undo the worst excesses of this process, while still emphasising the importance of self-control. Alternatively, when the economy requires willing consumers, there might be social pressures to socialise babies more indulgently, to make fewer demands on them to conform with parental expectations. These social movements cannot, however, be precisely orchestrated so it is likely that different currents will co-exist in any epoch.

Feelings as signals

But emotional regulation is not about control or the lack of it. It is about using feelings as signals to alert the individual to the need for action, in particular to help sustain needed relationships. A child's anxiety when mother goes out of the room is useful because it helps mother and child to stay close, promoting the survival of the child. Smiley, happy moments are a signal for more of the same. Anger communicates that something is badly wrong which requires urgent attention. When people pay attention to these signals, they are more likely to be adjusting to each other's and their own needs. Just like the simpler internal physiological signals of thirst, hunger or tiredness, they motivate action to keep the organism in optimal condition. Parents who respond to their baby's hunger signals by feeding on demand tend to have slimmer children who grow up better able to regulate their food intake (DiSantis 2011; Daniels et al. 2013). Those who learn instead to ignore their own hunger signals are more prone to overeating or under-eating.

Similarly, individuals who are aware of their own emotions are in a better position to use them constructively. It may not be helpful to ignore your own anger, because that anger can help you to defend your social position or allows you to challenge things that harm you. However, if you express your anger without awareness of its impact on others, failing to notice either their signals or to play your part in regulating them, then the social system becomes unco-ordinated and antisocial behaviour breaks out.

The attitude towards feelings is crucial. If they are seen as dangerous enemies, then they can only be managed through exerting social pressure and fear. Alternatively, if every impulse must be gratified, then relationships with others become only a means to your own ends. But if feelings are respected as valuable guides both to the state of your own organism as well as to that of others, then a very different culture arises in which others' feelings matter, and you are motivated to respond. There is a very different assumption that anger and aggression can be managed and kept within limits because they will be heard and responded to. They can be used to sustain the relationship. The emotionally secure person has this belief, a basic confidence in being heard, which facilitates inner control. This confidence in others helps him to wait and to think rather than to act impulsively. But if anger and aggression are taboo, the individual will be in a state of high arousal without any means of soothing himself, forced to rely only on his fear of others to hold back: a precarious strategy which may fail, ending at times in destructive dysregulated behaviour and the destruction of relationships.

As social creatures, we need to monitor other people as well as our own internal state, to maintain the relationships on which we all depend. Babies do this from the start – noticing facial expressions and tones of voice, highly alert and responsive to other humans even as newborns. If you watch parent and baby together, you will see them improvise a dance of mutual responsiveness as each takes turns in sticking out their tongue or making a sound. Later, as babies start to move around under their own steam, they manage their growing independence by checking back to the parent's face for cues about how to behave. Should they touch this dog that has just come into the room? Or smile at this stranger? The attachment figure becomes the touchstone, the source of social learning.

Emotional life is largely a matter of co-ordinating ourselves with others, through participating in their states of mind and thereby predicting what they will do and say. When we pay close attention to someone else, the same neurons are activated in our own brain; babies who see happy behaviour have activated left frontal brains and babies who witness sad behaviour have activated right frontal brains (Davidson and Fox 1992). This enables us to share each other's experience to a certain extent. We can resonate to each other's feelings. This enables a process of constant mutual influence, criss-crossing from one person to the other all the time. Beatrice Beebe, an infant researcher and psychotherapist, has described this as 'I change you as you unfold and you change me as I unfold' (Beebe 2002). In the next chapter I describe how the brain itself is subject to such influences.

3

Building a brain

Form emerges in successive interaction.

Susan Oyama

The basic brain

It is a beautiful spring morning. My cat lounges on a stone bench in the sun after breakfast, stretching himself to his full extent with evident pleasure. This is an image of simply being alive, a moment when the experience of existing and the sensory pleasures of sun, air, full belly are enough. But if a large dog should come past, the cat would also defend his own 'being' and would shoot off the bench and hide, or, if cornered, would hiss and snarl with his fur up to frighten off the dog. Likewise, if pangs of hunger alerted him to his need for more energy supplies, he would make sure to keep his 'being' going by pursuing a mouse or vole. He may not have self-consciousness or verbal communication, but he has a range of basic feelings and reactions which prompt his behaviour and ensure his survival.

This is where human beings start too. We share with other mammals a core brain which ensures survival. A newborn baby has a basic version of these systems in place: a functioning nervous system which enables him or her to breathe, a visual system which allows him to track the movements around him and to see faces close up, a core consciousness based in the brainstem which reacts to sensory experiences and assesses them in terms of survival. The baby also has some basic reflexes such as the ability to root for a breast and to suck milk to nourish himself, sad or angry cries to attract mother's attention, and a defensive freezing behaviour when threatened. As Jaak Panksepp (1998) puts it: 'the emotional systems that have been identified in animals correspond nicely to what are deemed to be basic emotional systems in humans'. But what distinguishes humans from other newborn mammals is the human baby's responsiveness to human interaction. Human beings are the most social of animals.

The recent discovery of mirror neurons in the brain has made it clear that we are connected to other people from the start of life (Iacoboni 2009; Kohler et al. 2002). Even very young babies have some capacity to understand others' behaviours or to feel their emotions. Before the 'higher' brain is fully developed, babies' brains are already resonating to other people's behaviours, using their premotor cortex, anterior cingulate cortex and insula. The mirror neurons in these areas automatically fire up when they observe (or hear) other people doing things. For example, the sight of someone in terrible pain is likely to make us flinch, or the sound of people laughing happily can make us feel mildly light-hearted. It's no accident that babies are closely watching facial expressions and noticing body language from the start of life, or even imitating a parent's facial movements. Their observations are providing a felt experience of the social world of emotions as well as helping them to understand other people's intentions (Iacoboni et al. 2005).

The primitive brain that we are born with basically ensures that the organism 'works'. The 'oldest' structures in evolutionary terms, such as the brainstem and sensorimotor cortex, are the parts of the brain which are most metaboli-cally active in the newborn. The new baby's priority is the internal regulation of body systems; adaptation to external conditions, which is largely managed by his emotional responses, soon follows. The active baby seeks out interac-tion with others, turns away from others when overwhelmed, freezes when he feels at risk; he already has the rudiments of emotion and self-regulation. Emotions are first and fore-most our guides to action: they are about going towards things or going away from them.

Getting away from danger is probably the most essential response for survival, and it is not surprising that the fear and self-defence system based in the amygdala is one of the first parts of the emotional brain to mature. Although the basic structure of the amygdala is complete at birth, it goes on developing – most rapidly during the post-natal period and up to 4 years old (Tottenham 2011). Although the amygdala is active in many emotional experiences, its primary function is to act as a sort of emotional radar, a social surveillance tool which is an important part of our survival system. The radar scans other people's body language, in particular picking up cues from their eyes; it detects emotional signals, especially anything that might be threatening and reacts to it automatically. As Joseph LeDoux, the amygdala expert, describes it, when you see a twig on your path that looks like a snake, you jump back fearfully, or freeze – you act first, think later (LeDoux 1998). But although these sorts of reactions are hard-wired and automatic, LeDoux suggests that they are also open to learning and memory. We adapt to local conditions by noting and unconsciously remembering the particular experiences that generate fear in early life, using them as cues which tend to become an 'indelible', unconscious, primary repertoire of fear reactions. If you have bad experiences with a shrill-voiced babysitter in infancy, you may shrink from shrill-voiced people for the rest of your life without knowing why. These underlying emotional systems generate the overall state of the organism, and the basic meaning we attribute to situations. Approach or avoid, live or die.

But Jonathan Turner suggests that these basic emotions of anger and fear are far too negative to be the basis for a social way of life (Turner 2000). They may work for cats who interact largely to defend their individual territory, but they do not work for a species which bands together in social groups. Living a social life as humans do involves a degree of sensitivity and responsiveness to others, which other animals don't on the whole need. Human beings, however, need a lot more than fear and anger to live together co-operatively.

Turner suggests this is why fear and anger were elaborated into more complex states such as sadness, shame and guilt – all feelings which help us to control our behaviour to meet social goals. At the same time, the basic emotion of satisfaction was enlarged into the more intense feelings of love, pleasure and happiness which have the capacity to bind people together. As layer upon layer of these more complex emotions developed in human interaction, they also took shape physiologically in the structure of the brain itself. Since Paul MacLean suggested in 1970 that there was a 'triune' brain, or three-brains-in-one, there has been general recognition that the brain is structured by evolution, starting with a reptilian brain, on top of which developed a mammalian emotional brain, and finally a human neocortex. As Reg Morrison vividly described it, the human brain is 'like an old farmhouse, a crude patchwork of lean-tos and other extensions that conceal entirely the ancient amphibian-reptilian toolshed at its core' (Morrison 1999). The most basic functions of life are found in this 'toolshed' at the base of the brain, above which the emotional reaction systems develop. Beyond and around those systems lie the prefrontal cortex and cingulate, which have been thought of as the thinking part of the emotional brain, where emotional experience is held on line and alternative courses of action considered (see Figure 3.1).

The social brain

Turner suggests our rationality and our language abilities grew out of 'our ability to be so emotional' (Turner 2000: 60). As the emotional brain developed, and we became more emotionally complex and sophisticated, more alternatives and choices arose in our interactions with others. This then required a capacity to think and reflect on our emotions, and thus led to the expansion of the pre-frontal area of the cortex (which is situated next to the emotional and survival-oriented areas of the subcortex). The prefrontal cortex has a unique role in humans with big brains. Faced with a huge range of sensory and motor information about the complex world we live in, humans need a way to prioritise information so that they can make decisions about how to act. The pre-frontal cortex is well placed to help with this. It can organise our lives because it is

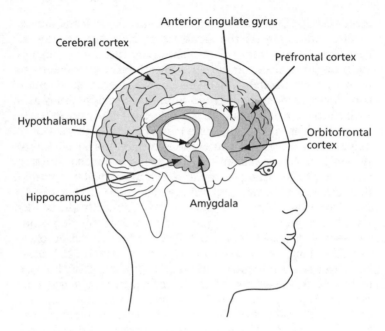

Figure 3.1 **The human brain.**

so well connected – it 'gets' the subcortical emotional systems as well as gathering together all our sensory information about the outside world; it is also linked to all the motor and chemical responses of the brain. This puts it in a unique position to 'eavesdrop' (as Damasio (1994) put it) on the activities of the whole organism and to co-ordinate all the information we have, both from inside and outside the body.

The first step towards emotional awareness is the maturation of the anterior cingulate during the first few months of life. This region of the brain encircles the emotional core, the structures of amygdala and hypothalamus (see Figure 3.1). Interestingly, its first priority seems to be to achieve an overview of the infant's *internal* emotional states in relation to other people. It registers what relationship experiences will bring pain (rejection, separation, or conflict for example) and what will bring a more rewarding feeling (parental soothing and holding). Expectations are soon formed, and within the first few months, the baby's anterior cingulate can already start to 'detect errors' – to alert the infant to situations that don't seem right or aren't as rewarding as previously expected. Over time, the anterior cingulate becomes expert at handling a wide range of competing or conflicting information; it specialises in a sort of cost–benefit analysis, figuring out what kind of behaviour works best and adjusting behaviour accordingly. As children get older, they draw on this ability to change behaviours to help them master their own impulses and to develop self-control. (Rothbart et al. 2000; Posner et al. 2007; Rushworth and Behrens 2008).

These emerging capacities are enhanced by the rapidly developing orbitofrontal part of the pre-frontal cortex. (This is found behind the eyes, also connected to both the amygdala and anterior cingulate, see Figure 3.1.) The orbitofrontal cortex is a big part of our story as it plays a key role in emotional life. Through studying what happens when this part of the brain is damaged, neuroscientists have put together a picture of its functions. If the orbitofrontal area is impaired, social life is undermined. People with brain damage that affects the orbitofrontal area can't relate to others sensitively. They become oblivious to social and emotional cues – they can even be sociopathic. They may be prone to dissociation if their orbitofrontal cortex is not able to integrate information from the environment with inner states. So the orbitofrontal cortex, together with other parts of the prefrontal cortex and anterior cingulate, is probably the area of the brain most responsible for what Daniel Goleman called 'emotional intelligence' (Goleman 1996).

The capacity to empathise, to vicariously experience what other people experience to some degree and to have an ability to infer their state of mind, requires a developed orbitofrontal cortex. It is particularly linked to the right side of the brain, which is specialised for grasping the general feel of things, the whole picture, and which is particularly involved in visual, spatial and emotional responses. In fact, according to Allan Schore, the orbitofrontal cortex is the controller for the entire right brain, which is dominant throughout infancy (Schore 2003). It is also larger on the right side of the brain. This may be where our capacity to identify distinctive feelings is processed, including some of our aesthetic experiences involving the flavour of food, the pleasure of touch, and the recognition of beauty (Rolls 1999). It has the highest level of opioids in the cerebral cortex and is highly involved in rewarding, pleasurable experiences of various kinds, including social attachment. The Japanese neuroscientist Yasuko Minegawa-Kawai has observed how when a mother watches a video of her baby smiling, her orbitofrontal cortex is activated and when the baby views his mother's smile, so is his (Minegawa-Kawai et al. 2009).

But the orbitofrontal cortex does not just respond to other people and their emotional cues; it is also involved with *managing* emotional behaviours. Connected to the amygdala, it quickly picks up on the emotions in facial expressions and tones of voice, but its role is more reflective: it considers what kind of response would be most appropriate and most likely to bring reward (Rolls and Grabenhorst 2008). Following on from that, it (together with the anterior cingulate) plays a part in holding back impulsive action and controlling emotional responses. This managerial role is achieved through its strong neural connections with the subcortical emotional systems such as the amygdala where intense emotions are generated.

Acting as a sort of control centre, the orbitofrontal cortex holds back what LeDoux calls the 'fast and dirty' emotional responses by activating more thoughtful, complex motivations. Through its connections to the more primitive brain systems, it can inhibit rage reactions, switch off fear, and generally apply brakes to feelings that arise in the subcortical areas.

This ability to hold back and defer immediate impulses and desires is the basis for our will-power and self-control, as well as our capacity for empathy. But the orbitofrontal area really works as an accessory to the emotional impulses. It can only 'fine tune' the deeper areas of the brain while they are activated. It doesn't work on its own. In the past, this part of the brain may have been neglected due to what Don Tucker has called 'cortical chauvinism' (Tucker 1992), an overvaluing of the 'higher' cortex and a neglect of this area linking cortex and subcortex.

How the social brain develops

I was surprised to discover that we are not born with these capacities. There are parents who hit their baby in the vain hope that he will stop crying or will eat the soggy carrot mush they have been trying to get him to finish for the last half an hour. But it is no good trying to 'discipline' a baby or to expect a baby to control its behaviour, since the brain capacity to do so does not yet exist. A baby cannot thoughtfully consider his mother's frustration and decide to eat up to keep her happy. His social capacities are mostly potential, not actual at birth. What needs to be written in neon letters lit up against a night sky is that the orbitofrontal cortex, which is so much about being human, develops almost entirely post-natally. This part of the brain develops after birth and doesn't begin to mature until toddlerhood.

Nor is it just a matter of waiting patiently for your baby to develop an orbitofrontal cortex as a matter of course. There is nothing automatic about it. Instead, the kind of brain that each baby develops is the brain that comes out of his or her particular experiences with people. The orbitofrontal cortex connects up through social stimulation: through play, and touch, and interaction. By adulthood, those who have wide social networks and see other people regularly have a larger orbitofrontal cortex (Powell et al. 2012). This brain structure is very 'experience dependent' as researchers put it. This means it is built up through experience, probably for a good evolutionary reason: so that each new human can be moulded to the environmental niche in which he finds himself. Precisely because we are so dependent as babies, and our brains at this stage are so 'plastic' (that is, easily changed), we can learn to fit in with whatever culture and circumstances we find ourselves in. The way I have come to think of it is that, in effect, when we are babies, our brains are socially programmed by the older members of our community, so that we adapt to the particular family and social group we must live among.

So the first 'higher' brain capacities to develop are social, and they develop in response to social experience. Rather than holding up flashcards to a baby, it would be more appropriate to the baby's stage of development to simply hold him and enjoy him.

Unfortunately, without the appropriate one-to-one social experience with a caring adult, the baby's orbitofrontal cortex is unlikely to develop well. It has been found to be smaller in volume when early relationships go badly wrong, particularly when children are emotionally or physically abused or neglected (Hanson et al. 2010; De Brito et al. 2013). Stressful early relationships also make it more difficult to establish the important neural pathways between the amygdala and the prefrontal cortex. When those connections are weak, the pre-frontal cortex cannot do a good job of holding back the amygdala's fearful responses, or of correcting earlier fear conditioning that is no longer appropriate, such as an early childhood fear of dogs or of red-haired people. This can leave the individual prone to anxieties and fears. In fact, poor amygdala–prefrontal connectivity is significantly correlated with both depression (Dannlowski et al. 2009) and anxiety (Kim and Whalen 2009).

Timing may also be crucial. Although a precisely timed 'sensitive period' has not been identified in humans as yet, there is evidence to suggest that there is a critical window of opportunity in growing this social part of the brain. In one early experiment, the primate researcher Harry Harlow found that if he isolated monkeys for the first year of life, they became effectively autistic and lost the ability to relate to other monkeys (Blum 2003). More recently, work done with Romanian orphans has shown that those who were cut off from close bonds with an adult by being left in their cots all day, unable to make relationships, had a virtual black hole where their orbitofrontal cortex should be (Chugani et al. 2001). When social relationships are denied during the period in which this part of the brain is maturing (up to the age of 3), there is little hope of fully recovering these lost social abilities or of developing this part of the brain adequately. Even after years of living in adoptive families, at the age of 9, these deprived children still have a less active orbitofrontal cortex as well as abnormal pathways between the orbitofrontal cortex and amygdala (Eluvathingal et al. 2006; Chugani et al. 2001).

A baby can't develop an orbitofrontal cortex on his or her own. It depends on the relationships with other people that are available and whether or not they are available when it counts most. It is hard to imagine how a baby could make himself a social person if he lived in conditions of social isolation. The case of Genie, a little girl kept in one room by her parents for most of the first 13 years of her life, showed how difficult it was to recover from such a beginning. Genie was almost certainly neglected from birth. Her older sister had been left in the garage so that her parents did not have to hear her cry; she had died aged 2 months of cold and neglect. From the age of 20 months, Genie herself was kept alone in a back bedroom, tied to a potty chair. She could not move or see out of the window. When she vocalised her needs, her father came upstairs and beat her with a wooden stick. This incredible deprivation continued until she was 13. Her rescuers found her to be incontinent, slow to react, unable to talk, with the motor skills of a 2 year old, obsessed with objects, and trained by fear to suppress all emotional self-expression. When she felt angry, she would attack herself, scratching at her face, blowing her nose and urinating. She craved affection but made no lasting relationships when last documented in her late twenties (Rymer 1994).

In a sense, the human baby has to be invited to participate in human culture. The first step in the process is to get the baby hooked on social interaction itself by making it highly pleasurable. In my work with mothers, fathers and babies, this has become a sort of benchmark – if the parent is finding pleasure in her relationship with her baby, then usually there is little to worry about, even if there are some problems. When the relationship is dominated by pleasurable interactions, the parent and the baby are, without realising it, building up the baby's prefrontal cortex and developing his capacities for self-regulation and complex social interactions. Most families do enjoy their babies in this way. But the mother-and-baby system is a delicate one, and can be easily derailed by a lack of inner or outer resources. The stress of low socio-economic status (SES) or a lack of emotional support, past or present, can interfere with a parent's ability to relax and pay attention to her baby. Fortunately, the relationship can often be put back on track with the right help at the right moment.

One mother I worked with, Sarah, was a highly successful professional who came to me in a very agitated and anxious state when she had her first baby. She was having great difficulty in breastfeeding. She had come to motherhood late and desperately wanted to get it right, but the tension between mother and baby was palpable. The baby had a flat, dull expression and turned away when her mother came near. Sarah resented her so much that she confessed she could not pass an upstairs window without having fantasies of throwing her baby out. Yet this situation was improved in a matter of weeks as the mother learnt to follow her baby's lead and let her baby tell her what she needed. Soon she started to relax, the baby started to relax, and before long the positive mutual feedback increased to the point where Sarah came in to see me with her baby, shining with love, and adoring her baby, while the baby smiled back at her. Pleasure had been restored.

The first sources of pleasure are smell, touch and sound. Babies can recognise their parents' voices from the start, and prefer them to any other. Being lovingly held is the greatest spur to development, more so even than breastfeeding. It is no accident that the image of Madonna and child has become an icon in human culture. In mother's or father's arms, where it is safe and warm, muscles can relax and breathing can deepen, as tensions are dispersed by gentle stroking or calm rocking. The baby's heart rate has been found to synchronise with the parent's heart rate; if she is relaxed and in a coherent state, so will the baby be. Her autonomic nervous system in effect communicates with her baby's nervous system, soothing it through touch. When we are physically held, we know that we are supported by others. There is a moment in Ashley Montague's film *Touching* which conveys this movingly: a distraught and distracted patient in a mental hospital, being interviewed by a psychiatrist, seems much more able to focus on the psychiatrist's face and engage with him when the psychiatrist reaches out and grasps his hand to convey his concern for the patient. These deep satisfactions of touch remain part of adult life, as bereaved people are comforted by a hug, partners communicate how 'in touch' they are with each other sexually, or people let go of the stresses of their daily life with a massage.

The power of a smile

As the world comes into focus, vision plays an increasingly important part in relationships. Eye contact now becomes the main source of information about other people's feelings and intentions: feelings are seen on the face. This reliance on faces may have evolved on the African savannah where it was necessary for our primate ancestors to communicate silently so as not to alert predators. This was done through visual means, developing a wide repertoire of facial movements and body language to convey information (Turner 2000). Certainly attentiveness to faces is hard-wired into human beings and is evident even in newborns.

By toddlerhood, the human child has started to use his mother's and father's faces as his immediate guides to behaviour in his particular environment. Is it safe to crawl out of this door? Does Dad like this visitor? This is known as 'social referencing', with the infant using visual communication at a distance to check out what to do and what not to do, what to feel and what not to feel, using the parent's facial expression as his source of information (Feinman 1992).

But according to Allan Schore, looking at faces has an even more powerful role to play in human life. Especially in infancy, these looks and smiles actually help the brain to grow. How does this work? Schore suggests that it is positive looks which are the most vital stimulus to the growth of the social, emotionally intelligent brain (Figure 3.2).

When the baby looks at his mother (or father), he reads her dilated pupils as information that her sympathetic nervous system is aroused, and she is experiencing pleasurable arousal. In response, his own nervous system becomes pleasurably aroused and his own heart rate goes up. These processes trigger a biochemical response. First, a pleasure

Figure 3.2 Positive looks are the most vital stimulus to growth of the social brain.

neuropeptide called beta-endorphin is released into the circulation and specifically into the orbitofrontal region of the brain. 'Endogenous' or home-made opioids such as beta-endorphin are known to help neurons to grow, by regulating glucose and insulin (Schore 1994). As natural opioids, they also make you feel good. At the same time, another neurotransmitter called dopamine is released from the brainstem, and again makes its way to the prefrontal cortex. This too enhances the uptake of glucose there, helping new tissue to grow in the prefrontal brain. Dopamine probably also feels good, insofar as it produces an energising and stimulating effect; it is involved in the anticipation of reward. So by this technical and circuitous route, we discover that the family's doting looks are triggering the pleasurable biochemicals that actually help the social brain to grow (Schore 1994).

The baby's brain is doing a lot of growing in the first year – it more than doubles in weight. The enormously increased glucose metabolism of the first two years of life, triggered by the baby's biochemical responses to his mother, facilitates the expression of genes. Like so much else about human development, genetic expression frequently depends on social input to become manifest. The hippocampus, temporal cortex, prefrontal and anterior cingulate are all immature at birth. But the success of their growth and genetic development depends on the amount of good experiences the individual has. Lots of positive experiences early on produce brains with more neuronal connections – more richly networked brains. We have all our neurons at birth, and we don't need to grow any more, but what we do need is to connect them up and make them work for us. With more connections, there is better performance and more ability to use particular areas of the brain.

In particular, between 6 and 12 months, there is a massive burst of these synaptic connections in the prefrontal cortex. They achieve their highest density just when the developing pleasurable relationship between parents and baby is most intense, and attachment bonds are being consolidated. This growth spurt in the prefrontal cortex reaches a final high pitch in early toddlerhood, when the novelty of being able to move independently creates elation in the toddler and pride and joy in his parents. In effect, the baby has now become a social being, with the beginnings of a social brain. But it takes most of the first year to reach this point.

Towards the end of the first year, the preparatory phase of infancy comes to an end. In some ways, the human baby now reaches the level of development that other animals achieve inside the womb. But by doing it outside the womb, human brain building is more open to social influence. This extended human dependency outside the womb enables an intense social bond between caregiver and child to develop. This generates the biochemicals that facilitate a high level of neural connections and brain growth which will never be as rapid again. However, connections do carry on being made throughout life. One demonstration of this was seen in Einstein's pickled brain, which was examined a few years ago by researchers in Canada. They compared Einstein's brain with other brains of men who died at a comparable age, and found that Einstein's brain was 15 per cent wider in the parietal area than the other brains. The parietal area is the part of the brain involved in maths reasoning and visual–spatial thinking. The message here is: the more you use it, the more it develops. However, if you don't use it, you lose it – the absence of activity tends to make neurons atrophy like wasted muscles.

The infant navigator

The first year of life is mostly building up these mental 'muscles'. Connections are made at a rapid rate providing a dense network of possibilities, the raw materials from which the mind will emerge. Then, experience begins to 'commit cells to their ultimate fates' (Greenough and Black 1992) as they take up their position in the whole system and start to die off if not used. This is known as 'pruning'. The brain keeps what is useful and lets go of the surplus connections that are not going to be needed for this particular life. Out of the chaotic overproduction of connections within the brain, patterns start to emerge. The most frequent and repetitive experiences start to form well-trodden pathways, while those connections that lie unused begin to be pruned away. The brain takes shape.

It does this through unconsciously registering the patterns that form when a group of neurons are active simultaneously. (Individual neurons cannot make patterns.) Patterns are formed by the ensemble of neurons as they rise into activity, respond to each other and to environmental stimuli, and then fade away, creating a 'cocktail party' of chatter in the brain (Varela et al. 1996). It is during the time when a brain region becomes metabolically active that it contributes to the behavioural repertoire of the individual (Chugani et al. 2001), suggesting that our social intelligence is particularly sensitive to the experiences we have between 6 and 18 months. Once neurons are formed into patterns, they can be used to organise experience and make inter-actions with others more predictable. As Daniel Siegel put it, the brain is an 'anticipation machine' (Siegel 1999).

It is designed to help us navigate our way, providing expectations of likely outcomes and holding knowledge of our environment.

In effect, the baby's brain slowly begins to categorise his or her experiences with other people, by noticing unconsciously what its common features are, what happens over and over again. If her father always bursts into the house every evening, bangs the door, quickly picks her up and kisses her on the nose, the baby will start to form an expectation that this is what daddies do. If her mother always wrinkles her nose in disgust and grumbles when changing her nappy, pulling it off roughly, the baby will form the expectation that nappy changing is an unpleasant experience and maybe eventually that her bodily functions are a source of displeasure to others. It is the repeated and typical experiences that structure her brain – generating basic emotional categories much like 'dog' or 'table', but in a highly sensory form. The inner image will be of a prototype episode: how the other person's face looked, how I feel in my body when they do that thing. If an experience is not likely to recur, it does not need to be remembered because it is not of much use as a predictor.

Unless they are highly traumatic, one-off experiences leave little trace. The exception to this rule is that very highly charged and arousing experiences will be registered in the amygdala which is responsible for instant reactions to situations of danger. Faces with expressions of fear and anger will be registered there and will provoke an automatic response. These situations may be emergencies and need a very fast reaction.

These pathways and internal images provide a practical guide to interaction. We draw on them when some feature of the current moment triggers them. They don't get put into words because they don't need to be put into words. They simply underpin our behaviour and our expectations of others without our realising it. In fact, it seems that mostly we prefer our expectations to be confirmed, even if they are unpleasant (Swann 1987).

However, humans have developed a way to revise those inner images if circumstances change. This is the option of conscious self-awareness, which is offered by the prefrontal cortex and anterior cingulate. These parts of the brain enable us to 'hold' our thoughts and emotions, extending them in time, allowing us to reflect on experience and consider alternatives before acting. For example, the inner image and feeling of disgust and rejection which is triggered by nappy changing may persist in later situations which trigger the same constellation of neurons – perhaps being given an enema in hospital. Instead of reacting automatically to this trigger, the prefrontal cortex can effectively press a pause button and consider whether it is really so shameful and disgusting when it is a necessary procedure to protect one's health.

The power of the image

As the orbitofrontal cortex starts to mature towards the end of the first year, through the toddler period to about 18 months old, the child starts to develop a capacity for storing images. The orbitofrontal cortex has specialised neurons for recognising faces, while another part of the brain (the temporal lobe), which also starts to mature at the same time, processes the visual side of faces. At first, these are like 'flashbulb' images, but as situations with other people get repeated over and over again, they become lasting images invested with emotion, images of self with other, not grounded in time or place, but etched in memory. This is a significant moment in human emotional life, because it is really the sketchy beginning of an inner life – an inner library of images that can be referred to that will become increasingly complex and loaded with associations and thoughts as the child grows up. These emotionally loaded images are probably quite close to the psychoanalytic idea of an 'inner object' or internalised mother.

The inner images also become an important source of emotional self-regulation. In future situations with similar types of emotional arousal, they can be used as a guide to behaviour in the absence of the caregiver. But without effective internalised parental strategies for soothing and calming high arousal in the right brain, the individual is vulnerable to stress, which can more easily escalate into overwhelming distress. At the same time, this capacity to hold emotional images of people and their expressions in mind, and to return to these images, underpins the building up of a complex human world of meaning that goes beyond a purely transient response to the moment.

Negative faces

However, this intense engagement with faces has its down side. Negative looks and interactions are also remembered and stored. A negative look can also trigger a biochemical response, just as the positive face does. The mother's disapproving face can trigger stress hormones such as cortisol which stops the endorphins and dopamine neurons in their tracks – and also stops the pleasurable feelings they generate. These looks have a powerful impact on the growing child. They have enormous power in babyhood and toddlerhood because the child is so dependent on the parent for regulation of his states, whether physiological or psychological. Anything that threatens this regulation is very stressful because it puts survival at risk. It does not make much difference whether the lack of regulation is caused by being emotionally isolated from the caregiver or physically isolated by separation. What a small child needs is an adult who is emotionally available and tuned in enough to help regulate his states. The well-documented harmful effects of separation are, I suspect, mostly due to being emotionally cut off and unregulated. One study of nursery school children showed that it was not the mother's absence in itself that increased stress hormones such as cortisol, but the absence of an adult figure who was responsive and alert to their states moment by moment. If there was a member of staff in the nursery school who took on this responsibility, their cortisol levels did not rise. Without such a figure, the child became stressed (Dettling et al. 2000).

However, the toddler's brain actually needs a certain amount of cortisol to complete its development at this time (Schore 1994). Increased levels of cortisol facilitate the growth of norepinephrine connections from the medulla up to the prefrontal cortex. This delivery of norepinephrine helps the orbitofrontal cortex to mature further in toddlerhood, by increasing blood flow to the area and by forming its links (via the hypothalamus) with the parasympathetic nervous system. The parasympathetic nervous system is vital to the growing child, because this is the inhibitory system which enables the child to stop doing something and to learn what behaviour is unacceptable or dangerous. As the toddler explores his local domestic world, the parent now issues a prohibition such as 'No! Don't do that!' every nine minutes on average (Schore 1994). For the toddler, this is sobering. The world is no longer his oyster. There are dangers round every corner, there are limits on his joyful exploration of the world. He discovers that the wonderful parents who spent 90 per cent of their time in positive interactions during babyhood, making every effort to tune in to his moods, now can be horribly unattuned. They convey this through their cold tone of voice and their negative looks. Like the horse whisperer's technique with horses, the toddler's parents get him into line by giving him the cold shoulder. They actively withdraw their attunement and convey to him that he has to fit in with the group's norms or he will be socially isolated. For a highly social creature such as the human toddler, even more so than the horse, this is punishment indeed.

These disapproving or rejecting looks produce a sudden lurch from sympathetic arousal to parasympathetic arousal, creating the effects we experience in shame – a sudden drop in blood pressure and shallow breathing. I recall this feeling so clearly when, at the age of about 7, I was summoned to the headmaster's office. I admired and loved my headmaster and arrived with positive anticipation. But his face looked grim as I walked in – and what on earth was my mother doing there in the middle of the school day? She had apparently gone to see him to pass on a trivial complaint I had made to her when she came to say goodnight to me in bed the previous night. I had not been selected for the school relay race and thought I should have been. I remember the shock and humiliation of being called to account for my whingeing. I felt the blood draining from me and became extremely faint and nauseous, as momentarily things went black. I am now aware that what may have been happening was that the links between my orbitofrontal cortex and my vagus nerve (via the hypothalamus) had been strongly triggered by my shame, and my sympathetic arousal took a sudden nosedive.

Shame is an important dimension of socialisation. But what matters equally is recovery from shame. It is important to have a 'dose' of cortisol, it seems, but an 'overdose' is extremely unhelpful, as I will discuss further in the next chapter. Just as the child produces cortisol in response to the parent's face, so too does the dispersion of cortisol depend on a changed expression on the parent's face. The young child can't do this for himself, so if parents don't restore attunement and regulation, he may remain stuck in a state of arousal. The benefits of cortisol in helping the orbitofrontal cortex to inhibit emotional arousal may then be lost.

The verbal self

The final stage of the early emotional development of the brain is the development of a verbal self. We have seen how the baby's means of communicating with others gradually becomes more complex: starting with touch, moving into visual dominance, and then in the second and third years of life, finally including verbal communication. Each new mode of communication is added to the previous one, yet none are lost. We become more complex by building upon and adding to the previous stage of development – not by excluding it.

Once the orbitofrontal cortex is established, with its growing ability to manage feelings, the right and left sides of the orbitofrontal cortex start to knit together, linking the expression and management of feelings. There is a shift from right brain dominance towards the development of the left brain. The left brain has different modes of operation and is specialised for sequential and verbal processing – one message at a time, unlike the right brain's intuitive grasp of many modalities and the whole picture. As this shift occurs, the brain becomes more stable and less open to change. It seems as if the left brain creates a higher order operation based on the achievements of the right brain. It monitors the organised self that has emerged from the right brain's activities, it asserts the self and it expresses that sense of self to other people.

The last part of the pre-frontal cortex to mature is the dorsolateral prefrontal cortex. This is where we play around with our thoughts and feelings, where we think about them. The dorsolateral cortex is the main site of what is known as 'working memory'. By extending the activation of neuronal patterns in time, it can hold on to memories and thoughts and compare them. This capacity to hold things in mind is a key aspect of our ability to plan, to evaluate experience and to make choices. It gives us more flexibility and the opportunity to correct thinking and behaviour in line with current experience. In fact, because of its strong connections to the premotor areas of the cortex, as well as to the basal ganglia, it has been suggested that the dorsolateral area may be central to how the prefrontal cortex exerts its control over behaviour (Miller and Cohen 2001). Certainly, those people with a damaged dorsolateral cortex have a problem adapting; they tend to be rigid in their behaviour as well as stuck on old ideas.

However, the dorsolateral cortex's talents lie primarily in adapting to new situations by juggling information and re-directing attention – rather than by directly managing the subcortical emotional systems in the way that the orbitofrontal cortex does. They have different tasks.

The second year is notable for the increased linguistic ability that now develops, based in the left brain. Both the dorsolateral cortex and the anterior cingulate, to which it is linked, are involved in speech production and verbal fluency. (According to Panksepp, if the anterior cingulate is damaged, the *urge* to talk, or motivation to communicate feelings such as distress, is lost.) As these parts of the brain develop, words now start to play as big a part as looks. Emotions can be communicated verbally as well as through touch and body language. This conscious attention to emotions opens up a wider range of possible responses. Instead of relying on the automatic habits and expectations generated by the templates of past experience, there is now some room for manoeuvre. Ways of doing things and ways of thinking can be examined. More subtle or complex solutions may be arrived at, often through discussion with other people. Parents can now teach social rules in a more explicit way: 'We don't snatch other people's things' or 'If you eat up your fishfingers, I will give you your favourite yoghurt.'

This is a major shift from the previous way of registering experience in 'anticipatory images' of recurrent situations with people. However, that earlier non-verbal form of images, based largely on feedback from other people's faces and body language, continues to inform our emotional responses. But now there is a new verbal form of feedback from others to be mastered. The quality of this feedback matters. If caregivers are well attuned to the child, they will be able to acknowledge the child's current emotional state and to symbolise it accurately in words. This allows the child to build up an emotional vocabulary that can identify feelings accurately and can differentiate between different states – to know that feeling sad is different from feeling tired, for example. But if caregivers don't talk about feelings, or if they represent them inaccurately, it will be much more difficult for the child to express feelings and to negotiate around feelings with others. And if feelings remain unsymbolised, then emotional arousal cannot be managed in a more conscious, verbal fashion – such as 'talking oneself out of it' in a low mood. Instead, states will be processed through the old non-verbal channels, and will not get updated by new feedback and reflection. This means that the child's sense of self will also remain rather undifferentiated.

The sense of self is strongly affected by another part of the brain, the hippocampus, which has its most rapid phase of development in the first two or three years. Once again, however, its development is affected by the quality of parenting. Supportive parenting enables the hippocampus to grow better (Luby et al. 2012).

The hippocampus has a finger in a few pies, as do so many parts of the brain. Through its links to the hypothalamus, it plays a role in managing stress. But it also has links to the prefrontal cortex and plays a central role in memory, albeit in a different way from the dorsolateral cortex. While 'working memory' keeps current experiences in mind for a temporary period, the hippocampus has the role of selecting the more significant elements of current experience and holding on to them until they can be stored in long-term memory. It also brings information together from various sources in the brain and situates it in time and place, giving it a context. This means that it is now possible to remember a sequence of personal events: first this happened, then that happened to me. There is a before, during and after. This enables the child to start to create a personal narrative and to have a past and a future – to have a narrative self, not just a self who lives in the moment. Parents can now talk to their child about the future – 'Cheer up, we're going to the park to see the ducks later this morning' – and they can refer to the past – 'Remember when you took off all your clothes at Uncle Bob's wedding!'

Probably, the reason that we cannot remember our early infancy is because the dorsolateral prefrontal cortex and its links to the hippocampus have not fully developed at that time. Perhaps this is because in early life individual events are not so important as the gradual emergence of pattern and form from the hubbub of ordinary daily life. The most highly emotional memories from infancy are stored instead in more primitive systems such as the amygdala, or in other brain pathways, and either way are not accessible to consciousness. They are the background to our life. But as we grow up, we may need to remember more specific information to guide our decision making. The hippocampus has this task of remembering where and when particular, significant events happened – the context and the place – and can make them accessible to conscious recall.

This whole left-brain dominated formation of dorsolateral prefrontal cortex, anterior cingulate and hippocampus together play a major role in the development of a social self who has an autobiography and who communicates with others verbally to sustain this sense of self. Surprisingly, the development of this verbal, narrative self has itself been found to be crucial to emotional security in adults. An important researcher in the field of attachment theory, Mary Main, has worked on attachment patterns and has devised a way of measuring attachment security in adults. What she found was rather unexpected. She discovered that when adults talked about their emotional lives and their important relationships in growing up, it didn't matter whether they had a 'happy childhood' or not. Their current emotional security depended much more on having an internally coherent and consistent narrative than on the actual story they had to tell. The people who were in trouble emotionally were those who either found it difficult to talk freely about their feelings, or those who talked too much in a rambling and incoherent way. For example, on the one hand, if an adult took the view that he had had a wonderful relationship with his mother, yet could recall no memories of good moments that he had enjoyed with her, his narrative would be regarded as internally inconsistent (Dismissing). On the other hand, if an adult could not convey a coherent narrative about her past without getting caught up in painful, tangled memories and feelings, she would equally be regarded as insecure (Preoccupied) (Main and Goldwyn 1985). It is not clear to me whether the story itself plays some crucial role in creating a secure sense of self, or whether it is a by-product of the attentive relationships and good feedback from others which have produced a secure sense of self. Certainly, when emotions are either blocked from awareness or are out of control, there will be less possibility to reflect on them using the left brain's resources.

Genie – the child reared in isolation – had a relatively undeveloped left frontal cortex. In an era before the recent scanning techniques were in use, researchers used psychological tests on Genie. These tests revealed that she was not using her left brain for language, nor could she complete any left-brain tasks. Of course, she had not received any emotional feedback except the instruction to shut up. Yet her right brain was a remarkable non-verbal communicator according to those who spent time with her. She could grasp the 'gestalt' of a situation in an 'uncanny' way. She could draw what she could not say. Susan Curtiss, one of the researchers involved with Genie, recalled the way that she made her desires and feelings known to strangers without a word. Genie had an obsession with plastic objects and would notice and covet anything plastic that anyone had:

One day, we were walking – I think we were in
Hollywood. I would act like an idiot, sing operatically, to
get her to release some of that tension she always had.
We reached the corner of this very busy intersection, and
the light turned red, and we stopped. Suddenly, I heard
the sound – it's a sound you can't mistake – of a handbag
being spilled. A woman in a car that had stopped at the
intersection was emptying her handbag and she got out
of the car and ran over and gave it to Genie and then ran
back to the car. A plastic handbag. Genie hadn't said a
word. (Rymer 1994: 95)

These right-brain abilities may have been amplified in
Genie's case, but they do persist in all of us alongside our
left-brain verbal capacities. What seems to be most important for optimum emotional health is that the left brain's
operations should be well connected to the right brain's
information. If these connections are weak or are blocked in
some way, the left brain is quite capable of spinning a story
that is not anchored in emotional reality. Lacking information, the left brain simply guesses and fills in the gaps as
best it can. This may be the tendency of the Dismissing man,
outlined above. Somehow, the left brain has become dominant but has lost touch with the right brain. However, in the
case of the Preoccupied woman, it seems as if the right brain
has not adequately established its links with the left brain's
reflective and narrative capacities. The success or failure of
these connections may depend on what happens in the
child's important relationships during the second and third
years, and whether adult caregivers have facilitated the
connections between hemispheres and levels of the brain, by
responding and talking to their child in a way that enables
his emotions to be integrated into higher functioning.

It seems to be the process of putting feelings into words
that enables the left and right brains to become integrated.
When words accurately describe feelings, they can then be
blended into a coherent whole. Eugene Gendlin's therapeutic
work around the concept of 'focusing' describes this process
of how people can learn to listen to their bodily 'felt sense'
and express it carefully in words, thus linking the right

brain's 'felt sense' and the left brain's verbal account. Gendlin suggests that this is very different from the flatness of simply expressing your 'position' and hearing the other person's 'position' on something at a rational level. He describes how words that 'flow out of a feeling' are the kind that make you say *that's what it's all about!* and produce a 'body shift' which always feels good (Gendlin 1978). These links may be important because they allow the maximum information to flow freely between the two hemispheres. The mind is no longer trapped in unregulated emotional arousal, but is able to use all its resources, particularly those of the left brain, to regulate feelings.

4

Corrosive cortisol

The nights were the worst. There were nights when, hearing him start at three or four in the morning, she would have welcomed anything that would let him stop and rest – paregoric, a sugar-tit, any of those wicked things. During her pregnancy, Priss had read a great deal about past mistakes in child rearing; according to the literature, they were the result not only of ignorance, but of sheer selfishness: a nurse or a mother who gave a child paregoric usually did it for her own peace of mind, not wanting to be bothered. For the doctors agreed it did not hurt a baby to cry; it only hurt grown-ups to listen to him. She supposed this was true. The nurses here wrote down every day on Stephen's chart how many hours he had cried, but neither Sloan nor Dr Turner turned a hair when they looked at that on the chart; all they cared about was the weight curve.

Mary McCarthy, *The Group*, 1963

Women send out messages like this from time to time, sometimes disguised in novels, sometimes in the first person – describing their experience of being alone with a baby day and night, with little adult company. The experience is often bleak, as the high incidence of 'post-natal depression' testifies; it is estimated to be suffered by one in ten new mothers. For them, there is a feeling of 'energy gone underground, flatness and grayness above ground; devastation, silence, withdrawal from life. .. How the baby perceives this withdrawal as the cloud moves over the sun, we can only guess'

(Welburn 1980). These days we can do more than guess. There is a wealth of research which reveals a great deal about the experience of babies living with mothers who feel depressed or angry, almost always because they are insufficiently supported. Cut off from their usual sources of identity and support, these are stressed women. Yet they are expected to find the inner resources to manage a vulnerable newborn baby's delicate nervous system and to keep him or her free from stress. Unfortunately, when mothers themselves get so stressed that it becomes a struggle to cope with their babies, the baby's own capacity to cope with stress can be adversely affected. This chapter explains what important new research has to tell us about the development of the stress response in babyhood and how it can affect future emotional life.

The stressed brain

Stress is a word that we now use so casually that it has lost its impact. 'You're stressing me out' moans the teenager over the slightest disagreement with parents. Magazines offer quizzes to test your stress levels. Popular culture is awash with stories of exam stress, stressed executives, the stress of moving house. It would be easy to dismiss the whole concept as overblown psychobabble. Yet the way that we manage stress is actually at the heart of our mental health. It deserves to be taken very seriously indeed, but to do that, perhaps it would be helpful to focus less on the events that are thought to be stressful and to understand more about the internal factors involved in coping with stress.

In a sense, managing stress is the extreme end of emotional regulation. Stress can be defined as any situation that overwhelms our ability to cope. When experience proves to be too challenging, and threatens our normal homeostatic mechanisms, the body's stress response may come into play. The first step is for the amygdala to alert the hypothalamus to a potential danger. The hypothalamus then responds to its distress signal by setting off a particular cascade of chemical reactions known as 'the stress response'. This has two phases.

The first and most immediate response to stress is the almost instant 'fight or flight' mechanism. This activates the sympathetic nervous system and triggers the release of the stress hormone epinephrine (adrenaline) which gets the heart racing and the blood pumping to the muscles to generate prompt action to deal with the threat.

The second stage of the same process is the release of a different stress hormone, cortisol. Scientists refer to this second stress response as the 'HPA axis' (hypothalamus triggers pituitary which in turn triggers the adrenal glands). This could be described as the back up plan. It takes about ten minutes to kick in, but then it enables the body to find extra energy to meet the challenging situation. While this sounds like a helpful and straightforward process, it can have some very unhelpful side effects if the stress is not resolved or if the stress response is not working properly and production of cortisol continues.

In recent years, scientists have discovered a great deal about cortisol, which has turned out to be a key player in our emotional lives. Discovering that they could measure cortisol in the saliva, with much the same accuracy as a blood test, has been a boon to researchers. It is much easier to collect saliva samples throughout the day than blood samples and, as a result, many new studies of stress have been undertaken, looking at what causes stress and how active an individual's stress response is. These studies are underlining the importance of our biochemical responses in our emotional lives.

Every day of our lives, our internal biochemicals are fluctuating outside our awareness. All sorts of emotional and physiological responses are taking place automatically. Waves of hormones come and go through the day, adjusting and responding to events outside the body, or inside the body. They are involved in the daily rhythms of sleeping and waking, processing food, and keeping warm, mostly under the management of the hypothalamus in the core limbic area of the brain. These chemicals set off gene expression, changing behaviour in a way that will hopefully help the organism to maintain a good state. Serotonin helps us to regulate our moods and to calm distress, norepinephrine to be alert, while cortisol usually rises in the early morning to help generate energy for the day, and sinks to a low level in the late afternoon. These rhythmic flows of inner chemistry are important to our daily moods. They impart particular qualities to experiences. Candace Pert suggests that these biochemicals in the body are a kind of unconscious emotional vocabulary (Pert 1998) – particularly since each one rarely acts alone, but is combined with others into sentences. When we try to translate these body events into actual words, we may be trying to describe the complex chemical cocktail of the current moment.

All the major systems of the body are linked by this neurobiological information, our 'chemical intelligence'. However, our scientific understanding of these biochemicals has developed relatively recently. In the 1950s, at about the same time that Watson and Crick were cracking the genetic code by unravelling the chemical structure of DNA, others were beginning to identify the chemical structure of hormones such as insulin. By 1970, the action of neurotransmitters – chemicals made within the body that have their main effects in the brain – was finally established and recognised. Gradually more of these biochemicals, some with more general effects in the body, began to be identified. So far, well over 100 neuropeptides and neurotransmitters have been identified. The process of identifying them carries on apace, the most recent being the discovery of endocannabinoids.

Since the brain plays a major role in monitoring experience and orchestrating responses to it, many biochemicals are concentrated there, particularly in the prefrontal cortex and the systems of the subcortex involved in emotion (Figure 4.1).

Bill's divorce

One of the major stressors, by common agreement, is divorce. When Bill, a solid middle-aged man with a sophisticated intelligence and pleasant manner, came to see me for the first time, he struggled not to cry. He told me his situation. Caroline and Bill had been a much envied couple for 20 years. Attractive and sociable, their parties were legendary.

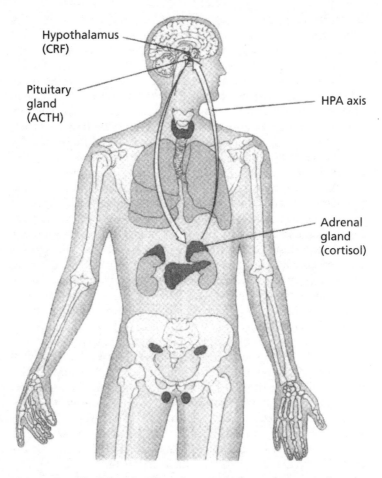

Hypothalamus
(CRF)

Pituitary
gland
(ACTH)

HPA axis

Adrenal
gland
(cortisol)

Figure 4.1 Each of the glands produces and releases hormones into the bloodstream. The arrow shows the hypothalamic pituitary adrenal (HPA) axis, which controls the release of the stress hormone cortisol.

They always seemed so mutually supportive and had both built up glittering careers in different fields of journalism. But suddenly they had shocked their friends and colleagues by separating. It transpired that Caroline had been having an affair with a younger man for several months.

Bill had come for psychotherapy to try to manage his complicated feelings. He revealed that in fact he had not felt close to Caroline for years. He felt that she only ever wanted to talk about work, and he could never get her to deal with the minor conflicts that arose between them. She would tell him how much she loved him and reassure him that everything was fine, yet he never felt his concerns were addressed; he felt palmed off by her 'niceness'. Yet discovering the affair was a terrible shock to Bill and had made him feel physically ill. He had always believed that Caroline was such a reliable, sensible person who always acted responsibly. He couldn't take in the change in his perception of her. Worse still, she had fallen madly in love with someone he despised – a charmer who lived off his inheritance, gambled and partied, and had five children by different wives.

Bill was suffering from one of the worst stresses known to humans – the loss of an attachment relationship. He was in pain. He had difficulty sleeping and he didn't feel like eating. He didn't know what to do; one minute he was thinking up ways of getting Caroline back, the next he was dreaming of burning down her lover's flat with her in it. Even though, as it happens, Caroline and Bill did not regulate each other's feelings very well, he was desperately afraid of being alone, afraid of never being loved again, and having no one there for him at all. He no longer felt secure.

Inside Bill's body

The uncertainty and fear of Bill's situation has triggered his stress response via his amygdala. His hypothalamus is doing overtime, struggling to keep his systems in balance. It has sent out a message to provide extra energy for Bill to meet this crisis in his life by producing extra cortisol. This message goes in stages, first in the form of corticotropin-releasing factor (CRF) to the pituitary, which in turn produces adreno-corticotropic hormone (ACTH), which then triggers the adrenal glands to produce cortisol.

As soon as the cortisol level rises in Bill's body, it starts to communicate with a whole range of his body systems. The cortisol puts brakes on his immune system, his capacity to learn, his ability to relax. In effect, the cortisol is having an internal conversation with other bodily systems which goes a bit like this: Cortisol: 'Stop what you're doing, guys! This is an emergency! Don't waste time fighting bugs. Don't waste time learning or connecting new pathways. Don't relax! I want all your attention on this problem.' This is useful as a short-term expedient. The cortisol breaks down fat and protein to generate extra energy and puts other systems on hold, temporarily. When the situation is over, the cortisol is gradually reabsorbed into its receptors or dispersed by enzymes. The body returns to normal.

But if the stress persists, and high levels of cortisol remain in the body over a longer period of time, then it can begin to have a damaging effect on other parts of the body. It can affect the lymphocytes of the immune system, making them less responsive, or even killing them off and stopping new ones from forming (Martin 1997).

In the brain, it can particularly affect the hippocampus. Although at first cortisol has a useful function in an emergency, activating defensive behaviour such as freezing the body's movement (which is co-ordinated by the hippocampus), it is less helpful as time goes on. If the level of cortisol remains high, the receptors for cortisol can close down and make the hippocampus less sensitive to cortisol, and less able to provide important feedback to the hypothalamus to tell it when to stop making more cortisol. Normally, the hippocampus informs the hypothalamus that a certain level has been reached and no more is needed. Hippocampus: 'I'm drowning in this stuff, please stop pumping it out. I've had enough cortisol.'

Without this feedback, the stress response can get stuck in the 'on' position. This can be a real problem for the hippocampus because if the cortisol continues, it can actually damage the hippocampus. The effect of too much cortisol can be to let too much glutamate get to the hippocampus, starting a process of neuron loss (Mogghadam et al. 1994). Eventually, the hippocampus may start to malfunction. If the stress goes on for a very long period, Bill might start to get forgetful, as the hippocampus is central to learning and memory. As the saying goes 'Stress makes you stupid' (Goosens and Sapolsky

2007; Radley and Morrison 2005; Chambers et al. 1999; McEwen 1999).

But the amygdala gets a buzz from all this cortisol. It gets more and more revved up and excited by the cortisol, and keeps releasing norepinephrine, which itself triggers yet more cortisol production (Makino et al. 1994; Vyas et al. 2002). In effect, the amygdala is an overexcited child with somewhat primitive reactions. Amygdala: 'This is such a bad situation! I must remember this and next time I see someone lying to me, like Caroline did to Bill, I will be in there like a shot!'

Only the medial prefrontal cortex, particularly the anterior cingulate, has the ability to control or override the amygdala (Kern et al. 2008). But the longer the stress continues, the more the neurotransmitters that normally power the prefrontal cortex are affected. Dopamine and serotonin levels fall there. Cells may also eventually start to die there.

The prefrontal cortex says wearily: 'I just can't cope with these organs. They are too hyped up. I can't stop them. I just don't have the strength. I'd better keep away from people, I can't deal with them right now.'

The sensitive nervous system

If these are the effects of stress on Bill's adult brain, consider what impact stress might have on a developing brain. How would stress affect the baby's hippocampus, prefrontal cortex and stress response? Just as the brain is customised by specific local experience and culture, so too are its biochemical systems, including the stress response. Like a car or a house, each individual is a system with basic features in common with other individual bodies, but also with its own history and peculiarities. Just as my home has rather poor plumbing and a tendency to leak, so too one individual might have many such 'tendencies': to have a weaker or stronger bladder than others, to react to the slightest difficulty with great anxiety, or to sail through life with confidence.

We tend to think of these human differences as genetic. It is hard to shake off the mechanical idea of the body as something which develops like clockwork to the dictation of genetic programmes, particularly our physiological responses which appear to be so automatic. We are not accustomed to thinking of these as socially influenced, particularly by the quality of our early relationships which may seem a sloppy and unscientific notion.

Yet the picture emerging in modern science is that genes provide us with raw ingredients for a mind – and each one of us comes with slightly different ingredients – but the cooking, particularly in infancy, is what matters. Even as genes are identified and linked to various human difficulties, the links are demonstrated over and over again to be necessary but not sufficient. In other words, there may be a genetic predisposition to depression, schizophrenia, obesity or other ills, yet it is impossible to say that these genes 'cause' the malfunction. Most genes are expressed in response to environmental triggers and in combination with each other. In early life, 'environment' mostly consists of the human beings who take care of us.

With the human nervous system, the very early stages of cooking make all the difference. Things can go wrong in many ways. A lack of good nutrition in the womb, a lack of oxygen during birth, or a lack of emotional support in infancy – all can have a tremendous impact on the assembling and developing organism. Early care actually shapes the developing nervous system and determines how stress is interpreted and responded to in the future.

One way of putting this is to say that the kinds of emotional experience that the baby has with his caregivers are 'biologically embedded' (Hertzman and Boyce 2010; Hertzman 1997). They get written into the child's physiology because this is the period of human life when regulatory habits are being formed. This is when our automatic emotional and physiological responses are set up in the brain. Although we do remain open systems and can still change our habits, it is also true to say that as we get older our internal systems stabilise and become relatively fixed. As anyone who has tried to create new eating habits or to change themselves emotionally knows, it is an uphill struggle to create new regulatory habits. It is hard to remember to behave differently and it takes a long time before new ways of doing things become automatic. Compared to that, infancy is an incredibly open period of life in which change can happen very rapidly.

In particular, these early experiences set up physiological expectations as to what our 'normal' levels of biochemicals are. In this way, they affect our baseline levels of serotonin or cortisol or norepinephrine, and the 'set point' that our body regards as its normal state. They will also affect the amounts of chemical we produce in response to particular situations. Stress in infancy – such as consistently being ignored when you cry – is particularly hazardous because high levels of cortisol in the early months of life can also affect the development of other neurotransmitter systems whose pathways are still being established. They are still immature and are not fully developed even by weaning time (Collins and Depue 1992; Konyescsni and Rogeness 1998). Babies of withdrawn mothers, for example, have lower norepinephrine, epinephrine and dopamine than other babies (Jones et al. 1997). When stressed, these various biochemical systems may become skewed in ways that make it more difficult for the individual to regulate himself in later life.

Human babies are born with the expectation of having stress managed for them. They tend to have low levels of cortisol for the first few months, as long as caring adults maintain their equilibrium through touch, stroking, feeding and rocking (Hofer 1995; Levine 2001). But their immature systems are also very unstable and reactive; they can be plunged into very high cortisol levels if there is no one responding to them (Gunnar and Donzella 2002). Babies cannot manage their own cortisol.

Gradually, however, they get used to distressing situations once they are confident that they will be managed by an adult caregiver, and cortisol is less easily triggered (Gunnar and Donzella 2002). Once their sleeping patterns become more stable, between about the age of 3 and 6 months, the normal rhythm of an early morning peak in cortisol as the baby wakes is established. However, it takes most of early childhood (until around 4 years old) to establish an adult pattern of high cortisol in the morning and low cortisol towards the end of the day.

There is still great confusion about how to manage distress in small babies. Not picking up a baby and leaving him or her to 'cry it out', as in the quote at the beginning of this chapter, is still common practice. Such distress is probably inevitable from time to time, but as a regular way of managing a baby it leaves a lot to be desired. A baby whose stress (and therefore cortisol) is not kept at a manageable level may eventually be seriously affected. However, stress is most likely to reach a toxic level only in unsupportive situations where there is no stable caregiver who can calm and soothe the baby and buffer the baby's stress.

When high levels of cortisol persist, they can shrink and reduce connections in the orbitofrontal cortex (Hanson et al. 2010; De Brito et al. 2013) and the medial prefrontal cortex, including the anterior cingulate (Radley and Morrison, 2005) – making them less effective in managing the more urgent reactions generated by the amygdala.

At the same time, an amygdala that has to deal with a lot of stress in early life tends to become more reactive. It responds to chronic stress by working harder and growing larger (Arnsten 2009; Liston 2006). The unfortunate end result is that while the person becomes more sensitive to stress, the structures that manage and suppress the stress response are weakened.

The hippocampus also plays a part in this chain of events. While babies who are touched and held a great deal have an abundance of cortisol receptors in the hippocampus as adults, stressed babies exposed to too much cortisol have reduced numbers of hippocampal cortisol receptors (McEwen et al. 2012; Caldji et al. 2000). This means that when cortisol levels rise during a stressful event, there are fewer receptors to receive it and the cortisol can flood the hippocampus, affecting its growth. A damaged hippocampus is then less able to give feedback to the HPA stress system and to stop the release of further cortisol.

But the kind of stress that matters most to young children is a lack of support from their parents. A recent study used magnetic imaging to look at the brains of young children at the low end of the social scale. The study found that it was not poverty nor their parents' poor prospects and low level of education which most affected the growth of the hippocampus. Instead, it was parental hostility that made the hippocampus shrink (Luby et al. 2013).

Stress shapes the stress response

Essentially, the effectiveness of the stress response system is affected by how much early stress it has to deal with, and how well the system is helped to recover. It seems that what you put in to the system is what you get out – a well-resourced and well-regulated infant becomes a child and adult who can regulate himself or herself well, while a poorly resourced and poorly regulated infant becomes a child who cannot regulate herself well. The way that Bill, for example, manages his crisis will be influenced in part by the robustness or otherwise of his stress response.

If he is a 'high reactor' to stress, he will produce a lot of cortisol at the least provocation. He may be easily depressed, easily panicked and prone to overeating. Without Caroline, he may fall into depression and put on weight. These types of stress response systems have been linked to having had less than optimum early mothering, with an inexperienced or depressed mother, or an unpredictable mother, who is sometimes available and sometimes not.

However, if he is a 'low reactor', he may have a flattened cortisol response. He may give the impression to his colleagues that he is coping, appearing not to have a strong reaction, but they may be surprised to see his occasional outbursts of aggression. This stress response is more often linked to having grown up in conditions of more or less continuous emotional unavailability. This may equally result from a parental 'stiff upper lip', or from more overtly hostile parents who used physical punishment to curb their son's emotions. At the extreme, this state may be found in orphans.

Nature or nurture?

As we have seen, the baby's vulnerability to mishandling can start even earlier, in the womb. Even at the very earliest stage of life, the elements of the brain responsible for responding to stress are among the most open to influence. In particular, the HPA axis is already forming during gestation. Then again, birth itself can be traumatic for a baby. A difficult forceps delivery or a use of suction during labour raises the baby's cortisol levels in a way that neither normal nor Caesarian delivery do, and this has an effect on the baby's stress response for at least 8 weeks, maybe longer (Taylor et al. 2000; Gitau et al. 2001b).

Babies exposed to these sorts of experiences in the womb or during birth are more likely to appear to be 'difficult' from the start. Of course, some babies are also born with a more sensitive temperament for genetic reasons. There is currently a broad consensus that babies' temperaments differ and that some are more temperamentally demanding than others. Although there are more subtle ways of describing temperament, the broadest categories describe two main types: the less reactive and the highly reactive baby. The reactive baby (thought to make up about 15 per cent of babies) possibly has more sensitive sensory equipment; he cries more and tends to be more timid and fearful because he is easily overwhelmed by stimuli.

Whether highly reactive or super-sensitive because of temperament or pre-natal experience, such babies are more easily stressed and need very good parental management to keep them free of stress. They need more than average amounts of soothing and calming, through being held and fed frequently, to restore their systems to normal responsiveness. Since this is more difficult for their parents than dealing with an 'easy' baby, many of these super-sensitives will find their stress systems getting overloaded and may end up with an overreactive system, high baseline cortisol and a risk of emotional insecurity.

This modern view of temperament, focused on the sensitivity or robustness of the baby, is rather different from the classical psychoanalytic understanding of children, whose focus was on children's different levels of sexual and aggressive 'drive'. In Freudian theory, the strength or weakness of these drives was thought to make them more or less prone to neurosis. Early psychoanalysts tended to focus on how the individual child got through the different stages of early development; problems arose through becoming 'fixated' at the oral or anal stage. Although this approach recognised the importance of early experience in later outcomes, it did not adequately recognise how parents and other adult caregivers might be affecting their developing child. It was not until after the Second World War that psychotherapists shifted their emphasis to the actual interactions between people and began to focus more boldly on the links between the experience of harsh, unpredictable or neglectful early parenting and later emotional difficulties. Subsequent research has indeed confirmed that parenting, at least as much as genes and innate factors, determines many outcomes.

For example, there is a strain of rats that is genetically predisposed to being more fearful than other strains of rat. Left with their biological mothers, these rat pups tend to be fearful and easily stressed. But when experimenters placed them for 'adoption' with non-fearful rat mothers, they found that these baby rats grew up without fear. Clearly, whatever the genetic tendency might be, it was the rearing that mattered (Francis et al. 1997). Similarly, rats from a 'low aggression' strain became aggressive when they were fostered to 'high aggression' foster mothers and vice versa (Flandera and Novakova 1974). But is the same true of humans?

Take a group of temperamentally reactive babies. Their genes appear to have destined them to be super-sensitive to stress. They are the whingers of the world, the crying babies who become neurotic adults. Indeed, research has confirmed that left to themselves they do tend to end up with insecure attachment to their mothers. However, the Dutch researcher Dymphna Van den Boom did not leave it at that. She wanted to find out if their mothers could learn to manage them in a way which calmed their stress. To this end, she designed a form of short-term instruction and support for mothers of sensitive babies which aimed to help the mothers to respond better to them. With this help, most of these more difficult babies did indeed grow up with secure attachments (Van den Boom 1994).

This kind of work makes a strong case that temperament does not determine outcomes. Emotional security
depends much more on the kind of care that babies receive,
and whether or not parents can rise to the challenge of
meeting the needs of their more demanding babies. As
attachment researchers have always pointed out, secure
emotional attachments are after all the product of a relationship, not of an individual temperament.

What is stress for a baby?

Most of us have an idea of what stress is for adults, perhaps
associated with working long hours and trying to do too
much, under pressure to achieve; or it may also be associated with the pressures of 24-hour-a-day parenting without
sleep or respite; or with the struggle to keep afloat in conditions of poverty and violence. What these ideas of stress have
in common is that stress is about being overwhelmed, lacking
sufficient resources to meet the demands life places on you
or trying to survive in particular environments without
sufficient support from other people. This is the adult version
of stress. But what does it mean in babyhood?

For babies, stress is probably much more to do with
sheer physical survival. Babies' resources are so limited that
they cannot keep themselves alive, so it is very stressful for
them if the mother is not there or does not respond quickly,
providing the milk, warmth or feeling of safety they need.
When these needs are not met by others, the baby may
become more aware of a sense of powerlessness and helplessness. Stress for babies may even have the quality of
trauma. Without the parent's help, they could in fact die. In
newborn babies, the stress response can be generated by
physical danger such as a forceps delivery or circumcision
(Gunnar et al. 1985a, 1985b), confirming its usefulness as a
way of meeting sudden threats to bodily integrity and the
need for survival.

A baby's cries of mental pain when distressed also
presumably have an important function. They successfully
create stress for the parent in turn, cutting through the
parent's dangerous inattention, to ensure a response – and

with it the baby's survival. In adulthood, we still use our stress response in situations that threaten our physical survival, like accidents, surgery or assaults. But in our less physically dangerous modern environments, the stress response is probably more often triggered by psychological threats. We are more likely to be stressed by losing a promotion or being caught with a prostitute than by being stalked by a tiger. This makes sense when we consider that in modern societies survival depends on social acceptance and social status; it is very stressful when these things are at stake.

In human society, there is a kind of stock exchange of the emotions of which cortisol seems to be a by-product. The more your social stock goes up, the more your cortisol comes down. Conversely, when your social stock goes down, your cortisol level will rise. Robert Sapolsky's work with baboons showed that the more social power you have, the less cortisol you have. Top baboons have low cortisol, while low-ranking baboons have high cortisol (Sapolsky 1995). We can see this most clearly in human society in the vicissitudes of emotional life in primary schools. When your young son or daughter experiences a painful demotion in a friendship, saying 'he was horrid to me, I hate him' one week, then rushes home in exhilaration saying 'he's my best friend' the next, we glimpse the process starkly. (Adults are perhaps better at hiding it, as well as better at managing these ups and downs.) But when children are also faced with social inequality in the wider sense, they are even more exposed to humiliations which can trigger the release of cortisol (Dickerson and Kemeny 2004).

Dangerous stress

Stress that comes and goes is the condition of life. But what really damages your mental and physical health is not passing periods of stress for a few hours or days, but persistent powerlessness and unrelieved, chronic stress. Short-term stress that is clearly over when the crisis has passed allows you to restore your internal systems to their normal state and does little harm. In fact, often people feel that a little stress is stimulating. But when you have to spend months or years worrying about your pension or your neighbour's loud parties, being unable to get the job you want or the partner you need, anxiety and helplessness at being unable to do anything about it can undermine your health.

To a large extent, stress is generated by what is unpredictable or uncontrollable. If you don't have the power to avoid a negative outcome or the power to get something you need, this is very stressful. For example, people who cannot get the treatment they need for an illness will be under extreme stress. However, it seems that people who are actually in the process of dying generate very little cortisol despite the threat to their body systems. Perhaps the slow decline of physical systems is accepted by this stage and no longer meets resistance and stress. But situations that are unpredictable, which take you unawares, which you want to resist but have little power to change, are the defining characteristics of stress. From this point of view, it is clear that babyhood can be extremely stressful without the support of tender, protective parenting.

Many sources of stress can be managed if there are resources to meet the challenge. If you are wealthy and have access to a team of lawyers and advisors, you may cope better with a pensions fraud than those who have no savings and little higher education. The same goes for inner resources – with enough inner confidence, many situations can be dealt with. The evidence is also that it makes a great deal of difference if the individual is supported by secure social bonds. With a network of support, stress may be manageable, whether in infancy or in adulthood. Researchers have shown that children with secure attachments do not release high levels of cortisol under stress, whereas insecure children do (Gunnar and Nelson 1994; Gunnar et al. 1996; Nachmias et al. 1996; Essex et al. 2002). There is a powerful link between emotional insecurity and cortisol dysfunction. So it is not necessarily the nature of the stress that matters, but the availability of others to help manage it, as well as the inner resources of the person experiencing it.

These inner resources are not always obvious. Researchers expected to find that children with rather timid, fearful temperaments would have high cortisol levels under stress, but this turned out not to be the case. They actually had normal cortisol levels under stress unless they were also insecurely attached to their parents. However, children who appeared on the surface to be cool and collected did have high cortisol levels under stress because they too turned out to be insecurely attached. It was the insecure attachment that mattered, not the personality style or 'persona', which is not always a reliable guide to inner emotional resources (Gunnar et al. 1996; Schieche and Spangler, 2005). By 1 year old, children who are in secure relationships that respond to their needs and regulate them well are unlikely to produce high levels of cortisol even when they are upset, whereas those in insecure relationships do (Gunnar and Donzella 2002). The key feature of insecure attachment is a lack of confidence in others' emotional availability and support.

Separation and dysregulation

Probably the most stressful experience of all for a baby or toddler is to be separated from his or her mother or caregiver, the person who is supposed to keep him or her alive. Early separation from the mother increases corticotropin-releasing factor (CRF) in the amygdala. This is thought, by some, to be the biochemical of fear, suggesting that even short separations from the source of food and protection are very frightening for any breastfed young mammals, including humans.

There is strong evidence that separation from those on whom we depend raises cortisol. Studies on both monkeys and rats have found strong correlations between early separations from the mother and high cortisol levels. Each time a baby squirrel monkey is separated from his mother, his cortisol goes up. If this happens repeatedly, even for only five hours a week, his cortisol feedback sensitivity increases. He becomes more clingy and easily distressed and plays less (Plotsky and Meaney 1993; Dettling et al. 2002).

Social conflict and threats from predators also raised cortisol levels. Primate studies have shown that cortisol levels rise when an individual is under threat from others in the group, in conflict with another member of the group, or cut off from the social group in some way, as well as more obvious episodes of physical separation from the mother in infancy. So it seems as if cortisol in general is a by-product of an anxiety about safety, survival and the social bonds which protect.

Recent work has linked these findings more directly to humans. In modern societies where women can potentially enjoy a variety of roles, children are increasingly separated from their mothers to enable them to go out to work. But arguments have raged for decades about the impact this has on their children. Andrea Dettling, a researcher in the USA, used cortisol as a way to measure the effect on their stress response. She went to an all-day nursery to study 3- and 4-year-old children who were separated from their attachment figures all day. What she found confirmed the fears of some mothers that their children do indeed find the experience stressful. They did not necessarily look stressed or behave as if they were stressed, but their stress response was activated and their cortisol levels rose as the day wore on, especially if they were children with poor social skills. By the afternoon, their cortisol was extra high – at a time of day when it was normally sinking in children at home with a parent (Dettling et al. 1999). These results have since been replicated, with some recent evidence suggesting that young children's cortisol levels in day care nurseries are most affected if they are looked after by nursery workers with an intrusive and overcontrolling style of care (Gunnar et al. 2010).

However, before leaping to conclusions about nursery care, Dettling asked some more questions about substitute childcare. She found that high stress levels were not inevitable. In a second study, she focused on children who were separated all day from their attachment figures, but were placed with childminders. Dettling found that what really mattered was the quality of the replacement caregiving and whether there was someone really paying attention to the child. Children who were placed with childminders who were highly responsive to them had normal cortisol levels (Dettling et al. 2000). Further recent work by Lisa Badanes has confirmed this picture. Her work in nurseries found that even securely attached children struggle to manage stressful experiences when their parent isn't available; however, if they have a secure relationship with an alternative parental figure such as the main caregiver in a nursery, this acts as a buffer against stress in much the same way as does a relationship with a sensitive parent (Badanes et al. 2012).

These findings strongly support the importance of emotional regulation and the absolute necessity for small children of having someone continuously available who notices your feelings and can help you regulate them. Her findings suggest that this person does not have to be a mother or a father, at least by the age of 3, as long as he or she is tuned in and emotionally available to the child. However, her studies do suggest that it is the lack of this consistent responsiveness and protection that is the mark of stress for a dependent child.

Stressed parent, stressed child

Sometimes, of course, it is not the mother's absence that is the problem for the child, but the quality of her presence. Even if children are at home with their biological parents, they may still be poorly regulated. For example, children of alcoholic parents have high levels of cortisol, probably as a result of having parents who may be physically present, but mentally unavailable to provide consistent regulation (Wand et al. 2001; Uhart et al. 2006).

Mothers who are themselves under stress are likely to have more difficulty in regulating their babies well. This was clearly demonstrated in primate studies of monkeys subjected to conditions where they did not know where the next meal was coming from. Known as 'unpredictable foraging', this turned out to be much more stressful for both mother and her offspring than conditions of consistently little food being available (Rosenblum et al. 1994). But having a stressed mother had a big effect on her offspring. The young monkeys themselves had high corticosteroids and high norepinephrine. We might imagine that a mother who is worrying about where the next meal is coming from would be less likely to be focused on the regulation of her offspring. As a result, the infants themselves couldn't relax. They too had to stay alert and anxious. These monkeys ended up behaving in a depressed fashion. It is not hard to imagine that human parents coping with unpredictable conditions of life, particularly those living in low social and economic strata, will experience similar responses. Current research suggests that this is indeed the case. One recent study looking at the impact of the 'Great Recession' of 2007–9 found that people's uncertainty and anticipatory worry about the economic situation created more stress – and more harsh parenting – than actual adversity. The moment when unemployment was *rising* rapidly was the most stressful time for vulnerable families (Lee et al. 2013).

It is ironical that our modern way of life itself involves putting the chief carers of babies under enormous stress themselves. Rachel Cusk describes the contradictions well:

> To be a mother I must leave the telephone unanswered, work undone, arrangements unmet. To be myself I must let the baby cry, must forestall her hunger or leave her for evenings out, must forget her in order to think about other things. To succeed in being one means to fail at being the other. (Cusk 2001: 57)

The most painful aspect of the situation seems to be the isolation coupled with total responsibility. She feels like 'a deserted settlement, an abandoned building in which a rotten timber occasionally breaks and comes crashing to the floor' – an image far from the earth mother of popular fantasy whose abundant breasts and maternal love will soothe her baby's every stress. As a result, both mother and baby are caught in the same trap, both lacking the support that they need to manage their stress.

While animal research has well documented the impact of early stress (such as repeated brief separations from the mother) on the infant's developing systems – such as a highly reactive stress response, together with a lifelong tendency towards anxiety, depression and loss of pleasure (Francis et al. 1997; Sanchez et al. 2001) – the links to human behaviour have taken longer to achieve. One of the first studies to provide direct evidence that humans as well as other animals are equally vulnerable to the effects of a stressful early environment was undertaken by Marilyn Essex and her colleagues at the University of Wisconsin (Essex et al. 2002). It was a convincingly rigorous, 'prospective' study. Based on a large sample of 570 families, it followed them all the way through from pregnancy to age 5 years. This substantial piece of work provided clear evidence that the experience you have as a baby predicts your later responses to stress.

When she measured the stress levels of children at the age of four and a half, she found that those who were currently living with stressed mothers had high cortisol, but only if their mothers had also been under stress or depressed when they were infants. In other words, they were only vulnerable if a difficult babyhood had affected their developing stress response or HPA axis. These children would be liable to produce more cortisol under pressure than other children who had experienced an easier babyhood. As they went through childhood, they had been left with a legacy from the early tensions in their relationship with their mothers – a tendency to react more strongly to difficulties in life. (Such vulnerable children don't have a constantly high level of cortisol. While there was no current stress, their level of cortisol was not raised.)

A more recent prospective study following a group of healthy, but low income, children from birth into adolescence found that their cortisol reactivity as teenagers was still related to how warm and responsive their parents had been in their early childhood (Hackman et al. 2013).

Work with Romanian orphans has also suggested that there may even be a critical period during which the HPA stress response system is being set up. Babies from these orphanages who were adopted after the age of 4 months continued to have high levels of cortisol, even when they were adopted, while those who were adopted before the age of 4 months seemed able to regain a normal stress response (Chisholm et al. 1995; Gunnar et al. 2001). Although this may have something to do with the mother's ability to bond more easily with a younger baby, there is other evidence to suggest that the HPA system adopts its 'set point' by the age of 6 months. During the earliest months, the cortisol response is variable, but after that age it seems to stabilise and remain consistent (Lewis and Ramsay 1995).

In the last decade, many studies have confirmed the importance of early experiences on the developing HPA axis. But new work on epigenetics is also opening up the possibility of being able to inherit an altered stress response in the womb. Environmental influences which have affected the mother's genes and her HPA axis can be passed on to her foetus; even more extraordinary, this altered stress responsiveness can be transmitted by the foetus to the next generation too (Matthews and Phillips 2010; Tarullo and Gunnar 2006). Some very new research findings with mice also add the possibility that traumatically stressed fathers could be passing on their altered genes to their offspring through their sperm (Gapp et al. 2014).

Highs and lows of cortisol

The whole period from conception to late toddlerhood is a crucial one in establishing the child's lifelong capacities for emotional regulation. What may start as a neurobiological vulnerability during gestation can be reinforced or ameliorated through the quality of early post-natal relationships. There are clear links between an individual's physiological coping strategies and his or her psychological coping strategies. Both are established in infancy and toddlerhood and tend to persist through life. Both are developed in response to the child's earliest relationships. As I have already outlined, secure early relationships are characterised by the presence of consistently responsive adults who seem to enable the child to organise himself or herself well, to be able to use others to help regulate stress when necessary, and in the process, to maintain a normal level of cortisol. However, insecure early relationships are more variable. They diverge in two broad directions: towards high emotional reactivity or low reactivity. A child who isn't feeling well regulated will normally be aroused and reacting, generating stress hormones such as cortisol. But, as I will describe shortly, sometimes an 'anti-arousal' mechanism will come into play if the child is under prolonged stress.

High cortisol

Children who are described in the attachment literature as 'resistantly' attached tend to dramatise their emotions. They do this in response to parents who are inconsistently emotionally available – whether distracted, absent-minded, busy, or frequently absent. They try to capture the parent's attention by amplifying them. But they never quite know if she will notice them or if they can get the comfort they need when they need it. Since unpredictability is one of the main factors which generates high cortisol, it seems probable that these may also be children with high cortisol levels. Certainly one study found these types of children to be the most fearful during infancy and toddlerhood (Kochanska 2001) and cortisol and CRF are the hormones of fear. However, there is little hard evidence that their cortisol levels are significantly high in this period. More research is needed to establish whether there are links or not.

High cortisol levels are linked to relatively high activity in the right frontal brain, the part of the brain which generates fearfulness, irritability and withdrawal from others (Davidson and Fox 1992; Kalin et al. 1998b). The right frontal area is specialised for processing stimuli which are novel and distracting, and it seems likely that children with an activated right hemisphere will be constantly on the alert. They may be children who live with unpredictable or unreliable caregivers who are driven to be emotionally vigilant and watchful as they attempt to read the parent's non-verbal signals.

We know that there are strong links between high cortisol and many emotional dysfunctions such as depression, anxiety and suicidal tendencies in adulthood, as well as with eating disorders, alcoholism, obesity and sexual abuse. Some of these links will be explored in subsequent chapters. High cortisol is not only implicated in psychological problems, but is also damaging to the body's systems. As Rosen and Schulkin put it, too much fear is 'metabolically costly'

(Rosen and Schulkin 1998). It can damage the hippocampus and capacity to retrieve information (perhaps making an 'absent-minded' or 'scatty' child), as well as affecting the ability of the prefrontal cortex to think and manage behaviour (Lyons et al. 2000b). It compromises the immune responses, making the individual vulnerable to infection; it compromises wound healing and even in some cases leads to decrease in muscle mass and to osteoporosis. It may play a part in diabetes and hypertension through increased blood glucose and insulin levels (which can also lead to overweight and fat tummies). The stress response is such an essential part of our organism's response to life that it appears to underlie an astonishing range of disorders. When it does not function well, we become vulnerable both physiologically and psychologically.

The mystery of low cortisol

But just as we are getting the measure of high cortisol and its impact on our lives, I must present another twist in the story. In some people, an unusually low baseline level of cortisol can be found, which is also linked with disorders of various kinds. This phenomenon of low cortisol is still somewhat mysterious. It is not yet fully understood, but is much more common than researchers thought. It is fairly clear that a child under stress will react with high cortisol. So why do some people have a consistently low baseline level of cortisol? One account is that if an organism experiences continuously high cortisol for a prolonged period, it will eventually react by closing down cortisol receptors. This is known as 'down regulation'. The physiological mechanisms involved in this phenomenon are not fully understood as yet, but researchers speculate that this is one way that the body deals with a prolonged exposure to cortisol. It may be a self-protective mechanism. Chronic exposure to high levels of cortisol is linked to potentially life-threatening illnesses. However, the trade-off in switching into a low cortisol mode is that the body is then more at risk of other symptoms instead – such as pain or fatigue (Fries et al. 2005; Heim et al. 2000a).

The switch into low cortisol mode also appears to be a kind of emotional defence mechanism. It is an attempt at disengagement from painful feelings through avoidance, withdrawal and denial (Mason et al. 2001); better to feel less than to cope with being constantly stressed. But this (unconscious) strategy can produce a state of emotional numbness, and even dissociation (Flack et al. 2000), which can make people feel empty and alienated from other people. Some children in this state go down a route of passive coping, which can make them less able to respond when they need to. For example, one study of children at a nursery school found that those with low baseline cortisol did not react to a highly stressful day by producing cortisol (Dettling et al. 1999). By some means, such a child is managing to deny the impact of painful or stressful events even to the extent of switching off his stress response. Unfortunately this may switch off feelings in general. These children may be less responsive to happy stimuli too, although they may often put on a cheerful face with 'overbright affect' (Ciccetti 1994).

Low cortisol has been associated with low grade, frequent emotional (and sometimes physical) abuse and neglect, as well as with unresponsive parenting. However, timing may be important. The age at which these experiences happen may be crucial in producing this low cortisol phenomenon. Andrea Dettling's research with marmosets (who are primates like us) has found that only the monkeys who were separated from their mothers in very early life (for up to two hours a day) developed low cortisol baselines. Their twin siblings, who had not been separated, didn't develop a low cortisol baseline, and nor did slightly older, semi-independent infant monkeys in another study (Dettling et al. 2002). Alternatively, it may be that the stress response only becomes blunted over a period of time and it is the length of exposure to stress that counts (Ruttle et al. 2011). Researchers continue to clarify the circumstances and timing which give rise to the low cortisol phenomenon, but very early neglect or deprivation of some kind do seem to be implicated.

There may well be overlaps with the category of avoidant attachment, too, although there is no clear evidence as yet.

Children tend to develop an emotionally avoidant style of relating when they experience negative attitudes towards them which may develop into hostility and criticism, or intrusive parenting which does not respect their boundaries. In return, these children feel angry, yet they live in a family culture which does not tolerate the child's self-expression, so find themselves obliged to suppress their own negative feelings. Unfortunately, suppressing feelings doesn't make them go away; in fact, it may actually increase arousal (Gross and Levenson 1993). This may be why such feelings eventually tend to burst out uncontrollably and unpredictably. Suppressed aggression may be stored until a relatively safe outlet is found which triggers its release. In children, it is often released with their peer group rather than with the parents who upset them in the first place.

It may seem paradoxical that the most destructive children are those who try to suppress their feelings. But the most aggressive boys at school are not those who are high in stress hormones, but low in them. There is increasing evidence that low cortisol levels are associated with impulsive forms of aggression (Feilhauer et al 2013) and with antisocial behaviour in general (Shirtcliff 2005). Their anger simmers beneath the surface, probably outside their awareness. It also probably arose from very early experiences of neglect, bullying or chronic hostility. Over time, these boys' bodies adjusted to an ongoing state of high cortisol and switched from a high to a low cortisol response (Ouellet-Morin et al. 2011). One important study (McBurnett et al. 2000) found that the earlier that antisocial behaviour develops in boys, the more likely it is to be associated with low cortisol. This suggests that the little terrors who are already upsetting others at nursery and primary school may do so because they have already had to develop a survival strategy to cope with low grade emotional abuse or neglect. Although they may appear 'tough' or strong because they seem to be insensitive to others and quite lacking in anxiety, their feelings are more suppressed than absent.

Children who show signs of aggression early on are different physiologically from boys who started to become aggressive only as teenagers. These later rebels, who behave antisocially as teenagers but hadn't done so as young children, are more in touch with their vulnerable feelings and still capable of expressing anxiety. Their high cortisol levels suggest that their teenage bad behaviour is a response (perhaps temporary) to the stresses of adolescence, rather than an outcome of early adverse experience.

However, those whose systems have adapted to stress early in life with a low cortisol defence are vulnerable to a host of disorders. In particular, there is a strong link between low cortisol and post-traumatic stress disorder (PTSD), which will be discussed in a later chapter. They may also be prone to conditions such as chronic fatigue, chronic pain, asthma, allergies, arthritis and seasonal affective disorder (Miller et al. 2011; Fries 2005; Heim et al. 2000a). Low cortisol has also been associated with a lack of positive good feeling. Although it is not an active state of feeling bad, like depression, it may produce a sort of flattened emotional life. This is very suggestive of a type of emotional life which has been named 'alexithymia' – a difficulty in putting emotions into words. Indeed, one researcher has found decreased cortisol levels in people with alexithymia (Henry et al. 1992; Henry 1993).

This way of being was first identified in connection with patients with classically 'psychosomatic' diseases, such as asthma, arthritis, or ulcerative colitis (Nemiah and Sifneos 1970), but its use has been extended to a much wider range of disorders. The difficulty in putting feelings into words probably originates in early parent–baby communication. If a mother figure does not teach her baby to put bodily experiences into words, then he may not develop the capacity to organise his feelings and contain tension through his own conscious mental processes without constantly relying on others. Indeed, those working with psychosomatic patients have found that they tend to depend heavily on one or a few other people, and when one of these key regulatory relationships is withdrawn or lost, they are vulnerable to illness (Taylor et al. 1997). This will be explored in Part 2 of this book.

One caveat against a neat division of people into those with 'high' and 'low' baseline cortisol is that we should probably not think of them as fixed states. Rather, a high cortisol state suggests someone who is currently engaged in struggling with stress in an active way, while a low cortisol state suggests that the balance between 'arousal and anti-arousal psychological mechanisms' (Mason et al. 2001) has tipped towards defending against feeling overwhelmed by stress. This perspective may help to make sense of some of the contradictory findings in the research literature; for example, the evidence that some sexually abused children have high cortisol levels while others have low levels. If Mason and his colleagues are right, this may have more to do with their way of adapting to the unique complexities of their current circumstances

The social nature of cortisol regulation

Clearly, the stress response is one key element of our emotional make-up. When we are regulating our emotional states, we are also regulating our hormone and neurotransmitter levels. However, the ability to do this effectively is strongly influenced by our parent figures and their own capacity to tolerate their baby's cries and demands and their way of responding. Psychotherapists might prefer to think in terms of the parents' 'unconscious defences' being transmitted to their children in the way that they navigate the stormy ocean of their baby's moods and needs.

A robust stress response is rather like a strong immune system; in fact, as Candace Pert has argued, they are interconnected. It provides 'host resistance' to the future stresses of childhood and adult life. But like the 'social brain', it too is shaped by the quality of contact between parents and babies. Good emotional 'immunity' comes out of the experience of feeling safely held, touched, seen and helped to recover from stress, while the stress response is undermined by separation, uncertainty, lack of contact and lack of regulation.

Above all, it seems to be vital to be able to switch off the production of cortisol at the right moment, without being flooded by it or having to suppress it. This seems to me to have clear parallels with the management of emotion in general: to be able to tolerate and accept whatever feelings come, knowing that when they start to become overwhelming there are ways of dealing with them – either through strategies of distraction, or of finding relief through other people. This is the secure strategy outlined by attachment research. But the insecure strategies are more problematic: the resistant pattern resembles the high cortisol situation of being overwhelmed by feelings, while the avoidant pattern of denial resembles the switched off low cortisol state. Both cause us continued trouble in emotional life.

There is a remarkably strong weight of evidence that has now accumulated in this field. It suggests very strongly that the HPA stress response can be programmed to be hypo- or hyper-responsive through early social experience, and that cortisol can have permanent effects on the developing baby's central nervous system. The way in which this manifests itself in particular individuals depends on the age at which their difficulties began, how chronic or intermittent they have been, and how intense. Research in this area continues, which will hopefully be able to make more specific links with various human conditions. However, there is little doubt that the stress response is one of the key indicators of the way an individual has learnt to regulate emotion.

Conclusion to Part 1

This part of the book has set out the scientific basis for understanding babyhood as a crucial time in emotional development. The basic systems that manage emotions – our stress response system, the responsiveness of our neuro-transmitters, the neural pathways which encode our implicit understanding of how intimate relationships work – none of these are in place at birth. Nor is the vital prefrontal cortex of the brain yet developed. Yet all of these systems will develop rapidly in the first two years of life, forming the basis of our emotional management for life. Although later experience will elaborate our responses and add to the reper-toire, the path that is trodden in very early life tends to set each of us off in a particular direction that gathers its own momentum. The longer we stay on a particular pathway, the more difficult it becomes to choose another and the harder it becomes to retrace our footsteps.

The weight of research now makes it quite clear that these biological systems involved in managing emotional life are all subject to social influence, particularly the influences that are present at the time that they are developing most rapidly. They will develop and function better or worse depending on the nature of these early social experiences. I have argued that the reason that our biological responses are so permeated by social influence is to enable us to adapt more precisely to the unique circumstances in which each individual finds himself or herself. If you live in a highly dangerous environment, it may be essential to survival to have a sensitive stress response; if you live with a hostile parent, it makes sense instinctively to learn to keep a tactful distance. However, the individual who is programmed like this in early childhood might find these tendencies a handicap in later life when circumstances improve. They may even become the source of psychopathology of one kind or another in adulthood, which I will now describe in Part 2.

PART 2

Shaky foundations and their consequences

> We are looking at the foundations of the human soul, those developments which are as essential as the foundation of a house, and as invisible when all is well.
>
> H. Krystal

The second part of the book looks in more detail at the links between various adult disorders and their roots in babyhood. What happens to babies who have a difficult babyhood? How does it affect their adult lives?

I will explore how a sensitive stress response, or a difficulty in regulating emotions, along with insecure attachments to others, can make individuals vulnerable to various psychopathologies. This does not imply that one 'causes' another, but simply that the likelihood of finding dysfunctional solutions to emotional dilemmas is increased. There are many well-trodden pathways to misery. People may choose to eat too much or too little, drink too much alcohol, react to other people without thinking, fail to have empathy for others, fall ill, make unreasonable emotional demands, become depressed, attack others physically, and so on, largely because their capacity to manage their own feelings has been impaired by their poorly developed emotion systems.

While few people fit into any pure typology, and others may appear to have come through unscathed, I believe that each pathway will be some sort of solution to the dilemmas posed by an individual's unique circumstances. Emotional behaviour is always a response to other people. Even those who seem to have found some remarkable inner resources and so to have regained their emotional balance, or developed 'emotional intelligence', will have done so in the context of particular relationship opportunities – since this intelligence is learnt with others and from others.

However, it is difficult to map out these pathways into adult emotional life with total confidence because they do so often overlap. The antisocial youth may also have a tendency to depression; the person vulnerable to psychosomatic ailments may have outbursts of rage. What they all have in common is an underlying lack of self-esteem, which may manifest itself in different ways. Although those in the caring professions may take this as a statement of the obvious, the notion that low self-esteem lies at the root of many disorders is anathema in some quarters. It is periodically fashionable for journalists to deride any talk of self-esteem as 'woolly' and unscientific, providing a licence for self-indulgence or liberal hand-wringing. So it is perhaps necessary to mount some defence of these concepts.

Those who have a basic confidence in dealing with the world and relating to others often assume that everyone feels the same, but unfortunately this is far from true. A great many people do not experience the kind of babyhood which provides the foundation for such confidence. One indication of the large numbers of people who do not get this start in life is provided by research on insecurely attached children. This research consistently finds that at the most conservative estimate, at least 35 per cent of children are insecure, in a variety of cultures (Van Ijzendoorn and Bakermans-Kranenburg 2009; Goldberg et al. 1995: 11). This is a very high proportion of the population. However, insecure attachment is not in itself a pathological condition. It only indicates something about the difficulty for such people of managing feelings well.

As I have already suggested, insecure attachments tend to come about because parents find it hard to respond adequately to their babies, for a variety of reasons. Mostly this is because their own difficulties in regulating their own feelings get passed on to their children. The parents themselves have not had their baby needs fulfilled, and so are unable to provide this for their own babies. The situation is like a prism in which you can look from many angles at the same thing. Whether you focus on the parent, the baby or the adult with mental health difficulties, the core problem remains the same: the insecure baby within.

It is pretty unpalatable for most adults to think of their 'inner baby' as many jokes about the 'inner child' attest. We all take pride in our social, practical and academic competencies, our independence and our grown-up status. But those whose work or family brings them in touch with the depressed, mentally ill, or criminal populations will be aware that there are people for whom being emotionally balanced is more obviously a struggle. There is an inner, invisible handicap which operates at both psychological and physiological level. In the past, this has been understood in terms of character flaws or genetic make-up, but we now have to take seriously the substantial contribution made by early experiences.

I have described in Part 1 the way that early relationships can affect both an individual's physiological responses – his distorted stress response, neuronal networks and biochemical functioning – and the psychological expectations of others that are brought to bear on daily life. These early experiences establish a framework for emotional life. If the framework is secure, it gives the individual a confidence in regulating the ups and downs of emotional life, with the help of others when needed. This is both a physiological capacity and a psychological one. But if the framework is shaky and insecure, then the person will find it much harder to cope effectively with stress, and will feel little confidence either in coping as an individual or in relying on others to help. This confidence in oneself and others is surely another way of describing self-esteem. Self-esteem is not just thinking well of oneself in the abstract; it is a capacity to respond to life's challenges.

Demanding adults

Those who lack self-esteem and the capacity to regulate themselves well may become very self-centred adults.

Without effective and well-resourced emotional systems, they cannot behave flexibly or respond to others' needs. They tend to be rather rigid, either attempting not to need others at all, or needing them too much. Because they have not had enough experience of being well cared for and well regulated, their original baby needs remain active within. In adulthood, this can in some cases be experienced as a kind of compulsion to get others to meet those needs. People who constantly fall in and out of love, who are addicted to foods or drugs of various kinds, who are workaholics, who are endlessly demanding medical or social services, are seeking something or someone who will regulate their feelings at all times. In effect, they are searching for the good babyhood that they have not yet had. From promiscuous celebrities to welfare shirkers, such people often provoke exasperation in others who wish they would 'grow up'. Even psychotherapists may take this attitude to adults whom they define as immature: 'In the groups I run, middle-aged people often feel and act like adolescents. If you listened to the material blindfold, you'd never guess their age. Many people grow older without growing up at all' (Garland 2001).

The paradox is that people need to have a satisfying experience of dependency before they can become truly independent and largely self-regulating. Yet this feels counterintuitive to many adults, who respond to the insecure with a punitive attitude, as if becoming more mature and self-regulating were a matter of will-power. Many therapists, frustrated at the slow pace of change, try to activate the client's will-power. For example, Neville Symington talks about 'choosing the life-giver' and 'saying yes to life' as a choice that a patient can make (Symington 1993: 53). It is very dispiriting when clients fail to make progress and seem unable to make positive choices. It can be hard to tolerate dependent and self-centred behaviour in adults who should be able to recognise the inappropriateness of their behaviour.

But it is not simply a matter of will-power. Even if willpower is invoked to bring about better behaviour, often this comes in the form of a 'false self' who tries to live up to others' requirements to act maturely. Unfortunately you cannot will genuine empathy for others, or a caring attitude to your own feelings, into existence. Imitating these postures is not the same as drawing on an inner experience of them. These are capacities that are internalised through experiencing them first-hand, from having had relationships with people who respond to your needs, help to regulate your feelings, and don't make premature demands on you to manage more than you can manage.

Good timing is a critical aspect of parenting, as well as in comedy. The ability to judge when a baby or child has the capacity to manage a little more self-control, thoughtfulness or independence is not something that books on child development can provide: the timing of moves in living relationships is an art, not a science. Parents' sensitivity to the child's unfolding capacities can often be hampered by an intolerance of dependency. This is partly cultural and partly the result of one's own early experience. Dependency can evoke powerful reactions. It is often regarded with disgust and repulsion, not as a delightful but fleeting part of experience. It may even be that dependence has a magnetic pull and adults themselves fear getting seduced by it; or that it is just intolerable to give to someone else what you are furious you didn't get yourself. As Ian Suttie put it: 'the indulgences we have been forced to renounce ourselves, we will certainly not permit to other people' (Suttie 1935: 71). Often, parents are in such a hurry to make their child independent that they expose their babies to long periods of waiting for food or comfort, or long absences from the mother, in order to achieve this aim. Grandparents only too often reinforce the message that you mustn't 'spoil' the baby by giving in to him.

Unfortunately, leaving a baby to cry or to cope by himself for more than a very short period usually has the reverse effect: it undermines the baby's confidence in the parent and in the world, leaving him more dependent not less. In the absence of the regulatory partner, a baby can do very little to regulate himself or herself other than to cry louder or to withdraw mentally. But the pain of being dependent like this and being powerless to help yourself leads to primitive psychological defences based on these two options.

Most of the adult pathways that I will discuss are more elaborate versions of these primitive responses. The dual nature of the defensive system seems to be built into our genetic programme: it's either fight or flight. Cry loudly or withdraw. Exaggerate feelings or minimise feelings. Be hyper-aroused or suppress arousal. These two basic strategies also underpin the insecure styles of attachment – the avoidant or the resistant. Whichever way the individual turns to find a solution (and these strategies may be used consistently or inconsistently), he or she will not have mastered the basic process of self-regulation and will remain prone to being overdemanding of others or underdemanding.

5

Trying not to feel

The links between early emotional regulation and the immune system

The avoiding reactions tend to spread . . . It can be carried to such a point that the individual is not only 'steeled against' the appeal and suffering of others, but he actually dreads appealing to their sympathy, and may, for example, conceal illness for fear of making a 'fuss' or 'scene'.

Ian Suttie, *The Origins of Love and Hate*, 1935

Hiding feelings

In western cultures, the withdrawn, underdemanding posture is more common. The English are famous for their 'stiff upper lip'. But North Americans too are dedicated to 'independence' at the earliest possible age, albeit in more extravert and friendly forms of self-sufficiency. This under-demanding or 'avoidant' style successfully conceals the baby's needs from the parent who seems not to want to deal with them. If such babies could speak they would be saying 'Don't worry, I won't bother you.' They sense that their dependence and neediness is unwelcome, so they learn to hide their feelings. In fact, they may grow up believing implicitly that they should not really have feelings, or perhaps only the 'nice' feelings that have received some positive response. Having lacked the kind of contingently responsive mothering that accepts the full range of the baby's feelings, they learn to suppress many feelings. This may develop into a difficulty in recognising one's own feelings. After all, if the mothering person is not interested in them, then how can the child be interested in them? If a parent has not identified and named the child's feelings, how can that child identify his own feelings and think about them? They will remain vague physical sensations of pleasure or displeasure that are undifferentiated and not well mapped in the higher brain.

People who grow up in this way are sometimes called 'alexithymic', meaning that they have not learnt to put feelings into words. They are often unaware of what they are feeling. Although they have feelings like everyone else, they ignore their feelings in much the same way that their caregivers ignored their feelings. Feelings don't become as subtly nuanced in the mind and treated as useful information about the state of the organism. They have not learnt to 'mentalise', as the distinguished British researcher Peter Fonagy put it. His concept is an important one which embraces a whole range of capacities including empathy, emotional awareness and emotional expression. Its key feature is the underlying ability to grasp that emotions motivate human behaviour. Alexithymic people, however, underplay the importance of emotion and tend to underuse those parts of the brain that are active in mentalising (especially the medial prefrontal cortex) (Moriguchi et al. 2006; Moriguchi and Komaki 2013).

Some may become pragmatic types who are focused on the external world and try not to dwell on inner states, whether their own or other people's. Very often they get by and do very well in a chosen field of work. They may be devoted parents too, who provide well for their children and encourage them to achieve, without noticing their children's inner states too keenly. To the superficial gaze, they may appear to be very normal and well balanced. However, they often rely heavily on the presence of a partner: someone just has to be there. They don't expect intimate relationships to be a place where subjectivities are mutually explored, but they are very dependent on the *presence* of a safe object for basic regulation. When this object is threatened – perhaps the partner leaves, or dies – there is an emotional disturbance that they do not know how to manage.

Emotions and illness

People who live in this way have been found to be susceptible to illnesses with a psychosomatic component, in the
sense that they are vulnerable when they lose their regulatory person, because their own regulatory capacities are
not well developed. In particular, they lack the inner
words to identify their feelings. They cannot express their
distress verbally, so find themselves giving distress signals
at a pre-symbolic level, through the body. The words that
could be used to interact with others to find soothing and
management of arousal cannot be found. When such people
experience separation or bereavement in particular, their
body systems, including the immune system, may not
function well.

I first became aware of the way in which emotional life
was implicated in physical illness when my mother became
ill with cancer at the age of 49. At the time, she was a woman
in her prime, a forceful, charismatic personality whose
beauty was mellowing from film-starry loveliness, Grace
Kelly without the chill, to a more contented, ripe beauty in
her late forties. I wanted to understand how someone so
apparently 'strong' could have been so vulnerable to disease
and I started reading about the 'cancer personality'. The
descriptions seemed to fit my mother well. Cancer personalities were thought to be too nice. They were co-operative,
thoughtful, concerned about others and never got angry and
negative. My mother too was relentlessly upbeat and tried to
search for the positives. She was very appreciative of others'
care and concern during her illness. Other people called her
'brave'.

Lawrence LeShan was a writer I read at the time who
identified a common pattern in cancer patients. He found
that a very high proportion (72 per cent) of those he studied
had had a difficult relationship with at least one of their
parents, which left them feeling emotionally isolated. He
noticed that many of these patients had then turned to a
strong emotional investment in someone or something else
as a young adult – and when it got taken away from them
they got ill. This pattern was found in only 10 per cent of his

control group (LeShan 1977). The pattern also fitted my mother. She left home at 16 to escape her difficult relationship with her own mother, married very young and after nearly 30 years of marriage was left by my father. A couple of years later, her illness was diagnosed.

At the time I wondered 'But how could feelings kill you?' I could see how exercise and nutrition were vital to a healthy body, but my mother was an athletic woman who played tennis, sang and kept her figure into middle age through attention to her diet. She did not look like a candidate for disease. Yet obviously, fatal illnesses could strike at the physically fit. What was it that had undermined her immune system?

Inflammation and the immune system

Researchers were beginning to suggest that the immune system was linked to emotions. People who did not express anger or negative feelings were particularly vulnerable. Lydia Temoshok, for example, found that the more a cancer patient was able to express her anger and negative responses, the more lymphocytes she had at tumour sites to deal with the tumour (Temoshok et al. 2008; Temoshok 1992). One explanation for this was that when anger is expressed, the sympathetic nervous system is aroused, a process that supports the production of lymphocytes and stimulates the immune responses, in the short term. However, when anger or distress are not expressed or dealt with in some constructive way, stress may become chronic and the stress hormone cortisol may remain in the system. As we have seen, this can end up with cortisol levels 'down-regulating'. The resulting 'hypoactive' or sluggish stress response can't then do its normal job of turning off the body's inflammatory response.

The inflammatory response is part of the immune system, usually mobilised to deal with bodily challenges such as an infection. But when cortisol levels are not high enough to turn off inflammation, a state of chronic inflammation can ensue, providing a fertile ground for all sorts of more life-threatening diseases such as heart disease and cancer to flourish (Miller et al. 2011; Danese et al. 2007).

Recent research is now suggesting that emotions can also affect the immune system more directly. Psychosocial stress itself can trigger the release of pro-inflammatory cytokines (Berk et al. 2013; Fleshner 2013). One intriguing study by George Slavich and his colleagues at the Cousins Centre for Psychoneuroimmunology in California looked at how being excluded from a game affected people. They found that the painful feeling of social rejection not only activated the brain's anterior cingulate and insula, but also increased inflammatory activity in the body (Slavich et al. 2010).

Certainly my mother had experienced a significant rejection before her illness. She also tended to hold back any expression of anger or negative feelings. Now other images came to me: of my mother retiring to bed in the middle of the afternoon, lying in a darkened room, as if the strain of maintaining her sociability, optimism and success at all she undertook was too exhausting. It struck me that she was trying to use sleep to regulate her stress. (Sleep can have a mild effect in reducing levels of cortisol.) But it also began to seem to me that the dread of vulnerability and failure, of sadness and anger – feelings which it seemed to me she had kept at bay all her life – had finally 'got' her. They had worked their own revenge for being ignored, by wreaking their own havoc within her body, setting off an uncontrollable process of inner destruction.

As an extravert 'avoidant' personality, a good actress who presented herself as cheerful and lively at all times, she could probably have been described as a classic candidate for psychosomatic illness. Like many people with alexithymic tendencies, her primary relationship was one in which the partner was simply required to 'be there'. During her illness, she described to me how she had had few expectations of emotional intimacy in her marriage, regarding my father as the 'background' to her life. This rather minimal approach to relationships was probably the way she learnt to regulate herself at an early age, with her own parents. Although highly articulate and vocal, she had a practice of not *talking* about her feelings to others, which seemed to me to have come out of her own babyhood experiences with my grandmother.

Granny was a Victorian character who expected much and gave little. She was physically unapproachable, critical and punitive. She left her babies crying outside in their prams, believing as many parents did at the time that it would 'strengthen their lungs'. In response, my mother took pride in being 'independent' from an early age, and tried to be as strong as Granny demanded. But it seems highly likely to me that she would have had a stressful infancy with a mother who disliked intimacy, touch and dependency as much as my grandmother did.

We know that high levels of cortisol during infancy can affect the parts of the immune system that are developing at that time, in particular the thymus and the lymph nodes. But just as the stress response is programmed by very early experience, so too it seems is the immune system. The more early exposure it has to psychosocial stress, the more exaggerated its future inflammatory response. The two systems are intertwined (Miller et al. 2011).

Some time ago, we learnt from primate studies that stressful early separations from the primary caregiver didn't just affect the stress response, but could also have powerful consequences for the immune system. They lowered the activation of lymphocytes and increased the speed at which an individual animal succumbed to disease (Laudenslager et al. 1985; Capitanio et al. 1998). Now the evidence is coming forward to show that early stressful experiences affect humans in the same way. In particular, researchers are finding that a harsh or stressful early upbringing programmes the baby's immune system.

Harsh parents can of course be found in every social class. Adults whose own sense of self-esteem is rocky are those who are most likely to devalue their child, whether by hitting or by putting the child down verbally. Harshness takes root in insecurity and stress, no matter what the living conditions (Katz et al. 2007). However, poverty itself is also a major source of stress. Living in overcrowded, noisy conditions, being exposed to violent behaviour or struggling with the powerlessness that a lack of income brings, increases the chance that parents will lash out.

Whatever the social context, such experiences leave their mark on the developing child. The Adverse Childhood Experiences (ACE) Study assessed over 17,000 adults and found that early exposure to negative behaviours such as violence in the home or abuse and instability had a cumulative effect on a child's future health. The more adverse experiences an individual ticked off, the greater his risk for a range of future health problems (Felitti et al. 1998). Current research increasingly links such outcomes to a compromised immune system. When such children grow up, they are likely to release twice as many pro-inflammatory interleukin-6 (IL-6) cytokines in response to current stresses as other non-abused individuals (Gouin et al. 2012; Miller and Chen 2010; Danese et al. 2008). Eventually, they become more vulnerable to a whole range of diseases in adulthood (Miller and Chen 2010; Miller et al. 2011; Ziol-Guest et al. 2012).

Conversely, a child who experiences loving and supportive parenting is not only buffered against stress but also has a more robust immune system. Being touched and held lovingly releases oxytocin in the lymph system, which protects against inflammation (Miller et al. 2011). Breastfeeding, in particular, releases oxytocin as well as passing on the mother's antibodies to the child (Schore 1994). Breastfeeding also passes on polyunsaturated fatty acids (PUFAs) such as omega-3, which play a part in protecting against stress by inhibiting the pro-inflammatory cytokines (Das 2001). So while separation and other forms of distress can undermine the development of the immune system, a warm early relationship helps to promote a robust immune system (Chen et al. 2011; Carroll et al. 2013).

The links between emotional and physical health are rooted in the experiences of infancy, the level of stress and the level of support available to deal with stress. As I have already suggested, early experiences can lead to children becoming 'high reactors' or 'low reactors' to stress. The low reactors often come out of families with harsh parenting styles, particularly with verbally critical and physically abusive parents. Whether it is the body or the psyche that is battered, they seem to have developed a tough skin, a kind of stoicism that lets the hurt wash over them. My grandmother had a special stick with which she beat her children and she believed in physical discipline. She was also constantly critical, as I experienced in my own childhood with her. I think it is likely that my mother became a 'low reactor' with low cortisol in response to this treatment, while at the same time developing an exaggerated inflammatory response to stress. This would fit with her tendency towards allergies, especially hay fever, and the beginnings of arthritis. Low cortisol is associated with a particular illness cluster – with auto-immune conditions in particular, such as asthma, arthritis, allergies, ulcerative colitis, fatigue and ME (Heim et al. 2000a). The so-called 'cancer personality', in other words, the capacity to endure trying circumstances with fortitude and few words of complaint, is also thought by some to loosely fit in this cluster. Clearly the strategy of suppressing feelings, and the low cortisol that results, can be a dangerous one which has knock-on physiological consequences.

Disease proneness

Today, the 'cancer personality' theory is no longer in vogue. The preferred theory these days is that of the 'disease-prone personality'. This is basically because such a wide variety of illnesses seem to have similar underlying roots in emotional suppression. The range of conditions which have been linked to this pattern is staggering.

Psychoanalytically informed doctors in the 1940s and 1950s were the first to identify and work with the classical 'psychosomatic' diseases (Taylor et al. 1997). They believed that they were caused by 'strangulated' or conflicted feelings that needed to be discharged. This was based on the psycho-analytic view that neurosis was caused by repressed sexual or aggressive drives which were in conflict with social morality. The cure was to bring them to consciousness.

The new paradigm of affect regulation offers the view that it is not so much the repression of our primitive sexual and aggressive urges that pushes us towards ill health, as a failure to experience and tolerate all our feelings while maintaining a state of organismic balance. The newer view is that human beings are self-regulating organisms, and failures of regulation can generate pathology.

Once you start to think of yourself as an organism with many interconnecting systems that provide feedback to each other and regulate each other, you can start to appreciate the part that feelings might play in physical illness. Emotions are central to self-regulation. They are the biological response of the organism to other people and situations, and this response can be a useful basis for reflection and a guide to action. But when emotional responses are suppressed, you are interfering with the flow of information. It then becomes much more difficult to behave flexibly. Adapting to people and situations becomes a matter of using external guidelines or abstract concepts rather than drawing on internal information, leading to rigid behaviour. It also impedes the flow of information between your various internal systems, making it more difficult for them to adjust levels of biochemicals and maintain internal equilibrium.

Feelings are always both biological and social. As a feeling happens, there are physiological changes taking place in a person's nervous system, endocrine system and other systems, along with thoughts arising in the mind. If these thoughts are pushed away, an important source of regulatory feedback is lost. For example, when you suppress anger, your body and its various systems remain aroused and biochemically stimulated. But if you refuse to become aware of your anger and don't express it to the person who has offended you, you lose the opportunity to put something right that is wrong – and to settle the biochemical, muscular and autonomic responses that have already been triggered (Carroll 2001). It makes it difficult to regain equilibrium and to calm arousal back to a normal level.

The bodily arousal within all these different systems is the underlying basis for what we describe as a 'feeling' about something that is happening to us. But the thought 'I feel jealous' (or sad, delighted, uncomfortable) is the way we consciously articulate this complex activation of body systems, in social terms. What we do not usually become aware of when we name our feelings is the internal signalling that is occurring within the body outside of consciousness.

The biochemicals of emotion

Candace Pert is a scientist who did groundbreaking work throwing light on how emotions might affect the immune system. An eccentric, warm character who linked the cool rational world of experimental science with New Age thinking about feelings, she suggested that the biochemical 'information substances' of our endocrine and neuro-transmitter systems are the molecules of emotion. When we have feelings, we are experiencing some unique cocktail of hormone, neuropeptide and neurotransmitter activation.

Pert's unique discovery was that this is taking place all over the body, not just in the brain. Although the brain, and its emotion systems, is a focal point of neurotransmitter activity, many of the same biochemicals communicate all around the body. Serotonin, opioids and dopamine receptors are present in locations such as the heart, the gut and down the spine. She argued that this means that we feel feelings with our bodies and not just with our brains. We may even feel things in our immune system, which not only responds to signals from these biochemicals but also releases them. As Deepak Chopra, one of Pert's admirers, put it: 'If being happy, sad, thoughtful, excited and so on all require the production of neuropeptides – and neurotransmitters in our brain cells – then the immune cells must also be happy, sad, thoughtful, excited, too' (Chopra 1989: 67).

Pert showed that these molecules of emotion communi-cate with each other across various systems of the human organism. The body's communication systems run along many interconnecting lines: in the blood; in the lymph system; along the nerves. For example, the fight or flight molecules which speed us up and make us more alert are carried round the body by the sympathetic nerves. The immune signals are carried through the blood, so that many immune stations around the body are aware of 'distress signals' such as those activated by an infection. Moreover, the immune system communicates with the brain along the vagus nerve, and this allows us to be aware of what is going on in our body.

Not so long ago, the immune system was thought of as a separate, self-contained bodily defence system. But Robert Ader made a startling discovery in the mid-1970s: he found that the immune system could learn from past experience. In one important experiment, Ader and Cohen established that the immune system has memory. Using rats, they had set up a mental association between an unpleasant drug and some pleasant sweetened water. The drugs made the rats feel sick and suppressed their immune systems. But they also gave the rats sweetened water every time they were given the drug. In this way, sweet water, feeling sick and an inner disabling of the immune system were linked in the rats' minds. Then, some time later, they did another experiment with the same rats. They found that all they had to do was to give the rats sweet water, and even without the active immune suppressive ingredient the rats' immune systems were suppressed. In effect, their expectations made it happen. The immune system inactivated itself when it remembered the taste of sweet water (Ader and Cohen 1981).

The immune system, then, has a history and a memory, just as other aspects of the self do. It has been called the 'body's brain' (Goleman 1996). Soon after this groundbreaking work, Ed Blalock made another important discovery – that the immune system could be affected by the hormones and neurotransmitters generated directly or indirectly by the brain (Blalock 1984). This meant that the brain could communicate directly with the immune system using neurotransmitters such as serotonin, or hormones such as cortisol. Whatever was going on in the individual's mind – current thoughts and feelings – could potentially trigger reactions of the immune system via the biochemicals that are triggered by extreme states of mind such as those occurring during situations of stress or depression. There are various regulatory systems involving our bodily chemistry which have an impact on the immune system – our autonomic nervous system and its neurotransmitters, as well as biochemicals such as prostaglandins and epinephrine which may also affect immune responses. But it is cortisol which seems to be the hormone that has the greatest impact on the immune system.

The effects of cortisol on the immune system are well documented (Cohen and Crnic 1982; Sternberg 2001). In essence, cortisol instructs the immune cells temporarily to slow down the immune response, allowing the body's energy to be focused on the crisis in hand. As a temporary measure, this is useful. However, when the stress is chronic and doesn't get resolved quickly, as in severe relationship conflict or long-lasting grief, then the continued release of cortisol can have a serious impact on the immune system. It can stop the white blood cells from moving around the body. It kills off lymphocytes, including natural killer cells, and stops new ones from being produced. These processes may underlie the massively increased frequency of cancerous tumours in mice subjected to prolonged stress, compared to those who were not (Riley 1975; Visintainer et al. 1982). More recent evidence suggests that stress may have a similar effect on humans. A meta-analysis by Yoichi Chida and her colleagues at University College London found that stress-related psychosocial factors were associated with a higher incidence of cancer, as well as with poorer survival rates (Chida et al. 2008).

My mother experienced these kinds of stress before her illness developed (she lost her husband and home, and then a little later her lover died suddenly and unexpectedly) and no doubt would have experienced an increase in stress hormones. But because she was not in the habit of turning to other people for comfort, she didn't have an effective means of regulating her overwhelming distress. Instead, as always, she took to her bed, deliberately avoiding people when her feelings became too painful.

The immune system's capacity to deal with cancerous cells in particular is thought to rely strongly on 'Natural Killer' cells, which are the general thugs of the immune system. But the level of NK cells has been found to be low in those who lack social support or who are under acute psychological stress (Martin 1997: 238). This suggests that those whose emotional style is one of suppressing feelings rather than expressing them and regulating them with the help of others, may have worse immune function. They do not seek social support. As I have described, the willingness to confide in others that has been found to be an important factor in good health is lacking in people with insecure attachment histories, but particularly with the 'avoidant' style, which attempts to be so emotionally self-sufficient.

In this sense, the regulatory patterns that are established in early life may not only affect your psychological well-being and the development of the 'brain' of the brain's emotional systems in the prefrontal cortex, but may also affect the 'body's brain' – the immune system and stress response which are also shaped by emotional experience. How cruel it is that those who were less well cared for in babyhood may also have a greater likelihood of suffering physical illness in later life.

The case of Dennis Potter

An emotionally suppressed infancy does not, of course, tell us which illnesses the person will succumb to. The pathways are many, depending on genetic inheritance, exposure to viruses and individual ways of managing feelings. The writer Dennis Potter, author of the innovative series *The Singing Detective* and other powerful television dramas, suppressed his feelings with somewhat different results.

It is impossible to reconstruct the precise effects of an infancy in retrospect, but the circumstances of Potter's babyhood are suggestive. According to his biographer, Humphrey Carpenter (1999), Potter's father was dangerously ill at the time of his birth. It is not unreasonable to speculate that his mother must have been under stress and may have passed on her cortisol to him in the womb. This – along with any genetic tendency – may have predisposed him to being a sensitive baby. It is also possible that a mother who was tending to a sick husband may have been less available to her newborn baby than otherwise. Whether or not that was the case, Potter's mother became pregnant again when Dennis was still only 4 months old. He would barely have been walking when his mother had another baby to care for.

We cannot know exactly what kind of early relationship Dennis Potter had with his mother, but the evidence of later childhood does strongly suggest that he too did not grow up with a confidence in turning to others for emotional support. At the age of 10, he was taken by his mother to live in London with relatives, and was separated from his father. There he was sexually abused by the uncle with whom he had to share a bed. It is telling that Potter did not express his horror to his mother. He justified his silence to his biographer on the grounds that he dared not tell her because 'it would be like throwing a bomb into the middle of everything that made me feel secure'. In other words, he did not see his mother as a person who would cope with the situation and who would help him to think about his feelings and to calm his distress. He felt he had to protect her from emotional arousal instead of expecting her protection and regulation. Instead he relied on her, as alexithymics do, simply to 'be there'. He got his feeling of security simply from her continued presence. As a result, he struggled to regulate the feelings this abuse aroused in him. He turned his distress inwards, blamed himself and felt 'totally invaded and swamped and warped for a while'. He stopped eating and explained this away to his mother by claiming to be homesick.

The person who learns in infancy to manage feelings by ignoring them can be thrown into crisis by demanding emotional events. Potter's next crisis came at a time when he was not happy with his work and was under pressure to work long hours to support his young family. He found himself compulsively visiting prostitutes to relieve his stress; whether through pleasure, or through power over others – both have biochemical effects. Again, he experienced disgust with his sexual 'pollution' but could not find a way to manage these complex feelings adequately with those he was close to. Instead, his chronic hypersensitivity to stress had an impact on his immune system and began to find expression in a physical form. He began to develop psoriatic arthropathy, a condition to which he was genetically predisposed. Potter believed that these attacks of skin shedding and joint inflammation were linked to his state of mind. Eventually, he put this into words in the mouth of Marlow, his best-known character in *The Singing Detective*, who said 'The temptation is to believe that the ills and poisons of the mind or the personality have somehow erupted straight out onto the skin.'

After his illness was diagnosed, Potter found a more satisfying life course by withdrawing from the demands of journalism into a more home-based life. He began writing plays for television, enabling him to explore a range of controversial feelings at one remove from his own life. In particular, he expressed – in visceral, passionate writing – the anger that he was not able to express in his own life, despite being perceived by others as a presence conveying 'tense, coiled anger'. Potter himself recognised a connection between this unexpressed anger and his ill health: 'I believe that we choose our illnesses. I was always angry, and I have the feeling that the anger in me was turned inwards.'

Addictions and self-medication

Trying not to feel can take many forms. Potter was also a heavy drinker and a chain smoker, and addictions of these kinds are common in people who lack regulatory skills. These failures in self-care may have contributed to his early death from cancer at the age of 59.

Handicapped by insecure relationship patterns, which prevent them from drawing comfort from others or problem solving with other people, many people turn to alternative sources to make themselves feel better. Their choice of addiction may be influenced by their parents' preferences. If father was a heavy drinker, and the person grows up with alcohol around, it may feel natural to turn to alcohol to relieve mental pain. Genetic factors may also play a part in facilitating the addiction. If sweet food was a 'treat' in your family, then overeating chocolates and biscuits may be a natural response to an emptiness or inner emotional conflict.

The substance of choice is something that soothes and in effect medicates the physiological disturbance of emotional distress. For example, we know that depression often involves low levels of serotonin. This may be why some people, finding their feelings difficult to manage, crave carbohydrates and sweet things, which can help to release serotonin into the brain. Sugar also stimulates the release of beta-endorphin, which again can reduce pain, both physical and emotional. Experiments with mice have shown that mice who are separated from their mothers cry less if given sugar water. They also respond less to physical pain caused by having their feet put on a hot plate, if given sugar water (Blass et al. 1986).

The person who chooses to self-medicate when feeling distress is attempting to restore some sort of internal equilibrium. But using substances such as food and drugs to relieve pain can lead to addiction. When you eat too many sweet things regularly, your beta-endorphin receptors close down, and then you need to eat more sweet things to achieve the same effect. Alcohol addiction works in a very similar way. Alcohol also releases beta-endorphin and alcoholics need to drink more to achieve the same pain relief.

The anorexic path

Surprisingly, not eating can also be as addictive a pathway as overeating or taking drugs. Like other addictions, it can become life threatening. Amongst patients with eating disorders, there is a high rate of attempted suicide (around 17 per cent (Butik et al. 2008)) as well as a tragically high death rate of approximately 5 per cent (Crow et al. 2009). Typically, this condition starts in adolescence or early adulthood with a diet to lose weight. As the diet progresses, the woman ignores messages from her body that it craves carbohydrates and moves into a phase of producing increased brain opioids which can make her feel high. Even though this phase of starvation makes her function at a very low level of activity and cuts her off from other people, she can then become addicted to the experience of starvation itself.

In the anorexic state, the woman finds some relief from feelings that she doesn't know how to manage. There is a numbing effect with the opioids. One patient wrote a letter to her parents from an anorexia clinic, saying:

The truth of the matter is that we focus on food and weight so that we don't have to feel any emotions or feelings that might be uncomfortable, such as anger, sadness, anxiety or guilt. We have been conditioned from childhood to suppress these feelings for various reasons, such as that it is not lady-like to express them

and that no-one wants to be around someone who is upset.
(Abraham and Llewellyn-Jones 2001)

The case of Nina

Nina was a patient of mine whose early family experience is
typical for the development of this particular addiction as a
solution to regulatory difficulties. Her mother was a fitness
enthusiast who ate sparingly and was concerned about
maintaining a smart appearance. Nina, an only child, grew
up as the focus of her parents' devotion; they adored her and
hoped for great things from her, but did not have a happy
relationship with each other. She was under pressure to
meet their needs – and in particular, it seemed to me, to
meet her mother's psychological needs. Nina tried to be a
good girl, and tried in particular to succeed at the sports that
her mother enjoyed. She was very scared of causing her
mother any hurt, disappointment or feeling of abandonment.
As a child, she felt she could not bear to stay overnight at a
friend's house in case it would make her mother feel left
out – she could not allow herself to have something good if
her mother didn't have it. Over and over again, she complied
with her parents' wishes to keep them happy – and perhaps,
to avoid any hint of negative feeling which seemed to be so
intolerable for this family.

In the process, Nina lost touch with her own wishes and
her own feelings – in a sense, they got 'swallowed'. The family
atmosphere was affectionate and even intense, yet the individuals within it did not clearly speak for themselves.
Father would say what mother felt, while the mother would
speak for Nina, and Nina would speak for her father, and
so on. Outsiders to the family were regarded with some
suspicion. This kind of family has been described as
'enmeshed' and Nina's personality often seemed to be merged
with her mother's. Being the focus of her parents' lives may
have had some value to her as a young child, but it certainly
proved problematic as she approached adulthood. She had
difficulty in growing up and separating from her parents
because they needed her so much. How would they survive
without her?

And how would she survive without them? She was terrified of the world, perhaps because she had so little ability to regulate herself. By adolescence, the pressure to regulate her own feelings and to engage with people outside the family was becoming much more intense. But the peculiarity of the anorexic family experience is that the child has learnt to cope with feelings by clinging on to her mother and remaining plugged in to her mother's psyche rather than manage them independently. As a teenager, Nina found that cutting out food was a way of preventing her own increasingly insistent feelings from surfacing. This method of suppressing feelings was a distorted way of regulating them by achieving a sense of emotional numbness and distance from them. However, as we worked on her problems, Nina began to eat more and she described to me how uncomfortable it was to become more aware of her feelings again.

One problem that emerged was that Nina's mother could not manage her own feelings and so had been unable to regulate Nina's states. Like Dennis Potter, Nina felt she couldn't tell her mother her problems because her mother might panic and overreact; her mother simply couldn't cope with, or 'contain', negative experience. Sometimes her mother would simply deny Nina's feelings. If Nina said she was lonely as her best friends had both moved away to another town, her mother would tell her 'You're not lonely, you have your family.' Her mother had difficulty in recognising Nina's true states. She attributed her own feelings to Nina. If the mother felt that a room was overheated, she would assume that Nina also must feel too hot.

Some research suggests that there may be a genetic predisposition to anorexia, which could be based in a tendency to emotional restraint or to other temperamental characteristics common in anorexics, such as compliance, perfectionism and worry (Woodside et al. 2002). But these characteristics could equally well be defined as a problem of regulating emotions. When you don't know how to manage difficult feelings, you avoid them. Lacking emotional confidence, you may become ambitious and perfectionist in an attempt to find self-esteem elsewhere. It may also be important to be perfect in every way so that you do not give offence or upset the people on whom you depend. Ironically, however, when the anorexic behaviour has taken hold, the anorexic individual in the grip of his or her addiction causes enormous distress to parents and provokes intense conflict and upset.

The roots of regulation lie in babyhood and, as we have seen, the stress response is a central aspect of regulation. In anorexics, the stress response is hypersensitive. The level of CRF and cortisol is high, and their adrenal glands have an exaggerated response to ACTH. This tends to be the case even after recovery, so it is not just attributable to the effects of starvation, which can itself raise cortisol levels (Hoek et al. 1998). Raised levels of CRF are probably the source of the common feelings of depression in anorexic individuals. The same high levels of CRF are also found in babies who are separated from their mothering person, and in adult depressives. It may indicate a basic fear about survival with parents who don't create a feeling of safety. Although they are constantly in the presence of the mother, they do not necessarily feel safely cared for by her.

Babies such as Nina are not genuinely allowed to have their own feelings. They come to believe that they will upset their parents if they have needs and feelings that the parent doesn't want them to have. Their parents need a child who is an extension of themselves or a source of comfort to them. This sends the Ninas of this world the implicit message that they must not become a separate individual with their own needs and feelings. As Henry Krystal put it, a daughter such as Nina does not 'own her own soul' (Krystal 1988). The hidden message is that her feelings do not really matter and are not to be taken seriously. The fact that feelings have so often been mislabelled makes it difficult for such a child to know her own feelings or to trust them. She has the feelings other people expect her to have. Feelings don't get accurately identified and differentiated into different shades of meaning that can be talked about. They remain rather vague, bodily sensations.

Drew Westen describes a range of research studies that have been done with anorexics using different tests and scales. The strongest and clearest finding of all was that a 'difficulty in recognising and accurately responding to emotional states and certain visceral sensations is a central deficit in eating disorder patients'. Severe anorexics typically have a 'constricted/overcontrolled' personality, and in particular have a difficulty in acknowledging or expressing anger or expressing their own wishes (Westen and Harnden-Fischer 2001; Westen 2000).

A susceptibility to illness and addictions is rooted in this estrangement from one's own body and in the resulting difficulties in regulating feelings. In particular, the attempt to escape from feelings has its origin in a babyhood in which the baby's feelings have not been identified and responded to in a contingent way. Babies in this situation can't take their own regulation for granted. They are confronted prematurely with their own raw needs, lacking the ability to meet them by themselves. This seems to leave a sort of unfinished business for the baby. As he or she grows up, the adult still longs to be properly taken care of, to be understood without words, to have all wishes fulfilled by magic, and to have needs anticipated without saying anything. People in this state are ultimately seeking the baby's experience of perfect unity and merger with an attuned mother.

As adults, they are prone to remain highly dependent on others, hoping that the magical other will make them feel all right. Some actively search for the perfect partner and go from one to the next in pursuit of Ms or Mr Right, in an endless quest exemplified by many film stars with their multiple marriages. Other more 'avoidant' personalities, who are afraid of depending on others who may abandon them, choose to persist in a low-key, often unsatisfactory relationship, making few demands in order to avoid abandonment.

These distortions arise when there has not been enough positive experience of dependence in infancy. Without an actively responsive and sensitive mothering experience, the baby can't identify with the parental attitude and apply it to him or herself. It isn't possible to generate the attitude of self-care and awareness of one's own feelings if someone else hasn't first done it for you. (That is why self-help books are of little use.) You need to have an experience with someone first – then you can reproduce it.

If the early relationship has not conveyed an acceptance of the full range of feelings, including 'negative' ones such as anger and sadness, then these feelings will be hard to tolerate and experience fully. If parents have not been able to convey confidence in handling such feelings, then the skills to manage them will very likely be lacking in their offspring. But relationships that steer clear of such feelings are brittle and lack resilience. They cannot flexibly respond to the ups and downs of experience, and provide a core feeling that relationships can be disrupted and then repaired – that attunement can be lost but it can also be restored.

Attempting to be too 'nice' or 'strong' is a dangerous course. It cuts off the flow of feelings which is essential for physical as well as mental health. As Candace Pert has suggested, we need this flow for the system to function well. Our feelings are a vital signalling system, both within each body and in its communications with others. Feelings are a source of useful information to which we should pay attention, using our biochemical signals to guide us in our more conscious negotiations with others. Feelings then do not have to be blocked or ignored or numbed. They can take their proper place as the core of the self, a self that can be elaborated in words.

6

Melancholy baby

How early experience can alter brain chemistry, leading to adult depression

> And did you get what
> you wanted from this life, even so?
> I did.
> And what did you want?
> To call myself beloved, to feel myself
> Beloved on the earth.
>> Raymond Carver, 'Late Fragment'

One of the most familiar mental health issues of all is that of depression. From Churchill's 'black dog' to William Styron's 'darkness', we think we know what it means even if we have not experienced the full-blown symptoms of a major depression. A typical depression scenario was described to me by my client Carys. She found the pain most intense in the early morning. When she woke up, she would become aware of a sick feeling in her stomach. Her muscles began to tense. She did not want to get up and face another day. What was the point? Nothing felt good, no one cared. There was a sharp feeling in her body, something like pain, without a specific location. A hollow feeling too, like hunger, yet she had no appetite for breakfast or anything else. She just wanted to curl up in bed and make the world go away, especially the images of failure and humiliation that endlessly circled in her head. The face of her employer when she had to tell him she'd made a dreadful mistake; her ex-partner's face and his words: 'It's not working, Carys, you are way too demanding.' She felt nothing would ever come right for her; she was a useless, bad person whom no one wanted in their life.

A striking aspect of depression is how physical it feels. This is perhaps why it is popular to describe depression as a biochemical imbalance, implying that it is a malfunction of the brain which has somehow appeared from nowhere, or possibly a result of genetic tendencies. Professor Peter Fonagy once asked 20 consecutive parents referred to his clinic what they thought had caused their child's problems. He was not surprised to learn that they all put brain chemistry at the top of the list, closely followed by 'bad genes' (Fonagy 2003). Scientific work has confirmed that depression does indeed involve biochemical changes in the brain's neurotransmitters. Depressed people do usually have some combination of low serotonin and low norepinephrine. Yet researchers have tried giving subjects doses of the neurochemicals involved in depression, and have found that on their own they do not make people depressed. Even if you create a serotonin deficiency by manipulating someone's diet, a normally balanced person will not experience this as a feeling of depression (Duman et al. 1997). Clearly, it is not the presence or absence of biochemicals alone which creates depression. In fact, it is more probable that these biochemicals are depleted as a side effect of an overactive stress response.

If Carys turns to the medical profession for help, she will almost certainly be offered drugs to correct these so-called biochemical imbalances in her brain. Antidepressants such as Prozac are now household names, and are often the first resort of those suffering from depression. In some cases, they are helpful in restoring equilibrium. Yet the medical approach is less confident than it seems. Drug treatments have benefits for some patients, but as few as a third achieve a full remission of their symptoms. Another third have some improvement but continued symptoms, and the final third no improvement (Tranter et al. 2002; Kirsch 2008). Drug companies have drawn a veil over this evidence by failing to publish the studies that show up such unsatisfactory results (Turner et al. 2007; Davies 2013).

Carys may also find some fatalistic satisfaction in learning that her depression may have a genetic component. Some twin studies have shown that identical twins are much more likely to have the same incidence of depression than non-identical twins (Andreasen 2001: 240), but there is little evidence of what exactly is being transmitted genetically. According to Willner, it may be as unspecific as a tendency to introversion that may culminate in depression in some circumstances (Willner 1985). In any case, whatever the genetic predisposition may consist of, it still has to be triggered by environmental factors to become manifest – the relevant genes are not inevitably or automatically expressed. This makes it all the more important to unravel the mystery of what these environmental factors might be.

Faced with a mounting epidemic of depression, with depression soon to become the second most prevalent cause of worldwide 'burden of disease' (Mathers and Loncar 2005), many researchers have attempted to identify its triggers. There are many angles: it is associated with a lack of B vitamins, a lack of omega-3 fatty acids, because of losing a parent at an early age, or caused by stressful life events such as bereavement or moving house. Clearly, it is both a biological condition and a psychological one. While Carys may well have low levels of certain brain chemicals that affect mood, along with inactive parts of her prefrontal cortex, her condition is also triggered by the images and thoughts in her mind. In particular, experiences of feeling rejected or abandoned by other people are the most common triggers for depression.

I believe that the core of depression is a fragile sense of self. It is a deep well of inner hopelessness, which brims over periodically when a vulnerable person's stocks of well-being are depleted – whether by a lack of essential nutrients, a lost relationship, a humiliation, an illness, or a burglary. It is an interesting fact that very few people who experience life events such as a bereavement or loss do actually become seriously depressed. They experience sadness and pain, but they do not become overwhelmed by it. However, such events often do trigger depression in someone who is already prone to it (Brown and Harris 1978; Carr et al. 2000).

Where does this fragile sense of self come from? Like many other depressed clients, Carys tells me the stories of her childhood that she remembers. Certain events and phrases stick in her mind: 'You are so selfish', 'Just get on with it.' I have heard the same phrases from client after client: 'It won't work, you know', 'I might have known you'd make a mess of it', 'You are pathetic', 'No wonder she doesn't like you', 'Your brother is so good with people – but you have no personality', 'You'll never be able to do that, you'd better let me do it', 'You don't have much common sense.' They may seem relatively innocuous, but they conjure up a certain kind of negative atmosphere in which the depressed person has grown up. Cumulatively, they convey the message that individuals such as Carys are inadequate and ineffective.

This leaves her in a state of longing for parental approval, for 'social reinforcement', love and belonging, while having little confidence in being able to obtain these things. But surely she should be able to get on with her life now that she is an adult? Carys is actually in her fifties. She has been married, had children and divorced. She has had affairs. She works part time as a receptionist – a job below her capabilities. But she still can't create satisfying relationships with other people that could sustain her emotionally. Underneath the surface appearance of living a normal adult life, she has unconsciously accepted the negative messages of her childhood that she is substandard in some way. In her early life, she developed an internal working model of herself as not good enough, or even 'bad', as she failed to live up to her parents' expectations or capture their attention.

This unconscious working model is very easily triggered by fresh cues from her environment. When her relationships go wrong – whether it is a neighbour criticising her for having her radio on too loud, or a lover ending the relationship – she falls apart. She feels suicidal. In her mind, it is all hopeless. She's a bad person and no one will ever really love her. Like Tolstoy's Anna Karenina, she is so insecure that misunderstandings are amplified and experienced as abandonment. In Tolstoy's novel, Count Vronsky just has to disagree with Anna and she thinks he hates her. She magnifies every slight into a cataclysmic abandonment, imagining the worst: "'He loves another woman, that is clearer still," she said to herself as she entered her own room. "I want love, and it is lacking. So everything is finished!" she repeated her own words, "and it must be finished"' (Tolstoy 1877/1995). Soon afterwards, Anna does indeed kill herself, as do around 15 per cent of seriously depressed people.

Why is depression on the increase?

Depression has been studied extensively because it is such a pervasive disorder and affects so many people. The latest estimates are that 19 per cent of the adult population in the USA will suffer an episode of depression at some point in their lives (Kessler and Ustun 2011). The rate of depression has increased dramatically since the 1950s, and is on a steady upward curve (Andreasen 2001). It may be coincidental that antidepressants were discovered in the 1950s, but it raises the question of whether the increase in depression is a greater willingness to be described as 'depressed' once there was a 'cure' available.

Most of the literature on depression is confined to its symptoms. The focus is on the adult's brain chemistry and the adult's cognitions, which are the target of treatments. There is remarkably little recognition that the adult's brain is itself formed by experiences starting in the womb, or that these may have contributed to a predisposition to depression. Yet there is abundant evidence that an overreactive stress response underlies chronic depression, as well as the involvement of other brain systems such as the immune system and endocrine system that are being orchestrated and fine-tuned in infancy. There is also evidence that a lack of emotional confidence and destructive internal working models can be set up very early in life. I will now turn to an exploration of these missing dimensions of the understanding of depression.

Madonna and child

In that time of early life celebrated by paintings and icons of the Madonna and child, mother and baby may, if all goes well, find themselves in a kind of cocoon of peace and love. Breastfeeding itself inactivates the mother's own stress response; her amygdala expresses less CRF, presumably removing anxious, fearful feelings; while the oxytocin generated by breastfeeding provides a feeling of tranquillity. The breastfeeding state of mind facilitates her ability to calm her baby and to manage his stress. Once established (and this is not always easy to achieve), breastfeeding can be a powerful source of sustenance for the mother as well as the baby.

She is then potentially more able to inhibit her baby's stress response and to ensure that his cortisol levels remain low. She brings this about through her presence, her feeding and her touch. The baby is protected from stress and discomfort and his brain responds by developing more receptors for cortisol on a variety of brain cells. A brain well stocked with cortisol receptors through this early experience will be better able to mop up this stress hormone when it is released in future. This furnishes the baby's brain with the capacity to stop producing cortisol when it has helped deal with a source of stress. The stress response will quickly be turned off when it is no longer needed.

But if the baby doesn't have this experience of being cocooned in a protective mother's arms (whether provided with bottle feeding or the breast), or if she is frequently unresponsive or absent for too long, then his stress response can kick in and become active prematurely. The baby may become flooded with cortisol and eventually the cortisol receptors will close down. This means that in the future he will have fewer cortisol receptors. The cortisol secreted at times of stress will not find enough receptor homes to go to, particularly in the hippocampus and hypothalamus, and will continue to wash around his brain, producing the high cortisol levels and the feeling that stress cannot be stopped. A reactive stress response will have been set up. There have been numerous studies linking depression with such a hyper-reactive stress response.

Neither Carys nor Anna Karenina were necessarily born to be drama queens, easily swept into misery by their self-centred view of the world. They may equally have had damaged stress response systems and depleted neurotransmitters because of their early experience as babies. Brought up by stressed or depressed mothers, or by childminders or nannies, they may have lacked the quality of attention that is necessary for small babies to thrive – the 'primary maternal preoccupation' described by the psychoanalyst Donald Winnicott (1992).

Human connections equal brain connections

Lacking these early experiences of blissful protected infancy doesn't just affect your stress response and your ability to switch off cortisol. A lack of positive rewarding interaction with the mother can have other negative effects on the brain's biochemicals. It can undermine the oxytocin system which is being built in the first year of life, leading to long-lasting effects (Feldman et al. 2013). Specifically, neglect or being deprived of the mother's presence is linked to low levels of norepinephrine, which make it hard for an individual to concentrate or sustain effort. This biochemical is usually dysregulated in depressed adults and it hampers the individual's ability to adapt, tending to keep a person doing the same old thing over and over again even if it is bad for him or her. An unhappy early relationship can also constrict the capacity for pleasure and reward in later life, due to fewer dopamine receptors and opioid receptors in the baby's brain, especially in the prefrontal cortex where they are usually very densely present. Early social deprivation or stress can lead to permanent reduction in dopaminergic neurons (Rodrigues et al. 2011; Martin 1997; Lagercrantz and Herlenius 2001), affecting the capacity for positive emotionality (Depue et al. 1994).

However, a child experiencing lots of rewarding contact, or one who is more successful in the genetic lottery, may end up with more dopamine synapses (Collins and Depue 1992). This affects the way that life is approached. With plenty of dopamine activity, the child approaches experience in a positive way. Dopamine flowing through the orbitofrontal cortex helps it to do its job of evaluating events and adapting to them quickly. It also helps the child to delay gratification and stop and think about choices of action. The child with fewer dopamine cells will be less aware of the positive rewards on offer, less able to adapt and think, may be physically slower, and may be more prone to depression and giving up.

Neurotransmitter connections are the way that our brains encode our sensory experiences within our neuronal pathways. Different experiences are reflected in 'alterations of neurochemical transmission at cortical synapses' (Collins and Depue 1992). A reduction in these neurotransmitters can also affect the connections between different levels of the brain. In particular, it may mean that the important regulatory connections between the prefrontal cortex and the subcortex are weaker.

Breastfeeding itself, which nowadays only a small minority of babies experience for longer than a few weeks, may play an important role in furnishing the baby's brain with the ingredients for a pleasurable life through the fatty acids provided in breast milk. Breastfed infants have higher levels of polyunsaturated fatty acids (PUFAs) than bottlefed babies. Although there are now formula milk products supplemented with PUFAs which can offer some of the benefits of breastmilk, they still cannot provide the complex range of benefits of breastfeeding. One of these is the breastfeeding mother's ability to provide tailor-made antibodies for her baby. As she nuzzles up close in skin to skin contact with her baby, she 'samples' the pathogens on the baby's skin, which triggers memory B cells specific for those pathogens. 'These B cells then migrate to the mother's breasts where they produce just those antibodies that the baby needs' according to the immunologist Lauren Sompayrac (Sompayrac 2012)

The essential fatty acids are also involved in producing neurotransmitters such as dopamine and serotonin, especially in the prefrontal cortex (Wainwright 2002). Animal studies suggest that if there is a deficiency of PUFAs in early life, this may have permanent effects. The brain may not fully recover if it does not get the nutrients it needs during the period before weaning, even if they are replaced later (Kodas et al. 2002). If this turns out to be true of human babies too, it may contribute to the way that the neurotransmitter balance is set in early life, including the serotonin and norepinephrine pathways implicated in depression. Interestingly, links between low PUFAs and human depression have been established (Golding et al. 2009; Maes et al.

1999; Peet et al. 1998; Bruinsma and Taren 2000). Low levels of omega-3 fatty acid in the brain also correlate with a lack of activity in the prefrontal cortex and anterior cingulate (Sublette et al. 2009). Conversely, PUFA supplements or a diet high in oily fish can help some individuals recover from depression (Lin and Su 2007; Peet and Horrobin 2002).

The power game

Babies who can't get the attention they need and who do not feel adequately protected from distress are forced to become aware of their own helplessness and powerlessness. But such awareness is premature because a young baby has virtually no capacity to regulate his own distress or act in his own interests. There is little he or she can do if no one responds to his protests and cries, except to try not to feel and to 'play dead'. This may be the safest course of action if his needs are an irritation to his caregivers.

Such passive behaviour is very like the behaviour of the rats that Martin Seligman studied in the 1980s. When they were put in unpleasant situations from which there was no escape, which they were powerless to affect, they gave up. They withdrew into a hopeless state. But what Seligman found most telling was that they carried on behaving in a powerless way even when conditions changed. When the stressful experience was over, they didn't even try to escape. He called this 'learned helplessness' (Seligman and Beagley 1975).

In this state of powerlessness and stress, high levels of cortisol are produced. As Sapolsky's work with baboons showed, it is stressful being at the bottom of the social pecking order. But it is equally stressful to be a baby who depends on parents who don't notice or meet your needs. In both cases, survival is at stake. As social creatures who depend on others, survival is not possible alone. It is frightening to be ignored, humiliated, threatened or trapped. It is not safe. Conversely, people (or animals) with social power feel safe, feel free to express themselves and expect to get their needs met. But without such power, the only safe course of action is to withdraw and submit to others.

Andrew Solomon, author of the masterful book on depression, *The Noonday Demon*, offered the intriguing thought that there is an evolutionary reason for withdrawal and depression (Solomon 2001). When subjected to attack by other more powerful members of the social group against whom he cannot win, the loser withdraws. He doesn't challenge his low social rank any more, in order to avoid a worse outcome – that of death. In the same way, in the family group, perhaps a child who is devalued and criticised will also accept his low status in order to survive. Our conflicts are played out at a more psychological level than those of our ancestors, but they are essentially the same defensive manoeuvres.

Cortisol is highest when the individual feels a loss of power or control over events, particularly if this cannot be predicted. The act of mentally preparing for an unpleasant experience does provide some protection against its stressful effects and results in the production of less cortisol. Presumably, the mental preparation provides some degree of control. Brier's research found that even depressed people have a normal cortisol response to stress when they have some measure of control over a stressor, but when they faced uncontrollable stress their cortisol levels shot up (Brier et al. 1987). This may account for the tendency of some depressed people to stick with low-risk relationships or job situations, which are predictable and familiar. It may be preferable to accept a low view of oneself than to risk social encounters which may raise one's status but may end in humiliation. It is particularly painful to reach out for affirmation and acceptance from other people and to fail to receive it.

Left and right brains

High cortisol levels are also associated with a highly active right brain and an underactive left brain. This is not the normal pattern. We know from the work of Tomarken and Davidson that most people have more active left than right brain hemispheres. They found that this was a stable characteristic – a 'trait' not a 'state' (Tomarken et al. 1992; Kalin et al. 1998b). An active left brain is linked to positive feelings, cheerfulness and a willingness to approach others with a kind of extraverted outlook. People like this who are shown amusing film clips tend to find them intensely positive. However, not everyone's brains are the same. There are also a lot of people who have a permanently more active right frontal hemisphere and they often do not see the joke. Instead, they are likely to have stronger responses to film clips which are negative and full of disaster (Tomarken et al. 1990). Depressed people are like this, and not just when they are currently depressed but all the time.

Depressed people seem to have a sluggish left frontal brain, incapable of managing when a storm of negative feelings erupts in the right frontal brain. In particular, during a depressive episode, they have less cerebral blood flow in the left dorsolateral and the left angular gyrus – a state which has been associated with apathy and 'poverty of speech' (Lichter and Cummings 2001). They also have some cognitive impairment correlated with decreased blood flow in part of the left medial prefrontal cortex (Bench et al. 1993; Drevets et al. 1997). Some studies in rats have shown that stress initially activates the left prefrontal cortex, and only activates the right prefrontal cortex once the stress becomes prolonged or uncontrollable. The left prefrontal cortex seems to be a sort of buffer that stops little stresses becoming big ones – a buffer that depressed people often lack (Sullivan and Gratton 2002).

How do some brains go one way and some another? It isn't certain whether some babies are in fact born with this tendency. Certainly there are babies with a hyperactive right frontal brain and a less active left frontal brain. But no study has established whether this is the case from birth or the result of experience. The fact that the left brain/right brain balance is a permanent, stable state suggests that something structural has taken place. One explanation would be that the architecture of the brain has been affected in early development. This is most likely to have happened in infancy when the brain is developing fastest, and indeed this is what research on the interactions between depressed mothers and their babies does suggest.

We know that babies of depressed mothers show this hemispheric tilt. They don't have the normal left hemisphere predominance that other babies have, even at times when they look quite happy playing. These babies with less left frontal activity have been described as less affectionate and less likely to approach their mother while playing. It may be that because the mother's own left frontal brain is less active, she cannot stimulate her baby's left frontal brain. She cannot pass on left-brain regulatory strategies either.

When they grow up, these babies of depressed mothers are highly at risk of succumbing to depression themselves. Some 40 per cent of them will experience depression before they are 16 years old – especially those who did not develop a secure attachment with their mother (Figure 6.1) (Murray et al. 2011).

But even as babies, there is reason to believe that they are already depressed. They are often withdrawn and they avoid making eye contact with people in general. This may be because they don't expect attention and positive responses from their depressed mothers. And it is sadly the case that many depressed mothers' brains don't respond very actively to their baby's cries; fMRI scans have revealed a relatively unresponsive prefrontal cortex compared to non-depressed mothers (Laurent and Ablow 2012).

There is no doubt that in turn, the lack of positive interaction can also have a big negative impact on their babies' brains. A recent study found that children aged 10 who have grown up with a continuously depressed mother have a significantly larger amygdala volume than other children (Lupien et al. 2011). But even when maternal depression only lasts during infancy, it can leave an unintended legacy for the baby; one study has found that some of these babies grow up with an altered stress response and are more prone to high levels of cortisol at the age of 13 (Murray et al. 2010).

Depressed mothers tend to behave differently from other mothers. One study (by Jeffrey Cohn and his colleagues) found that the normal state of play between a mother and baby is to fluctuate between positive and neutral interactions – about equally divided. But depressed mothers offer very few positive interactions. About 40 per cent of the time they are unresponsive or disengaged, while much of the rest

Figure 6.1 She's suffering from depression because her mother is.

of the time they are angry, intrusive and rough with their babies. When the mother is being overtly or covertly angry, these babies look away a lot. They can't actually leave the room, of course, but perhaps they would like to. For a baby, the most painful experience of all seems to be not being able to get mother's attention. Babies make the most protest when their mother's attention is switched off, as if this is even more unbearable than maltreatment. But either way, babies of depressed mothers experience more negative than positive feelings (Cohn et al. 1990).

Most babies of normal mothers experience very few negative states. This raises doubts about the Kleinian psychoanalytic theory that babies are innately full of envy and greed (Klein 1988). It seems more likely that a predominance of negative emotions is associated with abnormal experiences of the mother–baby relationship. Clearly, Klein's account resonates with many people, perhaps those who themselves experienced such infancies (and blame their baby selves for it). In my view, it is probably more accurate to think of the hostility and envy of the depressed mother towards her baby than vice versa.

Poverty and depression

Depression seems to go hand in hand with poverty and social exclusion. Certainly Brown and Harris found that those without economic resources were likely to experience more frequent triggers to depression, in the form of humiliations and frustrations. Yet like them, Karlen Lyons-Ruth found that it was not low income or multiple problems themselves which caused depression.

Lyons-Ruth analysed a sample of women living in poverty who were regarded as having difficulties in looking after their babies. Professionals who referred these mothers saw them as neglectful, apathetic or angry, but not as depressed. However, it turned out that they did have very high levels of depressive symptoms, often in a low-level, chronic form which Karlen Lyons-Ruth described as 'burnt out', their coping abilities stretched to breaking point. Other carefully matched women from the same poor communities who were coping all right with their children had far fewer depressive symptoms.

Lyons-Ruth suggests that the difficulties such women experience in parenting are not due solely to poverty or current problems alone, but have to be understood in the context of a life history of poor regulation, rooted in their own childhood experiences. What mattered most was whether or not they had a good relationship with their own mother in childhood. This was most predictive of depression and poor parenting (Lyons-Ruth 1992).

In my parent/infant practice, depressed mothers were the norm. Usually they were desperately in need of loving attention themselves. The majority described difficult relationships with their own mothers. For example, Benita had a mother who was disabled so she felt unable to make demands on her, Sally had an unpredictable alcoholic mother, Jill's mother was a career woman, busy and unavailable. Those parents who present a more positive account of their relationship with their mothers often aren't able to substantiate it. Many of these mothers did not get the attention they needed as babies and small children and now find it hard to provide it for their own babies. They feel helpless with their own babies, not knowing what to do, how to get the baby to stop crying, or to sleep through the night. They want the baby to grow up fast and not need so much attention.

Living with any mother who isn't emotionally available, for whatever reason, has much the same effect on the baby's brain as do more obvious deprivations such as complete isolation. Babies come into the world with a need for social interaction to help develop and organise their brains. If they don't get enough empathic, attuned attention – in other words, if they don't have a parent who is interested in them and reacting positively to them – then important parts of their brains simply will not develop as well.

This particularly affects the prefrontal cortex, the social brain. This is the part of the brain which has been strongly implicated in depression. In depressed people the prefrontal cortex is smaller, particularly on the left side. This has been found across a number of studies and has even been established with teenagers who are depressed (Steingard et al. 2002; Frodl et al. 2010). Unless it can be shown in subsequent studies that a small prefrontal cortex is genetically determined, this does provide powerful evidence that depression is linked with the poor development of the social brain in its most formative period of infancy and toddlerhood. In particular, there is a reduced density of neurons in the dorsolateral part of the prefrontal cortex, the area that develops in toddlerhood and is involved in verbalising feelings. The more depressed you are, the less activity there is in the prefrontal cortex, and with less blood flow in the prefrontal cortex, fewer neurotransmitters such as serotonin or norepinephrine are released. In particular, the orbitofrontal part of the prefrontal cortex is also less active, making it harder for depressed people to judge situations and control their reactions.

These effects could be the result of parental care or lack of it. Crying babies only reach high levels of cortisol if they are overwhelmed and unable to cope with their distress – if their regulatory partner does not do an effective job in reducing stress. Unfortunately, the way that babies are managed can have lasting effects. Babies who cry a lot at 4 months are the ones who show inhibited, withdrawn behaviour at 1 year. These are then the children who can be accurately predicted to become shy 4 year olds. At the most drastic extreme, Romanian orphans who have had virtually no mothering at all have brains with less active left orbitofrontal cortex, amygdala, hippocampus and temporal areas than comparable children of their age – precisely the areas involved in managing stress (Chugani et al. 2001).

The off switch

Numerous studies have shown that cortisol levels are high in most people with serious depression, but if you can get the cortisol level back to normal, the symptoms of depression will abate. As Andrew Solomon has described it, a state of high cortisol is like having the heating on all day even though the room is boiling hot. The stress response just keeps going even if there is no obvious stress around. Every little thing becomes a source of stress. The problem is that there is something wrong with the 'off' switch.

People who are vulnerable to these biochemical imbalances find that when unpleasant things happen to them, they cannot right themselves and tip the balance back to normal, as other people can. Their recovery mechanisms are damaged. Once again, this operates at both a biological and psychological level. At the biological level, the negative feedback loop within the brain is malfunctioning. When the level of cortisol is high for too long, it starts to affect the functioning of the hippocampus. This may be a particular problem in the developing brain. Recent research on monkeys suggests that high cortisol may be particularly toxic to the developing hippocampus, less so to the adult hippocampus. When researchers gave grown monkeys cortisol over a prolonged period, it had little effect on their hippocampi.

A malfunctioning hippocampus then fails to inform the hypothalamus that it is time to switch off the production of CRF. The hypothalamus, which is connected to many areas of the brain including the fear-generating amygdala, fails to use its 'off' switch. This means that the stress response goes on and on.

Recent thinking has added another dimension to the problem. A malfunctioning stress response may have an effect on the immune system too. Normally, cortisol turns off the inflammatory response within a few weeks of the initial trigger, which is usually either an infection or a stressful event. When it fails to do this, the inflammatory response can get out of control and production of pro-inflammatory cytokines such as IL–6 can double.

Intriguingly, this doesn't just affect the individual's health but also puts the individual at risk of depression. Some fascinating long-term studies have shown that adults with high levels of inflammation or pro-inflammatory cytokines are also those most likely to get depressed. One study of a very large number of Whitehall civil servants who were followed up over an 11-year period concluded that it was the cytokines which initiated depression, not the depression which triggered cytokines (Gimeno et al. 2009).

How come so many solid, middle-aged individuals had high levels of cytokines in the first place? For some, this seemed to be a response to current stresses – the male civil servants who felt aggrieved that their workplace wasn't just and fair turned out to have higher inflammatory markers (Elovainio et al. 2010). But for many others, it may have been the result of stresses much earlier in their lives. Unfortunately the study didn't enquire whether participants had a stressful early childhood. However, the researchers acknowledged that recent studies have shown that this can also set up an exacerbated inflammatory response (Danese et al. 2008; Miller et al. 2011; Pace 2006; Bilbo and Schwartz 2009).

At a psychological level, the high cortisol leaves the depressed person stuck in a state of anxiety, while the high level of inflammation can also bring a tendency to 'sickness behaviours' such as the urge to sleep or withdraw from others. In such a state, it is hard to shake off negative thoughts and feelings. The depressed person's most negative internal working models are easily triggered. George Brown and Tirril Harris found that depressive episodes in adulthood often start with a failure to get emotional support, or in some situation that involves a rejection or a loss of self-esteem (Brown and Harris 1978). Depressed people easily feel that they are ineffective or unwanted. This leads to negative thoughts about the self – 'I'm an idiot. I'm no good. I'm not worthy of attention. I'm pathetic.' When it is not forthcoming, the individual's need for positive feedback and attention from others feels shameful.

In their groundbreaking research of the 1970s, Brown and Harris pointed out that some people appear to be more vulnerable to current humiliations. They attempted to track down these vulnerable types and found that those who had lost a mother before the age of 11 were vulnerable, as were those whose attachments to others were generally insecure. They suggested that there was some missing element of self-esteem, which made it harder to believe that 'in the end, alternative sources of value will become available'. People vulnerable to depression had little ability to repair the tears in self-esteem caused by psychological injuries.

We might now describe this difficulty in recovering from psychological blows as a problem in self-regulation. Depressed people 'ruminate'. They cannot stop thinking painfully about their unmet emotional needs, yet they are unable to take smaller practical steps towards improving their situation. They struggle to avoid others' disapproval and rejection, yet feel helplessly disempowered and ineffective in winning the support they long for. They are in a self-regulatory bind, unable to give up their goals yet lacking the confidence to persist in achieving them (Carver and Scheier 1998).

Rupture and repair

Allan Schore has also drawn attention to this crucial dimension of the depressive experience. In a social context, hopelessness is the result of not being able to put things right. It is not just having negative thoughts about oneself – a crucial element of depression is that it also involves the feeling that there is no way of redeeming the self, of recovering others' good opinion or love. Carys often gave up on people or situations, believing that there was nothing she could do to improve her situation. On one occasion, she had forgotten to tell the doctor she worked for that a patient needed an urgent visit. This was a serious oversight. It could have had bad consequences for the patient. Carys just knew that she was going to lose her job and she would never find one as convenient. The doctor, whom she admired and who had always been friendly to her, would be so furious with her he wouldn't speak to her any more. And who could blame him? She was incompetent and stupid. She let people down. She was so tortured by guilty feelings that she failed to turn up to work. She couldn't face it. She made her situation worse, forcing the doctor to sack her. It didn't occur to her that she could explain and apologise, or that he might understand how exhausted she had been that day because her daughter had woken her in the middle of the night having a miscarriage. She gave up on her working relationship without attempting to repair it, or at least restore some mutual respect and understanding even if she had to lose her job.

Schore calls this the 'disruption and repair' cycle. When stress and conflict between people occur, as it inevitably will in every relationship, it is crucial to learn that the positive relationship can be restored. This is at the heart of the attachment between parent and child and is the core of emotional security and self-confidence. It is a repair system that is set up in a child's early life and is established by the age of 1 year. The secure child learns that the parent figures will soothe and comfort him when he is distressed; they won't leave him to suffer for too long. But if the child learns instead that he cannot turn to mum or dad for comfort when he is distressed, because they ignore him or punish him even more, then he will be stuck in stressful feelings, with cortisol running high, unable to turn it off. That is the parent's job in early life as the child has no capacity to regulate himself.

The child who experiences stress which isn't calmed by his parents grows up like Carys. He doesn't expect to be able to manage those painful feelings of conflict with others. But this isn't a personality trait that he was born with. It is a problem of regulation, which is learnt. More recently, attention has turned to the way in which depressed people regulate their feelings. Judy Garber made a series of fascinating studies of depressed people and their regulatory strategies (Garber and Dodge 1991). It was found that they have a dysfunctional style of regulation, based on the more primitive mechanism of 'fight or flight'. They seem to lack the more complex regulatory strategies that are associated with prefrontal development. Instead of actively solving problems with other people, talking things through, confident that some resolution can be found, they tend either to withdraw from people or attack them aggressively.

Megan Gunnar and Andrea Dettling's research on children with high cortisol echoed this finding. They found that high cortisol children don't expect to be able to deal effectively with other people's negative feelings. Their teachers rate them as less socially competent than other children for the very same reason – they manage negative feelings and difficult situations either by withdrawing or with aggression (Dettling et al. 1999, 2000).

This difficulty in repairing interpersonal situations is echoed by what is going on in the depressive person's brain, which is also having difficulty in repairing and regenerating its own neurons. This seems to be another unfortunate side effect of high levels of stress: overactive pro-inflammatory cytokines also have an effect on neurogenesis. The cytokines can inhibit the expression of brain derived neurotrophic factor (BDNF) (Lin and Su 2007) and hamper the ability of neurons to regenerate themselves after a stressful episode (Bilbo et al. 2012). Warm, supportive early mothering, however, *promotes* neurogenesis (Branchi et al. 2012; Luby et al. 2012; Lin and Su 2007).

Supportive parents are also parents who help their children to regulate their states of mind. Garber and Dodge (1991) discovered that depressed children have different expectations of their mothers from non-depressed children. They don't expect their mothers to be able to regulate them better than they can themselves. They don't expect to be able to alter their negative mood. This may be part of the reason why depressed people so easily fall into global negatives such as 'I'm stupid' or 'I'm bad'. As children they have tried to account for their experience of negative events. But from a child's perspective there is no way of knowing that their regulatory partner could act differently, so they tend to blame themselves and their own inadequacies for their misery. This dilemma, known as the 'moral defence', was described in the 1940s by Scottish psychoanalyst Ronald Fairbairn, who recognised that children were reluctant to admit that their parents were bad because it was safer for oneself to be bad than a parent on whom you depend for survival (Fairbairn 1952).

There is evidence to show that depressed parents, in particular, do offer less good regulation to their children than other parents. Their lack of attentiveness to their children's states may result in a failure to pass on good regulatory strategies. Their children may lack confidence that feelings can be managed jointly in co-operation with other people. However, children who are not depressed (and who do not have depressed parents) are much more able to respond to negative events by taking some sort of action.

They use active problem solving and deliberate distraction. When things go wrong, they draw the conclusion that they need to try harder, or perhaps give up and try something else. They don't assume that they are stuck, or that it must be their fault.

The passivity and apathy of the depressed may have a biochemical dimension, but at a behavioural level it is also the result of internal working models that are formed early in life. By early childhood the die may well be cast – children of depressed mothers have a 29 per cent chance of developing an emotional disorder compared to 8 per cent of children with a medically ill mother (Hammen et al. 1990). Recent research suggests that depressed *fathers* also have an impact on their babies, affecting their children's early behaviour and emotional development (Ramchandani et al. 2005).

These are children who don't expect support, who don't anticipate relief from distress as a result of contact with their parent, and who don't know how to regulate their negative feelings. Because they don't expect ruptures to be repaired, they don't turn to others. Because they have not been taught to focus on solving problems step by step, they cannot imagine any solution. They are truly stuck with negative feelings that they don't know how to disperse, other than by running away.

Unfortunately, depression is also cumulative. These kinds of thought patterns tend to get more easily evoked the more often the person feels hopeless. It has been found that the more often a person has a depressive episode, the more difficult it becomes to recover. Confidence that was not well established early in life may become progressively eroded as the individual fails to manage one situation after another. Brains that are emotionally underpowered by a lack of neurotransmitters and a less developed prefrontal cortex find it hard to generate new solutions, to find new ways of managing and calming the overactive stress response.

Clearly it is much more effective to prevent this vicious cycle from gathering pace. If it were recognised that baby-hood holds some of the keys to depression, it might seem more urgent to help depressed parents at the earliest opportunity. When mothers are successfully treated, and get better within 3 months, the outcome is good for their children (Weissman et al. 2006; Pilowsky et al. 2008). Conversely, stressed parents bring up stressed children, so it is vital to provide a more supportive environment for early parenting, and to find ways to enable parents to give their young children the regulatory skills and emotional confidence that they have lacked themselves.

7

Active harm

The links between trauma in babyhood and trauma in adult life

A plane crashes into the open countryside. Survivors stumble in a haze of smoke through a field of maize as tall as themselves, every footstep exquisitely loud. Each crunching step and laboured breath takes them back closer to the chaos of fire and bodies and panic surrounding the plane. This is the opening scene of the film *Fearless* and the hero of the film, acted flawlessly by Jeff Bridges, has a glazed expression as he passes a woman screaming for her baby, a child searching for his parents. He looks serenely at the scene of devastation, apparently oblivious to the roaring of flames, the wail of sirens and the human cries. Then he quietly appropriates a taxi cab and drives away from the scene.

The opening of this film draws the viewer into the state of mind of a traumatised person, following him over the months after the trauma as he comes to terms with the experience of still being alive – while his friend and business partner did not survive. His relationships are affected: he has difficulty relating to his wife and son, and starts instead to form a bond with another survivor who lost her baby. He has flashbacks of the crash, reliving the moments as the plane went down. He impulsively takes extreme risks with his body, walking blithely across a busy freeway. He is dissociated from reality.

These are indeed some of the symptoms that people experience after extreme traumas such as rape, mugging, car crashes, or war. Such experiences challenge an individual's coping skills to the limit, and most people find their resources temporarily overwhelmed. The psychiatric definition of trauma includes any experience which threatens your life or your body, or any harm which is inflicted on you intentionally (APA 2013). Experts have also found that it is traumatic even to witness this being done to someone else – or to be the perpetrator of harm or death to someone else oneself – suggesting that our identification with others' experience is something we cannot avoid. This is most acute and painful when we are closely involved with someone, and the loss of your own child is perhaps the most agonising loss of all. One autumn afternoon in 2002, when 10-year-old Nicky Fellows was going to visit a friend down the road, she was taken into a nearby wood where she was assaulted and murdered by a stranger. Her mother, Susan Fellows, described how it had affected her marriage at the time: 'We handled our grief differently, and we were accusing each other of not being there for her,' she says. 'I wouldn't let my husband near me ... I couldn't bear him touching me for a long time after. I tried to explain that it wasn't him, it was because of what had happened to Nicky – that she was sexually assaulted – kept flashing back in my mind' (*Guardian*, 25 November 2002).

Trauma is essentially a confrontation with damage to body or mind. It may be the body which is disabled or killed, or the psychological self which is hurt or destroyed. In either case, one person's subjectivity is denied by another person. This kind of hatred takes us to the edge of life – dramatised in Peter Weir's film by the image of the Jeff Bridges character literally walking perilously on the edge of the low wall that tops a skyscraper. Trauma is therefore also about fear in its most primal form. It is the fear of total helplessness, knowing that no one can save you or protect you or your loved one. The bonds that tie you to others are broken. Your physical and psychological integrity is breached. The world that you took for granted, the structure that underlies reality, is shattered. It doesn't look the same any more. It is no longer safe.

Post-traumatic stress disorder

The normal response to these kinds of traumatic experience is to be afraid. When this happens, an individual's amygdala will initiate a fight or flight response and kick various systems into action. The sympathetic nervous system will release adrenaline, and the heart rate and blood pressure will go up. The hypothalamus will then set off a chain reaction which results in the production of cortisol. All these effects normally die down and go back to normal within a few hours. But when the trauma is very extreme or very chronic, this might not happen. It can take as long as a year to recover from post-traumatic stress.

However, the label of post-traumatic stress *disorder* (PTSD) has become a recognised diagnosis of an abnormal reaction to trauma – one which goes on beyond the normal recovery period. When terrible things happen to people, psychiatrists accept that they will have difficulty in integrating the experience into their normal sense of self. The most common symptoms are intrusive thoughts of the trauma, distressing dreams, insomnia, irritability, anxiety, self-harm and a struggle to avoid talking about the trauma (Green 2003). Sufferers may experience flashbacks, panic or depression. They relive the experience over and over, vulnerable to reminders of the experience and hypervigilant and watchful for signs that something bad will happen again. But a person with normal emotional resources will have a chance to make some sense of it, or at least to draw comfort from others, and eventually find a way to live with it and resume a normal life to a large extent. As with any bereavement, the pain becomes more manageable and intermittent as time goes on. Most people recover their equilibrium within a year or so, but PTSD is the diagnosis for people who don't recover.

The reason that around 8 per cent (Russo et al. 2012) have a pathological reaction to adult trauma takes us back to babyhood. Many of the people who find it hard to recover from traumatic experience are those whose emotional systems are less robustly built in early childhood. Epigenetics has made it clear that early adversity can alter the function of the genes responsible for stress reactivity (Weaver 2007) and these altered genes can lead to a greater vulnerability to trauma and a predisposition to PTSD in adulthood (Seckl 2008; Seckl and Meaney 2006; Yehuda and LeDoux 2007).

Inevitably, people who have had difficulties in their past emotional lives, will be more likely to interpret current situations in a negative light. They are more likely to have an oversensitive response to stress, but also to interpret events more negatively. Their stress response may be more easily triggered into overdrive when they unconsciously assess a situation as threatening or unmanageable. Obviously, these assessments do play a very important part in the reaction to stressors. When we assess a situation as not very dangerous, the stress response is not going to be triggered. For example, one woman described by Bessel van der Kolk managed to cope very well with being raped, until many months after the event. She then discovered that her rapist had killed one of his victims. Suddenly, she developed full-blown PTSD symptoms as her interpretation of the danger she had been in changed (Van der Kolk and McFarlane 1996).

At the same time, survivors' powers of recovery will also be affected by their capacity to find the support they need; a capacity that is influenced by past experiences. Because of their lack of confidence in others' support, those who have had insecure or traumatised early lives may also be less likely to seek out support, and having current social support is a factor vital to recovery. Secure relationships help us to regulate feelings. Just holding the hand of someone you trust can reduce the activity of fear circuits in the brain (Coan et al. 2006). When the feeling that other people can keep you safe is lost, trauma can become overwhelming. The highest rate of PTSD in children is found when they have been physically or sexually abused by the very people they trust to protect them (and these also become the adults most likely to get PTSD when faced with traumatic experience) (Charuvastra and Cloitre 2008).

But equally, we all need to be able to feel trust in the wider social world. We need to feel safe within secure personal attachment relationships, but we also need to know that the social world we live in values other people. Some new work with veterans of the Iraq war suffering from PTSD found that their trauma was not predominantly to do with fear for their own well-being, it was to do with damage to their sense of belonging to a decent moral universe. At the start of the invasion, these marines had found themselves uncertain as to who was the enemy and had ended up killing civilians, including women and children. One marine called Lu Lobello could not erase a memory of a fellow marine walking round in circles, muttering and screaming 'We killed a baby! Lobello, we shot a baby!' These veterans suffered from 'moral injury' and were preoccupied with their shame, guilt and regret (Dokoupil 2012; Maguen et al. 2009).

The ability to recover from such intensely challenging experiences depends a great deal on the key systems that are established in early life – from the reactivity of the amygdala and stress response, to the hippocampus and prefrontal cortex control over emotional reactions. All are strongly influenced by the security of our early attachments. (However, it is possible that some traumatic experiences are so intense that they would disturb even the most well-regulated stress response system, as some traumatised survivors of the Nazi concentration camps describe having had warm, responsive families before their incarceration.)

Reactions to the Holocaust of the 1940s have been well documented by survivors and researchers. Victor Frankl, a camp inmate, felt strongly that it was possible to choose one's response to adversity (Frankl 1973) and that individuals could use their capacity to think (their frontal cortex, in effect) to hold on to meaning and a sense of agency even in circumstances that have stripped them away:

> Alternative attitudes really did exist. Probably in
> every concentration camp there were individuals able
> to overcome their apathy and suppress their irritability.
> These were the ones who were examples of renunciation
> and self-sacrifice. Asking nothing for themselves, they
> went about on the grounds and in the barracks of the
> camp, offering a kind word here, a last crust of bread
> there.

This behaviour he saw as the result of a 'spiritual attitude'. Others had great difficulty in holding on to value and meaning. For example, Roma Ligocka, at the time a child in the Polish ghetto – portrayed in Stephen Spielberg's film

Schindler's List as the little girl in a red coat – revealed in a recent interview that the horrors of that time in her life had not left her, despite a richly creative adult life as a theatrical designer. She said that she still suffered from fear, depression and sleeplessness – 'Time does not heal wounds' (*Guardian*, 16 October 2002). Such different responses may have more to do with an individual's early experience than with choice. Their internal systems may have become less robust because of their difficult early experiences or even through their *parents'* traumatic experiences being passed on to them. The extraordinary discoveries of epigenetics have highlighted the fact that once parents' own adaptations to life have resulted in altered genes, these can be inherited by their children, leaving them in turn more vulnerable to adversity (Yehuda and Bierer 2009).

The brain and PTSD

Various studies have found that the response of the amygdala, one of the more primitive areas of the brain conditioned by earlier fear experiences, is central to PTSD. Sufferers have amygdalas in a hyperactive state (Shin 2009; Etkin and Wager 2007, 2010; Liberzon et al. 1999). An amygdala in overdrive keeps a person in a state of vigilance, experiencing sympathetic nervous system arousal with rapid breathing, palpitations, cold sweats, nervousness and vigilance. Danger is around every corner. People in this state find themselves organising their whole lives around the trauma, usually trying to avoid any situation that might trigger associated thoughts and memories – although in some cases, such as with Jeff Bridges in the film *Fearless*, they may compulsively expose themselves to danger. Most sufferers will try every means at their disposal to switch off their arousal – avoiding people, trying to numb themselves with drink or drugs, often trying not to feel anything at all, since feeling nothing is better than feeling upset.

But they are handicapped in switching off their fear system for several reasons. One is that their amygdala may have been oversensitised to frightening experience in the womb or in early post-natal life. Another is that early childhood trauma or stress has affected the development of their anterior cingulate and medial prefrontal cortex, which, as we have already seen in an earlier chapter, play an important role in managing the amygdala. Several studies have found that the anterior cingulate is smaller in those who experienced early childhood trauma or stress (Woodward et al. 2013; Cohen et al. 2006; Bremner 2006). When these areas of the brain are sluggish and 'hypoactive' (Etkin and Wager 2010), they may be underpowered and less able to inhibit the amygdala and extinguish fear. This increases individuals' risk that PTSD might develop in future combat situations such as Vietnam (Shin et al. 2001; Woodward et al. 2013) – but also in any traumatic situation in adult life (Kasai et al. 2008).

There are other consequences of early stress which can affect the health of the amygdala and the circuits around it. Poor early attachment experiences can also lead to a lack of oxytocin, which also contributes to difficulties in suppressing the amygdala's fear responses (Fries 2005; Charuvastra and Cloitre 2008).

Early stress also reduces the amount of serotonin available to help the amygdala and anterior cingulate – and the neural circuit that runs between them – to function well. The younger a child is when he or she experiences stress, the less serotonin is available – and the more likely he is to be at risk of later PTSD (Murrough et al. 2011; Krystal and Neumeister 2009).

Many sufferers of chronic PTSD (though not all – it seems to be particularly associated with having experienced early childhood maltreatment (Schmidt et al. 2011)) also have low baseline cortisol levels. Since it is cortisol which switches off the emergency stress response, this may play an important part in the difficulty in recovering from flashbacks, and from states of high arousal. Low cortisol also allows the inflammatory response to flourish unchecked, bringing us back to the peculiar constellation of early stress leading to low cortisol leading to autoimmune illness. Recent research has suggested that individuals with PTSD have epigenetic changes in the genes related to inflammatory and immune responses (Beals 2010).

One expert who has long worked in this area of research is Rachel Yehuda in New York, who suggests that the lower cortisol found in PTSD sufferers may reflect an enhanced negative feedback by cortisol. Their glucocorticoid receptors become more sensitive and need less cortisol to react to stress (Yehuda 1999, 2001). When people whose systems have tried to defensively keep cortisol at a low level are hit with a fresh trauma, they react more strongly than others with a powerful wave of cortisol production.

Yehuda's recent work with New Yorkers who were pregnant at the time of the 9/11 attack on the World Trade Centre has shown that the women who developed PTSD as a result of this event had low cortisol. (Mothers who didn't develop PTSD didn't have low cortisol.) But the consequences were felt even by the next generation: when they were born, the babies of the PTSD mothers also had low cortisol, showing once again how a child's HPA axis stress system can be programmed even in the womb (Yehuda et al. 2005, 2009).

The role of the hippocampus

So cortisol, a stress hormone, can affect the stress response itself. But it can also affect another part of the brain which is involved with the HPA axis. This is the hippocampus, which through its influence on the hypothalamus (the H in HPA) can also help tone down the stress response. Unfortunately, when a child is under chronic stress, the cortisol that floods the brain is toxic to hippocampal cells and can eventually shrink the hippocampus over a longer period of stress (Moghaddam et al. 1994; McEwen 2001, 2010). Since the hippocampus plays a key role in organising our memories, a weakened hippocampus may also affect the ability to integrate memories into our personal history and to 'get things in proportion' as common sense would have it.

Cortisol is pernicious for the hippocampus also because it has ongoing effects on the possibility of recovery. Normally the hippocampus has great powers of regeneration. But too much cortisol can reduce levels of serotonin and BDNF, which may in turn affect the growth of new neurons in the hippocampus and its normally remarkable lifelong ability to recover (Karatsoreos and McEwen 2011; Chalmers et al. 1993; Pitchot et al. 2001).

Brain imaging studies have found that people with long-term PTSD have hippocampal shrinkage. Their hippocampi are about 8 per cent smaller than normal. In one study of Vietnam veterans who had been exposed to particularly intense and prolonged trauma, it was reduced by as much as 26 per cent (Bremner et al. 1997). This looked like a prima facie case that chronic exposure to the trauma of war was probably damaging these soldiers' brains. Their smaller hippocampi seemed to be the result of their terrible experiences in combat over a long period of time. However, other research has challenged this view. There is some evidence that the smaller hippocampi of these men may actually have preceded their time in Vietnam (Gilbertson et al. 2002).

Gilbertson and his colleagues at Harvard studied twins, one of whom had been exposed to the trauma of combat, while the other stayed at home. Following the established line of thinking, they discovered that the twin who had been exposed to trauma and who had developed PTSD had a smaller hippocampus than other veterans who had not developed PTSD. This fitted the thesis that stress itself had shrunk the hippocampus. The smaller the hippocampus, the more severe the post-traumatic stress. But then they found that the stay-at-home twin also had the same small hippocampus – implying that the small hippocampus had predated the stress of war.

Now it began to look as if it was the small hippocampus itself which had caused the combatant twin to succumb to PTSD. It is possible that without a fully developed hippocampus the stressed twins found it more difficult to process trauma than others with a relatively normal hippocampus.

Further research has confirmed that this may be due to their early experiences. Imaging studies have shown that children who are chronically physically or sexually abused may grow up to have the same reduced hippocampal volume in their brains (Bremner et al. 1997; Villareal and King 2001). Adults who suffer from major depression also have smaller hippocampi, perhaps as a result of their early experiences (Cole et al. 2011; Teicher et al. 2012; Bremner et al. 2000b).

The hippocampus may have a sensitive period when it is most affected by maltreatment or a lack of warm parental nurturing. The key period of development is thought to be between the ages of 3 and 5 years (Anderson 2008; Rao et al. 2010; Teicher et al. 2012). However, the picture is a complicated one. During early childhood itself, shrinkage is not in evidence. It only becomes visible in early adulthood. Researchers can't yet entirely make sense of these findings.

There may also be genetic predispositions involved. Recent discoveries include a link between a gene involved in memory (PKCa) and a gene involved in processing fear (Oprl1) both of which are thought to increase the risk of developing PTSD. However, the impact of genetic predispositions can't be separated from experience, particularly early experience. An individual with these genes who lives his life in a comfortable suburban existence may never get to use them. As Michael Meaney, a distinguished Canadian professor of medicine put it: 'Neurotransmitter and hormonal activity is profoundly influenced ... by social interactions, which lead to effects on gene activity, or expression. At no point in life is the operation of the genome independent of the context in which it functions' (Gonzalez-Pardo and Alvarez 2013: 10).

Putting shock into words

While the emotionally 'hot' amygdala stores powerful memories at an unconscious level and is not very open to change, the 'cool' hippocampus is involved in more conscious, verbal memory processes and is constantly updating its information. Together, the orbitofrontal cortex informed by the hippocampus can evaluate situations and anticipate their outcomes. This means that the hippocampus can play an important part in adapting to new circumstances. It can also alter memories and enable our personal narrative and sense of ourselves to move on with us. But in PTSD that isn't happening. With a less effective hippocampus, sufferers have a problem with integrating their traumatic experiences into verbal memory. They get stuck.

Rauch and his colleagues set up an experiment to find out what was happening in the brains of traumatised people when their traumatic memories were activated (Rauch et al. 1996). Using their own taped account of what had happened to them, he played back the tapes while scanning their brains using PET scans. What he found was that blood flow decreased in the left frontal hemisphere and Broca's area, which is involved in verbal organising – while blood flow increased in the right limbic system and visual cortex areas where emotions, sense of smell and visual images are activated. The traumatic memories were activating the global, sensory, emotional right brain but decreasing activity in the verbal left brain, as if the two were failing to connect. While highly aroused with areas of the right brain, the left frontal brain was unable to make sense of the experience and put it into verbal and narrative form. This may account for the phenomenon of speechless terror – that awful moment when you are confronted with something so overwhelming that you just squeak or can't get any words out at all. But without the verbalising activities of the left frontal brain, Broca's area and hippocampus, it is difficult to process and evaluate feelings normally. These left-brain activities would normally put experiences into a context and into a time sequence. But without their full participation, feelings never get into the past and can't be put behind you. They keep leaping into the present as if they were happening all over again, right now. This is the flashback state, which is a reliving of fragmented memories that have not been adequately processed by the hippocampus and other systems.

Recovery may depend on talking about it – on getting the appropriate parts of the left brain activated to put the traumatic experience into context. Putting stress into words has been found to be an effective way of coping with it, in many circumstances (Pennebaker 1993). Of course, this is not really an option for a small child. As I have outlined in earlier chapters, the left brain and the hippocampus do not become fully functional until the second or third year of life. Therefore, early stress in babyhood and in the preschool period is unlikely to be effectively processed in these areas of the brain. Stressful experience is more likely to be stored in the amygdala and the subcortical areas of the brain. However, without a fully developed prefrontal cortex at this time, the child has little chance of overriding the subcortical system with the orbitofrontal cortex. He will not be able to 'adjust his self-o-stat' as the TV show *The Simpsons* once put it (Van der Kolk and McFarlane 1996). Instead, he may get stuck in a constant appraisal of threat, with the amygdala in overdrive and a distorted stress response.

The continuum between trauma and abuse

Adults with robust stress responses and normal hippocampi can usually manage the pain and distress of extreme circumstances, although they may go through an exhausting psychic struggle to do so and need a great deal of support. But children, whose brains and body systems are still in the process of development, are much more vulnerable. They have fewer resources and at the same time, they are much closer to the possibility of death. They cannot survive alone and are highly dependent on adults to provide for their basic needs of food, shelter, warmth and comfort. Without the goodwill of adults, they could indeed die. In this sense, experiences that would not be a matter of life and death for an adult may well be experienced as such by a child. If the mother or carer so much as goes out of sight, there is a possibility that the child could be attacked or injured without her. Equally, if she is not disposed to protect the child, he is exposed to danger. Trauma as a confrontation with mortality in some form is in some ways then much more likely in childhood than in adulthood, particularly in comfortable societies where adults rarely starve, fight wars, or die in epidemics. But childhood trauma may also result from a much wider and more innocuous-seeming range of circumstances.

From an adult perspective, 'abuse' tends to mean the more gross and visible examples of maltreatment such as hitting and injuring children, or violating them sexually. It is much harder, I think, for some adults to appreciate that being told you are 'a stupid waste of space' or being left unattended and alone are also traumatic for dependent children. The essential aspect of trauma is that it generates doubts about surviving – either as a body, but equally as a psychological self. As one survivor put it: 'I had to believe I was hurt and hated because I was so bad, and so all these years I hurt and hated myself' (Chu 1998: 88).

Children demand a great deal of protection and care, but they reward us with their devotion to their caregivers. For them, adults are the centre of their world. In Western families, where there are few alternatives to the mother as the source of protection and nurture, and few opportunities to form loving bonds with other adults in the wider community, this dependence can be extreme. So much then depends on one central caregiver and her state of mind to create a safe world or a fearful world for her child.

The emotional world that parents create for their children is experienced with an intensity that tends to fade as the dependency lessens. The atmosphere of this world is conveyed by films such as Ingmar Bergman's *Fanny and Alexander*, which conjures up dazzling impressions of the sensory richness of Christmas in a large Swedish house where an extended family is gathering. We see the weirdness of complex adult relationships from a child's eye view. Childhood seems to pass in slow motion, in a world where every move the adults make is magnified in the child's mind. Adults loom large while children are acutely responsive to adult moods and often sensitive to every slight and every hint of praise. Although children can band together against adults, with great glee, most children dependent on their small nuclear families will feel the impact of rejection or neglect by their caregivers most painfully. Certainly it is now recognised that more extreme childhood abuse of various types can lead to a variety of serious later conditions such as major depression, borderline personality disorder, or symptoms of post-traumatic stress disorder.

Research tends to focus on those conditions that have been well defined and that have the most impact on later psychological functioning, but in my view there is a continuum between milder forms of neglect and emotional abuse and its more intense or sustained forms. They are essentially the same thing – a problem with emotional regulation within the parent–child relationship. In all cases, when regulation is problematic, the bonds between parents and children are thrown into question, leaving an inner residue of doubt about their safety and security. In less severe cases, this will be manifest as insecure attachments of the avoidant or resistant type that may lead to depression and anxiety, neurosis or narcissistic personality disorders. But in more dysfunctional parent–child relationships, anxiety may shade into outright fear. These types of relationships were identified relatively recently as a 'disorganised' type of attachment, where there was no consistent defence mechanism (Main and Solomon 1990).

The disturbed child

Toddlers who are defined as having these disorganised attachments are those who don't have a consistent pattern of behaviour with their mother. In experimental conditions designed to discover their attachment status, they react in a confused way to reunions with their parent – sometimes eager, sometimes frozen. I have seen video footage of children who are placed in this category. They are the children who bang their heads against the wall when the parent comes in, who move eagerly towards her but then swerve away, or who just sit on the floor looking at no one, making a weird high-pitched sound. They may have muscular tics, related to right-hemisphere dysfunction (Schore 2003). All these behaviours make sense as an expression of confusion, of not knowing whether it is safe or not to go to the parent. They are in the grip of what Jeremy Holmes has called the 'approach/avoidance dilemma' (Holmes 2002).

Most maltreated children end up with disorganised attachments (Schore 2003). These children are confused and disorganised because they simply don't know if they can trust parents who do sometimes hurt them, or frighten them. It is an exquisitely painful dilemma, particularly in childhood when you depend so much on your parental figures. The attachment system is motivating you to go to them but experience tells you it could be dangerous. Instead of comforting you, you fear they might attack you. This is similar in some ways to the experience of children in the 'resistant' category, who also experience parental inconsistency. The difference is that for children who become 'disorganised', their parents are positively frightening at times, either because of their aggression or because of their extreme vulnerability and anxiety. Either way, fear and love get mixed up. In adulthood, this pattern may be seen in people who get caught up in sado-masochistic relationships.

Many children with disorganised attachments will have experienced this poisonous concoction of love combined with harm. The degree of stress they experience in their family is reflected in their very high levels of cortisol, much higher than in other insecure children (Bernard and Dozier 2010; Hertsgaard et al. 1995). These are also the children who are most at risk of developing serious psychopathology in adulthood. Some go on to become diagnosed as suffering from borderline personality disorder (although not all).

The effects on the child's brain of early abuse and neglect are like other forms of stress; such experiences sensitise the stress response and generate high CRF and high cortisol. Early traumatic experience, such as maternal deprivation which is highly stressful for a dependent child (Hennessy 1997), can also affect the emotional circuits of the brain, pruning away the rapidly developing links between the orbitofrontal cortex, anterior cingulate and amygdala via the hypothalamus – the very system that has the power to restrain the impulsive amygdala (Schore 2003). It can also alter the balance between serotonin and dopamine in the orbitofrontal cortex and in the anterior cingulate (Poeggel et al. 2003). In fact, it appears to affect the volume of the brain in general, particularly the size of the prefrontal cortex. The earlier a child experiences severe abuse or neglect, the smaller the brain volume, particularly of the prefrontal cortex which is so vital in controlling and calming the more urgent fear reactions of the amygdala (De Bellis et al. 2002).

Children's brains are most vulnerable to stress at the time when they are developing fastest. In particular, the time when a brain region becomes metabolically active is the time when it contributes most to the behavioural reper-toire of the individual (Chugani et al. 2001). It seems likely then that trauma has its strongest effects on the stress response while the stress response is developing – up to the age of 3. High cortisol early in life may also be responsible for hippocampal damage, since cortisol increases the release of glutamates which are thought to damage the hippoc-ampus. These glutamates may interfere with feedback systems and with the adaptability of the brain. Timing also does seem to play an important part in setting the baseline level of cortisol reactivity. Where stress has been chronic very early on, the baseline is likely to peak, then drop below normal. Later stress, however, doesn't seem to alter the baseline level in this way (Lyons et al. 2000b; Dettling et al. 2002). Taken together, the effects of early stress appear to have the potential for considerable handicapping of the indi-vidual's capacities to respond to future stress.

Minor traumas

I don't want to leave the impression that trauma arises only from extreme or continuously difficult experiences. Attachment trauma can also arise from periodic episodes of neglect or abusive treatment, or as Jon Allen put it, 'the core failure is episodic unresponsiveness when the infant is in a state of heightened attachment needs' (Allen 2001). In other words, the attachment system is activated when a child is afraid and needs comfort, reassurance, safety and it is trau-matic when he or she does not get it. Those who manage such difficult attachment experiences with relatively effec-tive defences such as the avoidant or resistant ways of behaving are more likely to be vulnerable to emotional diffi-culties in a minor key: to narcissistic personality disorder, anxiety, neurosis or depression. Their early experiences rarely reach the intensity of overt abuse, but they do belong to the same continuum. The parenting that such children have received is also less than optimal. They have often been dependent on parents who are relatively incompetent in managing feelings. But because this end of the continuum shades into normality, and because many perfectly good parents are at times incompetent or out of control, it is harder to see how such chronic mismanagement of feelings can in fact deeply affect a dependent child. These children do not usually have the deep fears about their physical survival that more disturbed children will have experienced. Nonetheless, they are still exposed to fears about their *psychological* survival. They are left feeling uncertain about their worth and whether they have a right to exist.

Attachment literature has made it clear that children develop working models of relationships based on their own experiences, but that these are not simply models of how other people behave. They are models of one's self *with* another person; models of interaction between people, not static internal images of 'mother' or 'father'. This means that the inner pictures that we draw on to guide our behaviour are images that conjure up how it *feels* to be with another person. If the other person consistently treats you as if you were a fool, you feel like a fool. (You also develop the capacity to treat others as if they were fools.) If your parents show little interest in your states of mind, you feel as if your states of mind are not of interest to others (and probably have little interest in their states of mind either). Of course, as people develop they bring their internal working models to bear on other people too, but in early childhood they are still being formed and are largely shaped by the adults and older children in their life. From later childhood onwards, they will elaborate and rework these early models in various ways.

But in families which neglect or criticise their children too much, there can be a fundamental uncertainty about the worth of the self. The internal working model will be one of inner worthlessness or even badness anticipating a critical or neglectful other. These expectations inform behaviour and often draw others into confirming the expectations, setting up a vicious cycle which is hard to break. Just how difficult will be examined in the following chapters.

8

Torment

The links between personality disorders and early experience

> I looked upon myself like so much garbage, an anomaly, a disgrace, and, what was worse, I believed that I had allowed myself to be overrun by error because of an evil nature.
>
> Marie Cardinal 1984

Being the object of others' negative attention or being disregarded is like an acid which eats away at self-esteem. As we have seen, it can lead to depression or can create a vulnerability to depression if experienced early in life when the personality is forming. But there is a darker form of depression, which is linked to more extreme early experiences, particularly in infancy. This is known in the psychiatric trade as 'borderline personality disorder'. It originally described someone who is on the borderline of psychosis, prone to lose their grip on reality and liable to take their inner world for reality. For example, someone who is fearful of another person's motives towards him may believe that she is actually trying to poison him. Today, borderline personality disorder is more commonly seen as a disorder of emotional regulation.

There is a whole rainbow-like diagnostic spectrum of personality disorders (with acronyms such as ASPD, BPD, NPD, OCD etc.) which have been categorised to give doctors and mental health workers some sense of clarity and predictability in their encounters with people in mental distress. Real individuals don't always fit neatly into such categories. Although these terms are useful insofar as they provide a shorthand form of communication between professionals, I think it needs to be made clear that although couched in the language of disease, the personality disorders are not actual diseases of any kind. In fact, they merely describe typical features of various points on a continuum of difficulties in managing emotional life.

The other problem they raise for me is that there is always something demeaning about being described in such terms as 'narcissistic' or 'borderline personality'. The terminology carries a slight sneer, a whiff of contempt with it and to my mind conveys little compassion for the personal history that will inevitably have gone before. Despite all that, I will carry on using these terms because they do conveniently mark out certain territories.

Depression runs through the personality disorders, like a familiar theme in different pieces of music. In both the 'narcissistic' and 'borderline' disturbances of personality, individuals are prone to depression. They share a fragile sense of self that can be disturbed by experiences which more robust people would manage with little difficulty. But the depression of the 'borderline' is less a flattening of feelings and submission to fate than a terrifying roller coaster of emotions. Borderline behaviours are described in textbook terms as including self-destructiveness, impulsiveness, dissociation, hostility, shame, fear of abandonment and difficulty maintaining stable relationships. To others living better regulated lives, it is apparent that the borderline person has enormous difficulty in regulating feelings. Emotions are on the rampage, often quite out of control.

But the focus on describing the 'symptoms' of the person with a personality disorder inevitably results in distortion. These are not qualities the person was born with, nor are they the sum total of the whole personality. The symptoms are the end results of certain typical histories of parent–child relationships. On this continuum, to think in the most simplified terms, it is likely that the more hurtful these relationships have been, the greater the symptoms are likely to be. The situation is more complex than that, of course, since individual temperaments and circumstances play their part in the outcome, as well as the timing of various events, which can be crucial as we will see. But what can be stated quite categorically is that emotional difficulties such as these are the result of an individual's relationship history (Carlson et al. 2009; Agrawal et al. 2004).

In particular, the borderline experience may be a disturbance rooted in early infancy. Allan Schore sees the central feature of the borderline experience as growing up in a family which does not help the child to process his own emotional experience well. The child may have a mother there all day long, but the experience is one of 'neglect in the presence of the mother'. The child is buffeted by emotion, experiencing high levels of sympathetic nervous system arousal because his parent figures are in some way physically or psychologically absent or abusive. Recent research has confirmed the powerful effect it can have on a baby when a parent emotionally withdraws; it is in fact the biggest factor in predicting the development of borderline personality disorder, especially the likelihood of future self-harm (Lyons-Ruth et al. 2013). This may well be because a parent's withdrawal from close contact deprives the child of the regulatory partner that he or she needs to make sense of emotional experiences and to keep on an even keel through the day. It has been noticed by some commentators that in borderline family histories, the father as well as the mother is usually not well attuned to the child, leaving the child in a state of virtual emotional abandonment.

What kinds of parents do borderline people have?

Most often these are parents who have very few inner resources themselves and find it very difficult to be sensitive to their babies' cues, usually because they are so preoccupied with their own feelings. For example, a baby who is over-aroused by a noisy rattle being waved close to his face will turn his head away to signal that he has had enough of that particular stimulus. But the unattuned parent may be paying more attention, consciously or unconsciously, to her own inner state of anxiety or distress than to her baby's signal. She might shake the rattle more loudly, thinking that he has just lost interest, instead of responding accurately to the baby's signal and soothing him or offering him something else. As a result, she will increase his (unpleasant) arousal rather than regulating it back to a good state. Of course, such incidents are part of normal parenting and have little effect in a relationship which is mostly attuned, but if this is the chronic state of things, it can affect the baby's regulatory capacities. Worse, if the parent's inner state is one of turmoil and resentment or even hostility to her baby, her capacity to regulate him well will diminish even further.

Lacking self-soothing skills, such parents trying to cope with a baby will be highly stressed. Their nerves are jangled by the baby's crying. The baby's mess is intolerable. There is no time for themselves. Parents in this state who lack helpful family supports may react strongly against the baby, hitting or verbally attacking him, or they may avoid him altogether, leaving him to cry.

The parent of a potential borderline person is often very needy and sensitive to rejection. She may feel that her newborn baby doesn't like her because he is not yet smiling, or perhaps when her baby starts to take an interest in the world around him at around 4 months old, this parent can feel that he is rejecting her. He doesn't seem to need her any more. This can feel very painful since her own emotional needs are so powerfully felt, so unmet. She may retaliate by withdrawing from the baby. The problem is that anyone with powerful unmet needs of her own may find great difficulty in putting the baby's needs before her own, particularly if that does not provide any gratification for her. It can be very hard for her to be a parent in the psychological sense.

Often, such parents have had histories of being neglected or maltreated in their own childhood. They may reject their babies in ways that they too have been rejected. One curious piece of evidence showed that mothers who abuse their young children find it quite aversive to be with them. Alongside the more predictable finding that the mothers' abusive behaviour towards their babies was often triggered by the baby crying was another finding that was more surprising. These mothers had an unpleasantly high level of arousal not only when their baby cried, but also when the baby smiled at them (Frodi and Lamb 1980). Perhaps they found the demands of a relationship with a baby too much, living with a profound uncertainty about their capacity to regulate their own or the baby's arousal.

Even though such parents might have great devotion to their children, their difficulty in sustaining emotional availability because of their own inner preoccupations tends to make them erratic parents who frequently fail to respond to their baby's distress. As a result, their children often develop disorganised attachments. This can also happen sometimes in families which are not neglectful or abusive, but which have had a tragedy of some kind which has not been successfully mourned. Very often, this might be the death of a previous baby, or sometimes the death of the grandparent, which remains in the parent's mind, distracting her from living in the present and attending fully to her baby. The effect on the baby can be rather similar to living with a parent who can't pay attention because of a legacy of inner pain left from her own childhood. In either case, the salient fact is that the baby finds the parent's attention unpredictable and unrelated to his own needs. For example, she might go into a trance-like state, or flinch away from the baby as if the baby is going to hurt her, or suddenly loom into the baby's face too close – behaviours that are frightening to the baby but have more to do with what is going on in the parent's mind than a response to the baby (Solomon and George 1999: 13).

Fear is usually a component of the 'disorganised' baby's experience, perhaps partly because inconsistent care in the first year of life is itself potentially life threatening. Adult patients who may have had these sorts of experiences as infants often describe feelings of falling or disintegrating, suggestive of moments of total regulatory failure.

My clients Norah and her baby Ricky had a volatile relationship which generated these kinds of moments of fear for Ricky. Norah adored her baby when she felt all right, but when her boyfriend let her down and didn't call round when he said he would, she felt so lost and abandoned and enraged that she would treat Ricky viciously, feeding him roughly, shoving the spoon into his mouth in a sadistic fashion, or she would be playing with him and suddenly give in to the urge to pinch his ear very hard, making him cry. Later, she could feel remorse for her behaviour, but she seemed incapable of controlling it. She worried that Ricky wouldn't love her any more because of the way she treated him at times, but still experienced flashes of pure hatred for him as the embodiment of a world that didn't love her enough.

In effect, parents suffering from unmanageable internal pain create a barrier between themselves and their child. Norah's attacks on Ricky made him look at her with the wariness and anxious fearfulness that made her doubt whether he loved her. Such situations feed on themselves in a vicious cycle, which it is vital to break into at the earliest opportunity. Fortunately, Norah did seek help. By becoming more aware of her own history and the distress that could be so easily triggered in the present, she was able to see Ricky differently and to recognise that he was not the cause of that distress. Prolonged therapeutic work is often needed to help such parents to learn to manage their own states well enough to be able to focus on the baby's needs.

The 'disorganised' baby

But what is it like to be the baby of such a parent? It is very difficult for him to co-ordinate his developing systems with his mother as she is so unpredictable. He can't develop a coherent strategy or game plan with such a parent. He doesn't know whether to turn to her or keep away from her. He needs her, but she may make things worse rather than better. These are the features of a disorganised attachment, as I described in the last chapter.

Disorganised attachments are at the extreme end of the scale of emotional dysregulation, with corresponding effects on the brain. The child is simply not being taught how to manage feelings in any consistent way. He may not have the brain structures to calm himself and cope with distress. Small stresses may escalate into major distress because the orbitofrontal cortex cannot control the arousal of the amygdala and hypothalamus. He may find it difficult to hold back feelings or distract himself when it's necessary to achieve his own goals. This actually leaves the developing child in a rather helpless and dependent state, unable to trust his own responses, constantly looking to other people for cues about how to act and feel. Even though time passes and he looks as if he is growing up, internally he may remain a baby who awaits vital input that would give him the tools to cope with the world.

The kind of neglect that results from having parents preoccupied with their own emotional states can also be very frightening. It is hard to make sense of a world which has to be navigated without a reliable guide. But the parent may also be frightening because he or she is unpredictably violent, or verbally abusive at times when her own feelings spiral out of control.

According to Marsha Linehan, an American therapist who has pioneered a highly effective treatment programme especially for borderline personality disorders, the borderline person has experienced what she calls an 'invalidating environment' in childhood (Linehan 1993). Its essence is the parents' inability to recognise and respect the child's own feelings and experiences. They may be denigrated because they are an inconvenience to the parents. 'Shut up about that stupid toy, we're not going back for Mr. Squeaky' the parent will say. Because of her own inability to soothe herself, the parent cannot bear her child being upset. Instead of acknowledging what is wrong, the parent feels so uncomfortable that she says irritably 'stop being a cry-baby'. Such parenting behaviour in effect demands that the child manage his own feelings and punishes the child for a lack of moral fibre if he is not equal to the task. But it does not teach the child how to manage his feelings.

The requirement not to have feelings that your parent finds too demanding may also result in the production of a 'false self', a front which acts like a person but doesn't feel like a person inside. As Marie Cardinal, a French woman who wrote an account of her slow recovery from mental illness, put it:

I had been fashioned to resemble as closely as possible a human model which I had not chosen and which did

not suit me. Day after day since my birth, I had been
made up: my gestures, my attitudes, my vocabulary.
My needs were repressed, my desires, my impetus,
they had been dammed up, painted over, disguised and
imprisoned. After having removed my brain, having
gutted my skull, they had stuffed it full of acceptable
thoughts which suited me like an apron on a cow.
(Cardinal 1984: 121)

The narcissistic personality disorder

Patti was a patient of mine who felt that she too was an 'as
if' person. She was an active person who enjoyed walking
and travel, but had not managed to develop any of her interests into a career. She could not stick at anything long
enough to become good at it. She did not say so, but her
descriptions of her parents conjured up people who were
intolerant of her feelings and needs. They wanted her to
grow up as fast as possible and had not enjoyed her being a
dependent baby. She had not been breastfed. If she cried out
at night, her mother didn't come. Her mother's needs came
first. She could not wait to get away from the children, to
shop for nice clothes, have an affair, enjoy her holidays.
Someone else was always left on the beach with the children.
She was not very interested in them or their company. Worse,
when Patti inconvenienced her, for example, by knocking
over a special vase that her mother had forgotten to put
away, her mother would lash out with fury and hit her. She
was frequently punished. Patti grew up feeling she was
clumsy and stupid, and focused on trying hard to please
others by being helpful. She attempted to be a sensible,
grown-up person, yet inside she always felt like a little girl
in a world full of grown ups, Alice in Wonderland, lost without
the rule book. She would try to have the feelings she thought
were expected of her, but she had great difficulty in knowing
what she was really feeling. Her personal relationships
never quite got off the ground and soon fizzled out for one
reason or another. This story is typical of the experiences of
a 'narcissistic personality disorder' – the kind of experience
which might lead to a vulnerability to depression.

The narcissistic or 'neurotic' person is often described in terms of attempts to manage without other people. Various writers have attempted to define narcissism, but most agree on the typical symptoms of narcissism as:

- self-consciousness and shame (extreme reactions to being criticised)
- an inflated sense of self (grandiosity)
- not knowing who you are, being out of touch with feelings
- fear of others' envy
- the illusion of self-sufficiency
- sado-masochism and hidden anger (based on Mollon 1993).

Most of these categories involve the kind of instability involved in not being well connected to others and not being able to use them to help regulate feelings. Feelings of personal power and agency fluctuate, so that at times the individual feels capable of great things without any help, and at other times feels that others will hurt or destroy him.

Allan Schore believes that problems in the narcissistic spectrum have their roots in toddlerhood. He thinks that people with these sorts of difficulties probably had good enough care as babies to have a coherent body image and even to feel very good about themselves at times, as excited toddlers do, but he suggests that they have not had the kind of parenting that would help them to manage shame and the recovery from shame.

Many parents do well at the baby stage, unlike the parents I have just described as potential parents of 'borderline' people. They are able to enjoy their babies because they feel needed and powerful. The baby can be experienced as an extension of the mother's body and is largely under her control. However, when their child becomes a toddler with a mind of his own and a body that comes under his own control, they may not enjoy parenting as much. The mother wants a compliant child who fits in with her and meets her needs – possibly one who does not grow up and become separate. She does, in a sense, want to take over the child (see above, the narcissistic adult's fear of being taken over).

This kind of parent might forge an insecure attachment with her child. She may be an inconsistent mother who can be totally in tune with the child one moment, but withdrawn, bored, or unattuned the next; or she may be a more consistently resentful and reluctant mother, as Patti's seems to have been.

No matter what the attachment pattern, humiliation may be a central issue that links those in the narcissistic spectrum. Allan Schore thinks that its 'symptoms' arise largely from the poor regulation of shame, in particular. During toddlerhood, important aspects of socialisation are taking place, facilitating important brain development. As I have already described in Chapter 3, this is when the orbitofrontal area of the prefrontal cortex matures and comes online. As the orbitofrontal cortex starts to develop connections with the amygdala, it can stop the amygdala in turn from activating the hypothalamus and other autonomic structures (Barbas 2007). This enables the child to begin to be able to control his own behaviour in response to parental guidance and to choose not to react so impulsively. This is a key period when parents can start to convey their rules to their child.

One way they do this is by withdrawing attunement and positive feedback. As the orbitofrontal cortex develops, it gets more skilled at 'reading' faces and evaluating social situations and can now start to recognise disapproval and negativity on the parent's face. Through its connections to the autonomic nervous system, this can trigger the unpleasant 'gut' feelings of humiliation, leading to a drop in blood pressure, as well as the release of cortisol.

Although this process is an important route to learning social rules, it's equally vital for the ruptured relationship to be quickly repaired before the feeling of continuity of the good relationship is lost. This is a matter of judgement, and can perhaps be extended in time as the child gets older. But small children, who need much more continuous regulation, cannot afford to lose the thread of their regulatory relationship. At a physiological level, they need to restore the warm connection with their parent in order to disperse the cortisol and other stress hormones and regulate back to a normal set point.

Parents who are not good at regulating their toddlers may leave the toddler in a distressed state for too long. They may be parents who have difficulties in bearing negative feelings, so they may attempt to distance themselves from the child's feelings instead of entering into them and 'containing' them. These parents often tease or humiliate a child in a state of shame, saying things such as 'I can see why they picked on you in the playground' or 'Don't be so wet.' If the child is angry, instead of containing the anger the parent may escalate it – 'Don't you talk to me like that!' Equally, the parent may have difficulty responding to the toddler's excitement and joy, in meeting it and sharing it, and regulating it to a manageable level. With these kinds of regulatory difficulties, over time the child may lose confidence in his relationship with the parent and in its basic goodness and capacity to regulate him. As we have seen in the previous chapter, he may become prone to depression – easily plunged into dysregulation by a current humiliation or loss, because his stress response is oversensitised during toddlerhood.

Along the spectrum towards abuse

Although this was true of Patti's toddlerhood, there was also a deeper undertone in Patti's experience, which was more difficult to get at and to put into words. There were hints that her problems did not just originate in her toddler experience, but went further back to the beginning of her life as a baby. Her mother had found her difficult to breastfeed. She didn't hold her very much. There were incidents which suggested that her mother was actively hostile towards her early on – an incident of hypothermia when she had been left out in her pram for too long, being told she was an ugly baby. Later, at the start of her own adolescence, she became aware of her mother's continuing hostility when they were on a camping holiday and she was forced to wash her mother's blood-stained knickers in public. But such memories were few and her conscious awareness and ability to put these things into words was limited.

However, in her relationship with her therapist, Patti wordlessly conveyed many things about her early life, in particular her deep ambivalence towards women. Her wiry, restless body conveyed tension: she tended to treat the therapist as a social acquaintance whom she was chatting to at a bus stop, relaying the week's events, rather than as an intimate regulatory partner whom she could trust to understand and manage her more difficult feelings. She was critical of the therapy too, but a punctual, regular attender who tended to fall to pieces when there was a holiday break. She frequently toyed with the possibility of other therapies or threatened to break off the work because she couldn't afford it, echoing the fear of abandonment that her mother had generated in her. These experiences suggested that Patti had mildly borderline aspects to her history. With borderline patients, the therapeutic relationship is often the most potent evidence of the inner world that was created through this person's early life experience, since it is a *lack* of trust and a *lack* of expectation of regulation that is the painful core of the person's life.

Many researchers have linked the borderline condition with sexual abuse, which was not something that Patti had experienced. Although there does seem to be a strong link (Linehan suggests that as many as 75 per cent of borderline patients may have been sexually abused while other studies suggest much lower figures), it may not be the key factor in the borderline experience. Emotional abuse in particular, as well as physical abuse or neglect, is equally associated with borderline personality disorder (Widom et al. 2009; Posner and Rothbart 2000).

I would agree with Linehan that it is probably not the sexual abuse alone which derails people. Sexual abuse may be a side effect of a dysfunctional, invalidating family, or even a 'marker' of the severity of family dysfunction (Zanarini et al. 1997). As de Zulueta has pointed out, abuse is a 'specialised form of rejection' (de Zulueta 1993). What matters is that the child's emotional needs are not attended to – but the borderline state seems to involve the double whammy of the child depending on someone who isn't reliably there for him emotionally *and* who abuses or rejects him in some way. This is highlighted by the life story of the American poet Anne Sexton.

Anne was the youngest of three daughters, born to a prominent businessman father and a mother who liked writing and socialising – a wealthy, Scott Fitzgerald-type of party-loving, boozing family. But the parents were both extremely unpredictable emotionally. As Jane, one of Anne's sisters, said: 'Daddy was either drunk or he was sober, but you never knew, with Mother, when she was going to be horrible or nice. The minute you thought you knew where you were, she'd turn on you.' Anne also remembered how 'mean' Daddy could be when he was drunk: 'He would sit and look at you as though you had committed some terrible crime' (Middlebrook 1991). His put-downs included complaints that her teenage acne disgusted him: 'I can't eat when she's at the dinner table,' he said, while Mother disparaged her writing, sending her teenage poems off to an expert to check whether she was plagiarising someone.

From infancy, Anne and her sister were supervised by a nurse who was described as tough and reserved. She managed their appearance and their manners. They were dressed up to join their parents for dinner or to be presented at a party, but did not see a great deal of their mother, whom they adored. Anne grew up shy and lonely, describing herself as 'a nothing crouching in the closet'. Although she found it hard to get any positive attention from her mother, she did get negative attention and humiliation. When she was about 4 years old, her mother used to inspect her genitals 'saying how we had to keep it clean and mustn't touch'. Her bowel movements were also inspected on a daily basis and she was threatened with a colostomy at the age of 12 if she didn't 'go'. She ended up being hospitalised for severe constipation.

One relationship seemed different – with great aunt Anna, who had been closely involved with the family throughout Anne's childhood and was openly affectionate towards Anne. She moved in with the family when Anne was 11 and Anne spent huge amounts of time with her: eating lunch with her, playing cards in her room, doing homework with her, going to the movies with her after school, and having her 'daily cuddle with Nana' when they lay together in bed. The evidence appears to be that this was a sexual contact too; Anne later sexually abused one of her own daughters (Magai and Hunziker 1998: 384). Nana had no adult sexual partner and perhaps sought comfort from Anne which she could not find elsewhere, or perhaps she was seeking to discharge her sexual tension or her anger, using the child as a vehicle for some unresolved emotional dynamic of her own. Whatever her motives, the adult abuser fails to recognise the child's emotional needs, putting her own first. Of course children such as Anne who are emotionally needy and unprotected by their own parents are easy to manipulate into sexual situations.

One consequence for the sexually abused child is that she (or he) may feel that there is nowhere to turn for comfort, as Felicity de Zulueta has pointed out. The fact that sexual abuse is taking place within the family means that the child has lost the protection of both parents, not just of the perpetrator. An overwhelming, physiologically arousing event has taken place without any means of regulating it. Those borderline personalities who have experienced this kind of absence of support and regulation tend to have a hyper-reactive stress response (Lyons-Ruth 2011; Rinne et al. 2002).

Children such as Anne have to contend with high levels of negative affect and a hyperactive amygdala because of the physical or emotional abuse they suffer (Brendel et al. 2005). Yet the parts of the brain which could manage this emotion – the orbitofrontal cortex and anterior cingulate are not well connected to the amygdala. They are under-active and fail to 'come online' to deal with negative states as they do in more emotionally robust individuals (Silbersweig et al. 2007; New et al. 2007). Their right brains may also have a blunted capacity to regulate emotion because their dopamine receptors are less sensitive (Schore 2003). All this makes them prone to becoming overwhelmed by intense feelings such as anger. As Horowitz described it: 'Not thinking, all feeling. He wants to demolish and destroy persons who frustrate him. He is not aware of ever loving or even faintly liking the object. He has no awareness that his rage is a passion that will decline. He believes he will hate the object forever' (Horowitz 1992, quoted in Schore 2003).

Anne Sexton had lifelong problems of emotional regulation. When she felt overwhelmed by intense states, she either used alcohol or sleeping pills to tranquillise herself, or she went into 'trances' where she stared ahead for hours at a time, dissociated from her feelings altogether. Dissociation is one of the most primitive defences against mental pain – a crude attempt to cut off contact with other people who might generate further (unpleasant) sympathetic nervous system arousal. People in a dissociated state have activated the dorsal vagal complex in the brainstem, bringing about a physiological slowdown, with decreased blood pressure and heart rate, like animals who 'play dead' when caught by a predator. This is known to be a psychological defence often used by children with a 'disorganised' attachment. When you do not know whether to approach or avoid, you 'flee inwards' (Schore 2003).

Encouraged by her psychotherapist to write, Anne attempted to use her poetry as well as her therapy to regulate herself more constructively. Her poetry brilliantly articulated her intense and extreme feelings and she became a successful poet, winning recognition and even adulation from men and women, with whom she had many sexual affairs. The tensions involved in borderline histories often produce great creativity. But when her therapist abruptly terminated her treatment, she committed suicide, aged 46.

A child who suffers these kinds of experience is not only being physically harmed, but is also being poisoned with the parent's toxic beliefs about relationships. Survivors have testified that the physical harm that has been done to them is not necessarily the main impact of the experience. As one woman put it, 'I can accept that I was hit and raped, but I can't get over being hated' (Chu 1998: 12). The feeling of being a mere thing for someone else's use drains the self of meaning and value. If your parents don't love you, what are you worth? Anne Sexton gave voice to this feeling of having only transitory worth for others in one verse:

Let's face it, I have been momentary.
A luxury. A bright red sloop in the harbour.

My hair rising like smoke from the car window.
Littleneck clams out of season.

(Sexton 2000)

The black hole

Dehumanisation and lack of emotional value is at the heart of
the borderline relationship. From the start, the parents have
difficulties in recognising their baby as an intentional being
with mental states. Peter Fonagy has studied borderline
issues both from the perspective of attachment research and
from a clinical, psychoanalytic perspective. He places a great
deal of emphasis on what he calls 'mentalising' – the capacity
to recognise other minds. He suggests that the borderline
person grows up avoiding thinking and mentalising because
it would involve recognising this hatred or lack of love in his
parents' attitude to him. But blanking out the maltreatment
and thoughts about it makes it impossible for the person to
find any way of recovering from it (Fonagy et al. 1997).

Severely borderline people often have great difficulty
thinking about their experiences, particularly their experiences with their parents. It is unbearable to know that your
parents disregarded your feelings and may even have hated
you in some way. This makes the therapeutic process a very
difficult task. It is true that borderline people do need to
understand what has happened to them and they will find it
difficult to have a secure sense of self until they can face the
painful nature of their childhood experiences and find a way
of accepting them. Nevertheless, Fonagy's emphasis on
mind-mindedness and the verbal articulation of feelings
tends to underplay the importance of early infancy in my
view. It does not give sufficient weight to the basic difficulties with regulating feelings that people in the borderline
category invariably experience; difficulties that I agree with
Allan Schore originate in the baby's experience of being
unregulated.

The feelings that are experienced by borderline people
evoke the intensity and terror of a helpless, uncared for baby.
At its worst, the borderline sometimes falls into what has
been called the 'black hole of shame', a non-verbal state of

blankness: timeless, spaceless horror. It is linked to feelings of falling into the void – of not being safely held, contained, in a mother's arms. The borderline person is overwhelmed by negative feelings and tends to have what others experience as an exaggerated response. When things are going badly, everything is bad, there is no possible end to badness. He feels he himself is bad. His feelings are shameful since no one can understand them or wants to know them. He loathes himself. Past good feelings don't exist and can't be recalled. As Patti said to me once, 'I can't keep good experiences in.' Good feelings run through the fingers like sand, perhaps because nothing good can be trusted in a world where parents have been so ambivalent towards you. This inability to make use of advice or support is particularly characteristic of the borderline condition.

It's as if there is not enough of a 'self' there to process the experience – 'self' in the sense of a regulatory self. After all, 'selfhood' is very tied up with the ability to manage emotions in a consistent way that others can recognise and comment on. When others notice that 'you're always so calm, controlling, persistent, quick to act, absent-minded, stoical or practical', they are commenting on your style of emotional management. The sense of self is very dependent on this feedback from others. We need to know how others see us and to develop a consistent 'personality' or style of emotional management. But if the parental response is consistently negative or absent, we can feel 'wiped out', invalidated and basically bad. It becomes much harder to think about feelings without a framework of ongoing support and the sense of self becomes increasingly tenuous.

My patient Dilys was in her forties, yet lived in a state of near confusion and regulatory chaos. When she came to see me, she would endlessly question her behaviour, muttering at a fast pace, 'I shouldn't have come in a car, I can't afford the petrol, I should have walked. Why did I do that?' she would wail. 'My daughter wants me to get her a dress for her birthday but I don't know what to choose for her – I can't decide – I can't think. I thought I should get something pink but now I don't know if pink suits her. Is pink a good colour? Her father doesn't like pink. I should have got her to bed last night instead of watching the film. I'm stupid – the film wasn't that good. Her teacher looks down on me, she thinks Elly is always tired. I know I'm a terrible mother. I forgot to give her a bath this morning, but you don't need a bath every morning do you?' – and so on – and on. Dilys had no bearings on her own reality that were rooted in her own feelings. She acted impulsively and she spoke impulsively, without an organising principle that would allow her to prioritise her experiences and make choices about how to act. For most of us, the organising principle is our feelings and the meaning we attribute to them. But Dilys didn't know what she felt. Her constant attacks on herself were an invitation in a way to sort her out. She conveyed the helplessness of a baby, who needed someone somewhere to look after her and make sense of it all. She herself was the daughter of an alcoholic mother and a criminal father, and had been sexually abused by her uncle as a child.

Lacking adequate regulatory mechanisms, she was prone to panic, particularly when she felt abandoned by other people. The borderline person usually has a desperate fear of rejection or abandonment. Many borderline people (20–40 per cent) have in fact had a traumatic separation from a parent or parents in early childhood, something which had happened to Dilys too (Bradley and Westen 2005). But it's also possible to feel abandoned and uncared for when the parent figure is physically present, if they are not attentive or responsive. In either case, when key relationships are threatened, or he imagines they are threatened, it feels as if the world is falling apart. At this point, the borderline person has to rely on his own means of self-regulation, which are often very crude. He tends to act impulsively and often destructively. Because he has inadequate mental regulatory strategies, he tends to try to manage feelings through direct action – jumping in a car and driving 100 miles an hour to relieve inner tension, or slamming the phone down when angered by a conversation. He may cut himself to relieve the mental pain, or try to blot it out with sleep or drugs or alcohol. When Dilys's mother died unexpectedly, she kept going to the local railway station, thinking about jumping onto the rails.

Many borderline behaviours are self-destructive rather than destructive of others, although they often do impact on others' lives in a negative way. But in the next chapter, I will consider how criminal behaviour may also be a form of borderline behaviour in some instances, which manages the rage produced by early mistreatment very differently – by attacking others.

9

Original sin

How babies who are treated harshly may not develop empathy for others

The violent children of the future are now babies.

If you meet a teenage mugger on the street one night, the last thing that you will be thinking about is his infancy. But the fear and rage evoked in you are probably the same feelings that have been with him since babyhood, which have been instrumental in transforming this particular baby into an antisocial thug. His actions succeed in infecting his victims with his own fear and anger.

As victims or potential victims, we retaliate, with thoughts of punishment and imprisonment. The language we use conveys our rejection and repulsion. We refer accusingly to the yob, chav, vandal, thief, bully, hooligan, robber, murderer. They are words that conjure up fearful images of a foul-mouthed young man who spits, carries knives, menaces others and threatens our safety. Our attitude seems to be: he clearly doesn't care about other people – so why should we care about him? It is very hard to even bother to imagine that this menace was once a baby. The more serious his violence, the further away from human concern he gets. The young man who shoots a stranger in the street for his mobile phone or the teenager who stamps on an old woman's face to take her meagre savings are beyond our comprehension. How can they lose sight of the humanness of another person to such a degree? One answer, supplied by Peter Fonagy, is that they have not had the meaningful attachment relationships in early life that would allow them to identify with others (Fonagy et al. 1997). Other people's feelings do not seem real to them because theirs have not been real to the people who mattered.

It surprised me very much to discover, when I worked with teenage criminals in Tottenham, a poor part of north London, how vulnerable these boys often were beneath their sullen bravado. One young black teenager called Delroy – a tall, shy, gangly boy – was building up a criminal record for theft and mugging and becoming a familiar face in the Law Centre where I worked in the 1970s. I used to take statements from him, aware of his attempts to wriggle out of responsibility for what he had done. He was dismissive and seemed to think of his actions as minor peccadilloes, even though his latest adventure on the bus with his friend Manny had included casually threatening an older woman with a knife.

When he was arrested, he demanded in his stroppy adolescent way to see the policeman's identification and, according to him, was rewarded by the policeman grabbing his testicles and slapping him across the face so that his nose bled. He was then charged with resisting arrest. The day came for his court hearing, but he was still unaware of what his actions meant to others, expressing great reluctance to take the morning off his new job at Tesco to come to court. It was also the day of his seventeenth birthday. I still remember his expression when he got 'sent down' to Borstal, a term of imprisonment that he had never expected. He looked so bewildered and hurt as he was taken to the cells beneath the court, and so young. As his keys, lighter and penknife were taken from him, being told with heavy sarcasm that 'prison officers don't like being stabbed you know', he was crying. I suddenly became aware that he was someone's son and that he had barely left childhood.

What had gone wrong with Delroy? Was it his genes, his upbringing, or his own bad moral choices? This debate was taken up in Steven Pinker's book *The Blank Slate* (2002). In it, he argues that criminals such as Delroy are likely to be genetically different from the rest of us. Pinker argues that we have to 'consider the possibility that violent tendencies could be inherited as well as learned' (Pinker 2002: 310). He asserts: 'There can be little doubt that some individuals are constitutionally more prone to violence than others'; men, for example, and especially men who are 'impulsive, low in intelligence, hyperactive, and attention-deficient'. These traits, he suggests, 'emerge in early childhood, persist through the lifespan, and are largely heritable, though nowhere near completely so' (Pinker 2002: 315). Although Pinker does not claim that violence is only a question of genetics, this portrayal of violent offenders does tend to allow them to be written off as substandard products of bad genes.

Natural born aggression

Pinker's (qualified) emphasis on genes as a major source of aggression, criminality or antisocial behaviour drew on twin studies from the 1980s and 1990s which argued there was a 'substantial' genetic effect on criminal behaviour of around 60 per cent (Mealey 1995). Similarly, studies of adopted children from this same period also found that children of antisocial biological parents had a greater likelihood of becoming antisocial themselves, even when adopted into another family (Mednick et al. 1984; Cadoret et al. 1995). These findings appeared to be powerful evidence for the genetic inheritance of violence and criminality.

Despite this high level of heritability, geneticists have struggled to identify specific genes that would invariably produce antisocial and criminal behaviours. One recent 'genome wide' study could not find any genes that had a significant association with adult antisocial behaviour (Tielbeek et al. 2012). As the search goes on, it is clear that the process of passing on antisocial behaviour must be a complex one. After all, genes don't and can't code for socially defined behaviours. DNA codes for molecules, not for traits such as athleticism, fashion sense or depression (Meaney 2010). There simply aren't enough genes to specify all the connections in our brain and nervous system in advance; their role is a broader one of providing the basic structures that organise behaviour, such as knowing *how* to react with fear, but not defining *what* to be afraid of. Also, the self-same genes can give rise to different behaviour in different environments. One example that Michael Rutter gives is that a risk-taking gene might equally find expression in criminal activity or in great creativity (Rutter 1996).

In practice, our behaviour is the result of learning; our biochemistry responds to the specific environments in which we find ourselves. Genes don't act independently of environments, but interact with them in quite a flexible way, switching on and off when needed, often within minutes or hours. While the 'genotype' – an individual's genetic 'hard drive' if you like – evolves slowly over hundreds of years, it can give rise to many different 'phenotypes', or selections of characteristics, to suit the immediate demands of a rapidly changing world.

New thinking in epigenetics offers another perspective on how antisocial behaviour might be passed on down the generations. For example, when an individual lives in an impoverished and unsafe neighbourhood, she and her genes will adapt to those circumstances and those of her genes involved in responding to stress may get modified. One key process is known as 'methylation' – a biochemical process that inactivates genes or prevents them from being expressed. Surprisingly, these gene alterations not only last – often for a lifetime – but, as we have seen, they can also be inherited by her offspring (and possibly even by the following generation as well). Less surprisingly, although such epigenetic changes can take place at any time in the lifespan, they are likely to have their greatest impact during gestation and in response to early maternal care when the child's basic phenotype is in development, as we saw in the case of Yehuda's study of babies born after the 9/11 attacks.

Past research has sometimes failed to apply a developmental perspective and to take account of the enormous amount that happens in the womb and in the post-natal period. Many adoption studies, for example, do not clearly specify the age at which adoption occurred, leaving open the possibility that the child who is adopted may have already developed an oversensitive stress response or have acquired other altered biological systems by means of epigenetic transmission. Adrian Raine, a British researcher now based in California and an expert on the brains of murderers, highlighted the story of a man called Jeffrey Landrigan. As a baby, Jeffrey lived in a dysfunctional family, and at 8 months old was abandoned by his mother. He was subsequently adopted by a 'respectable' family, giving him a 'perfect new beginning', as Raine put it. The story ends with the revelation that in adulthood, Landrigan turns out to be a murderer, just as his father had been. Raine sees this as evidence for genetic transmission of criminality, discounting the time spent in his mother's womb or the 8 months of post-natal development (Raine 2013). However, Remi Cadoret, author of a major adoption study in 1995, recognised the flaw in much of the adoption research, acknowledging that babies are affected by their earliest experiences, and that studies need to begin in the first weeks of life.

Perhaps it is natural for geneticists to prefer explanations that put a baby's attributes down to genetic differences or 'temperament'. Anyone who has handled a number of different babies will confirm that babies certainly *are* born temperamentally different, in the sense of having a different propensity to respond to external stimuli. Some babies are eager to approach others and are open to new experiences, others are more cautious. Some are physically robust and active, others less so. Some find it more difficult to switch off from the stimulating environment than others do and these more reactive babies will have more difficulty with self-regulation. However, these characteristics aren't always the result of inherited genes nor are they necessarily stable; behaviour patterns are changeable during the first year (Sroufe, 1995).

At least some of these differences at birth have a great deal to do with the environmental influences that have already been at work for 9 months, during the period of gestation. These very early influences are increasingly playing a part in thinking about the propensity to criminal or antisocial behaviour. In particular, there are two aspects of pre-natal experience that have very strong links with later antisocial tendencies: stress and smoking.

The inhospitable womb

As I have already described in the first chapter, a pregnant woman suffering from chronic stress can inadvertently affect her foetus – though it's not yet clear exactly *how* her anxiety is passed on – whether through cortisol in the amniotic fluid, changes in the placenta, low birth weight or epigenetic changes (Glover et al. 2009; O'Donnell et al. 2009). Whatever the mechanism, babies of chronically stressed mothers are at greater risk of having a more anxious 'temperament' (Baibazarova et al. 2013), they cry more (Wurmser et al. 2005) and have a more reactive stress response at 3 months old (Oberlander 2008a); they may also have low levels of serotonin (Field et al. 2006; Van Goozen and Fairchild 2006). They run a greater risk of later behaviour problems such as becoming antisocial (Rice et al. 2010).

The developing serotonin system may also be affected by stress in the post-natal period. Recent research with monkeys has found that when they were deprived of their mothers early on, their serotonin decreased by up to 23 per cent in areas of the brain such as the amygdala and hypothalamus (involved in the stress response) as well as the anterior cingulate, caudate and thalamus (Ichise et al. 2006). They were also more likely to be impulsive and aggressive later in life.

Similar risks arise for babies who are exposed in the womb to nicotine, alcohol or other drugs, or whose mother is poorly nourished. Although some researchers have found direct links between a mother's alcohol consumption during pregnancy and her offspring's later antisocial behaviour, the findings are not regarded as definitive. However, there is an overwhelming consensus on the link between smoking over 10 cigarettes a day during pregnancy and future conduct disorder and aggression in her child; the more cigarettes, the more risk (Huijbregts et al. 2012; Cornelius 2011; Wakschlag et al. 2011; Brion et al. 2010). The effects are also long-lasting. Many researchers over the last decade have found a 'dose response' relationship between the amount of pre-natal smoking the mother did and the degree of later offending behaviour: most recently, Marie Cornelius and her team in Pittsburgh found that children of mothers who had smoked during pregnancy became 22-year-old adults who were more likely to be aggressive and to have been arrested by the police (Cornelius 2012).

How do stress and smoking in pregnancy have such a long-term impact on behaviour? As we have seen, stress alters cortisol levels and can affect other neurotransmitters. Similarly, nicotine affects the normal development of neurotransmitter systems and interferes with communication between nerve cells (Slotkin 1998). It can also lead to a loss of brain cells and in particular can have an effect on the thickness of the orbitofrontal cortex (Toro et al. 2008; Raine 2013).

There seems to be a direct link between these biological events and later antisocial behaviour. There is substantial evidence that low serotonin levels are strongly associated with aggressive behaviour (Douglas et al. 2011). This works in a variety of ways since serotonin is a multi-tasker and has influence in many systems. First, low serotonin levels affect the orbital and ventromedial areas of the prefrontal cortex (where there is a high density of serotonin receptors) and their ability to do their job of controlling and inhibiting aggression and anger (Phan 2005; Davidson et al. 2000). Second, when serotonin is low, it can't manage the dopamine system effectively or hold back excessive dopamine activation. In this situation the unchecked dopamine system can get overactive, promoting impulsive behaviour and aggression (Seo and Patrick 2008).

Even though these links between the foetal environment and later behaviour problems are very robust, genes may still play an important role. One suggestion is that the women who choose to smoke during pregnancy are different from other mothers; they are more likely to be aggressive and antisocial and to pass this on to their children (Ellingson et al. 2012; D'Onofrio 2008; Brion 2010). Another line of thinking is that there are specific genes which confer a greater risk of antisocial behaviour. This research has homed in on particular genes such as the MAOA-L gene, the dopamine genes DAT1, DR2 and DR4 and the short-allele serotonin gene. There has been some excitement about their links to social problems, with wildly exaggerated claims about aggressive 'warrior genes'.

In fact, these genes don't directly 'cause' antisocial behaviour. What they have in common is that they are all involved in emotional regulation (Buckholtz and Meyer-Lindenberg 2008). So researchers have found that children with the MAOA-L gene are twice as likely to have difficulty holding back strong emotional impulses or managing their responses to threat; children with the short allele of serotonin (the sensitive 'orchid' children) are more at risk of depression in response to the stress of rejection, loss or humiliation (Dodge 2009). In other words, these genes intensify a child's responses to other people. However, with good parental regulation, there is no evidence that they will be anything but fine. After all, around 40 per cent of the population has the MAOA-L gene and very few of them have ever committed any crime.

It is increasingly looking as if the possibility of behaving in an antisocial way arises within a matrix of interacting events. It may start with risky genes or with risky maternal behaviour or a combination of the two. But that is not the whole story. Post-natal factors are just as important. The poor emotional regulation that might arise as a result of any of these factors can still be put right in early childhood – or exacerbated, depending on the care which is available.

Factoring in the impact of parenting

Nicotine poisoning, inadequate nutrition or high levels of cortisol can all have an impact on the emotional regulation systems of the developing foetus. But after birth, some of these babies will be subjected to a double whammy if they also have caregivers who aren't able to respond to them and regulate them well, just as monkeys with sensitive temperaments run into trouble when they are reared by mothers who are themselves irritable, but do fine with calm mothers (Suomi 1999). A fascinating piece of research by Adrian Raine found that the established link between smoking and later antisocial behaviour only held if the mother felt rejection towards her baby and had considered an abortion or had had the baby taken into care during his first year (Raine et al 1997a); in other words, however neurobiologically vulnerable the baby was, the quality of care in the post-natal period was crucial to outcomes. Similarly, the child who is already vulnerable because of exposure to the mother's depressive biochemistry during gestation and who then experiences harsh or abusive parenting, has a 12 times greater risk of developing depression or conduct disorder (Pawlby et al. 2011).

The same two-stage process is involved in the realization of genetic predispositions. A landmark study by Avshalom Caspi in 2002 concluded that having the risky version of the MAOA gene did not lead to future violent or antisocial behaviour unless those children were also maltreated (Caspi et al. 2002). This study has since been replicated several times. Similarly, children with the dopamine gene variant (DRD4–7 allele), which predisposes to a relative insensitivity to social rewards and punishments, are more likely to act out their feelings of anger and frustration without holding back, but only if their parents treat them insensitively. When they have parents who care for them sensitively, they are least likely to do so (Bakermans-Kranenburg et al. 2008; Bakermans-Kranenburg and van Ijzendoorn 2011). Likewise, a child with the short serotonin gene only has a problem with managing his emotions if he or she is in an insecure attachment relationship, but can still be emotionally well regulated in a secure one (Kochanska 2009). Clearly, the impact of either neurobiological or genetic sensitivities is much greater when the parent–child relationship is not working well.

The negative spiral

Any kind of insecure attachment increases the risk of future antisocial behaviour. How does one lead to the other in practice? Again, the evidence points to problems with the parent and baby adapting to each other and learning how to tune in to each other. Many parents don't know how to pay attention to the baby's body language or are not skilled at regulating emotions. But without their help, how can their baby learn to develop his own capacity for paying attention or self-regulating? Indeed, those children who can't pay attention or self-regulate are the very children who are more likely to develop externalising problems (Belsky et al. 2007; Hill et al. 2006; Eiden 2007, 2009).

Recent research suggests that fathers may play an important role in establishing good emotional regulation early on. Paul Ramchandani's work at Oxford University has found that when fathers were distant and uninvolved, their babies had more externalising problems at the age of 1 year old (Ramchandani et al. 2013).

When a positive relationship hasn't been established in babyhood, the next stage of socialising the toddler into acceptable behaviour is made infinitely more difficult. The parent cannot draw on a secure bond laced with good humour and mutual understanding, and cannot make demands on the child to restrain his impulses for the sake of maintaining that good relationship. Instead, the child is already defensive and expects harsh treatment so he has little to lose in defying parental wishes.

The problem can be compounded by parents who lack self-esteem or a strong sense of self. These are the parents who find it most difficult to be 'authoritative' and to follow through on their demands of the child in a firm way. This unwittingly reinforces the child's negative and resistant behaviour. We have all seen what can happen next: parents at their wits' end who find themselves resorting to coercive tactics such as threatening, yelling or bullying the child to behave.

Hostile, coercive and harsh parenting is strongly linked to the child's difficulty in regulating emotions and increases the likelihood that a child will react and act out his or her anger (Sellers et al. 2013; Xu et al. 2009; McKee et al. 2008). Some gender differences have been found here as boys are more likely to express themselves in physical aggression (Hill et al. 2006) while girls may be especially good at what Hyun Rhee and Waldman (2002) call 'relational aggression', such as the malicious damaging of another's reputation, or excluding others from the peer group.

To put it bluntly, children who are not treated well are more likely to become antisocial. The whole range of 'adverse childhood experiences', from emotional abuse or neglect through to physical abuse and sexual abuse, is linked with an increased incidence of future antisocial behaviour (Teisl and Ciccetti 2008; Douglas et al. 2011). Although active adult hostility is most likely to provoke a strong reaction in the child, any sort of ineffective parenting, such as a parent who is withdrawn or 'haunted' by past hurts of her own, or who can't keep clear boundaries, will destabilise the child. When children experience any kind of hurtful or anxiety-provoking parenting, they have no safe haven to go to: the very person who should be soothing their fears is making them afraid (Madigan et al. 2006).

This leaves such children at very high risk of developing a disorganised attachment. In the average population, around 15 per cent end up with this most problematic form of attachment, but in maltreated children it is at least 51 per cent (Van Ijzendoorn and Bakermans-Kranenburg 2009; Cyr 2010). Lacking sufficient parental emotional support, these are the children who are most likely to develop 'externalising' behaviour problems, as well as more complex forms of psychopathology (Fearon et al. 2010; Cyr et al. 2010).

The tensed-up body

However, the impact is not just on a child's psychological development. Children who go through such experiences are also affected physiologically. The maltreated child ends up not only being more watchful and vigilant, but also has a more active right brain (processing negative feelings), and a much higher heart rate when provoked by his schoolmates (Lenneke et al. 2009). He tends to anticipate hostility from others, often interpreting others' behaviour as aggressive and antagonistic even when it isn't (Dodge and Somberg 1987).

The child who has had demanding, critical parenting linked to coercion and physical punishment may also be at risk of heart disease. Ray Rosenman and Meyer Friedman were the originators of the Type A concept, which has since been refined and adjusted by subsequent research. Its core aspect has been found to be an attitude of hostility to others, and an expectation of being mistreated by others which can result in paranoid, suspicious and impatient behaviour. According to the straight-talking Robert Sapolsky, biologist and author of the brilliant *Why Zebras Don't Get Ulcers* (2004), Friedman knew all about being a Type A. Sapolsky describes him as a 'driven, steamrolling son of a bitch' before he had a heart attack, although he turned into a gentle, 'courtly' man in old age.

As he grows up, the child learns to drive himself as harshly as his parents drove him. He can end up with an overactive stress response and overaroused sympathetic nervous system. High levels of norepinephrine are found in such people (and in antisocial criminals too). Norepinephrine can increase blood pressure and with it the workload of the heart, but it also damages the lining of the arteries which enables cholesterol to seep through to clog them up. The highly aroused overreactor, with his clenched jaw and readiness to react, has great difficulty in activating his parasympathetic nervous system which is responsible for calming him down. So this type of regulatory pattern has been strongly associated with heart disease. The high levels of norepinephrine also block the activity of part of the immune system, the macrophages, and may also explain findings that Type A personalities are also vulnerable to ulcers, migraine, cancer, herpes and vision problems.

But what has also been learnt in these early years is a mode of emotional regulation. An unusual study of older black men by Harburg and colleagues (1991) found that those who tended to act out their anger, who slammed doors and said aggressive things to others, were the ones with high blood pressure, while those who held back the expression of anger and attempted to solve their problems with others had significantly lower blood pressure.

The 'abuse excuse'

Clearly the child whom we experience as a social problem has not had the kind of support and care he needed. Most likely, he has experienced rejection or neglect in some shape or form. But Steven Pinker has little time for what he calls 'the abuse excuse'. He sneers at the claim that 'most people don't commit horrendous crimes without profoundly damaging things happening to them', and argues that only naive people parrot the 'mantra' that 'violence is learned behaviour' (Pinker 2002: 178, 308).

The story of Robert Thompson and Jon Venables, two 10-year-old boys who committed murder, challenges these assumptions. They abducted a 2-year-old boy from a shopping mall and took him to a nearby railway line, where they tied him down to the line, threw bricks and an iron bar at him, and left him to die. Their case aroused horror and revulsion, as child murderers do. How could children be so full of hate? To what extent were they responsible for their evil actions?

Steven Pinker plausibly suggests that violence is an instinctive human response to obstacles in our way, and that our basic instinct is to pursue our desires without considering other people. When other human beings are the obstacle, we are prone to reducing them to 'things' or to dehumanising them in order to free us to clear them out of our way. But the murder victim, James Bulger, was not an 'obstacle' to Robert Thompson and Jon Venables. They were not pursuing self-interest. They were venting their hatred on a safe object, someone weaker than themselves.

Where did this hatred come from? Hatred is not genetic, it is a response. Their past experience had created a store of hatred ready to find expression one morning when the two boys skived off school and hung around a shopping mall. Although relatively little has been written about the environments that they grew up in, I believe that they played a decisive role in the events of that day. Robert Thompson was the fifth son of seven children. In this large family of boys, Robert and his brothers were largely left to their own devices, especially after their father left home when Robert was aged 5 and their mother took to drinking heavily. The family had a lineage of violence. Robert's mother had been beaten throughout her childhood; in her terror, she was still wetting the bed at the age of 15. She escaped into an early marriage at the age of 18 – to another violent man. The brothers grew up with physical punishments and threats as the norm and exercised little restraint in taking their frustrations out upon each other, biting, hammering, beating and threatening each other with knives (Morrison 1997). One son actually asked to be taken into care and when he was later returned to the bosom of his family, he attempted suicide by taking an overdose of painkillers. Robert's mother had also attempted suicide. The misery of this household is hard to imagine. It seemed to lack a centre, without anyone able to take responsibility and to provide the loving attention they all needed. Robert's mother was rarely in court to support her 10-year-old son when he faced the ordeal of a trial.

The family of Jon Venables seemed to have been less chaotic, but has also been described as unstable and unhappy. The Venables parents were divorced. Although Mr Venables took care of the children for a few days a week, the press reported nothing about his care of them. However, Mrs Venables was depicted in the press as preoccupied with her appearance, searching for a new man, with a succession of boyfriends at the house. She had serious 'depressive problems' and had also tried to kill herself. Following experiences of neglect in her own childhood, she did not appreciate the concern of others who reported her to social services for leaving her young children alone in the house for several hours at a time. She believed she was a good parent because she provided for her children materially, but her misery apparently made her a harsh parent and Jon was reported to be afraid of her. Certainly his behaviour was highly disturbed. He had been known to slash himself, to hide under chairs, to stick paper on his face. He had been diagnosed as 'hyperactive' and had tried to strangle a boy at school.

Jon and Robert frequently bunked off school, shoplifted, and were involved in violent incidents. Neighbours reported after the event that the boys had shot pigeons with an airgun, had stolen charity collecting boxes and, in a chilling foretaste of what they did to James Bulger, had tied rabbits to a railway line. These kinds of cruel childhood activities are common in the histories of adult murderers. These were not children who had been taught how to manage their aggressive impulses. They were neglected, often physically abused, deprived of the positive relationships that could have helped them to manage their feelings. If they were born with sensitive temperaments, it is hard to see how their unhappy parents could have provided the good nurturing such temperaments require.

Pinker points out that we have a limited 'circle of sympathy' for others, and that morality depends on how far we extend our 'circle of sympathy'. Many crimes are achieved by dehumanising the victims and shutting them out of the circle of sympathy – most notably the Holocaust, but most wars, conflicts and crimes involve this denial of the other's humanity. Clearly, Robert and Jon failed to recognise the humanity of James Bulger that afternoon. Pinker believes that putting strangers outside the circle is the human 'default setting', for which he claims a certain evolutionary logic.

Yet the peculiarity of human culture is that it doesn't rely on such instinctive programmes for aggressive self-defence or aggressive pursuit of our goals. Whether violent behaviour is learnt by imitation or is our first instinctive reaction to obstacles, is not the issue. What matters is whether or not a culture of empathy is passed on from parents to children. Do parents recognise and respect their children's feelings? Do they teach their children how to manage conflicts and negative feelings? These are the key questions in transcending any basic wiring that can lead to violence and aggression. Yet instead of recognising the importance of parenting in passing on this vital aspect of human culture, Pinker seems to prefer to see the problem as one of individual will-power and individual genetic propensities. This is why he advocates punishment to keep people in line, rather than parenting classes. But in fact abusive families lack the regulatory skills that are needed to develop empathy with others. These have not been learnt by the parents and so cannot be handed down.

Some researchers have documented the particular skills that are needed to control impulses. The three main strategies are self-distraction, comfort seeking and seeking information about the obstacle to our goals. One study found that 3 year olds who were skilled in using all three strategies showed the least aggressive and externalising behaviour (Gilliom et al. 2002). They were able to control themselves sufficiently to turn away from the source of frustration and focus on something else, and were less likely to attack it. They could also ask questions about when the situation would be alleviated, which was very helpful in dissolving anger. Only when feeling quite distressed or overwhelmed did they use the comfort-seeking strategy. But children who did not have this repertoire and used only one strategy were found to be the most aggressive. These strategies are learnt – they are modelled by parental behaviour and encouragement, they are not genetic.

Poorly developed prefrontal cortex

Much of the skill involved is in inhibiting behaviour for the sake of others. But this skill depends also on brain development, on the good development of the prefrontal cortex which plays this inhibitory role. Yet in a circular fashion, the development of this part of the brain is very dependent on relationships – on the affectionate, tactile early relationships that will generate plenty of opioids which help the brain to grow. Parents who succeed in tuning in to their baby's moods and give him lots of feedback are helping to consolidate his self-awareness, which in time will be reflected in a well-connected, ventromedial prefrontal cortex (Mah et al. 2005; Kolb et al. 2012). Since this part of the brain helps him to quell fears and anxieties, it also plays an important role in self-regulation (Milad et al. 2005). On top of that, it helps him regulate his physiological responses since the ventromedial prefrontal cortex is linked to the nervous system and can increase or decrease blood pressure and heart rate (Hilz et al. 2006; Hansel and Kanel 2008). But the child's ability to manage his emotions in all these ways depends very much on experiencing warm, supportive parenting in the first place (Eisenberg et al. 2010).

As the baby's pre-frontal cortex develops, he can use his increasing self-awareness to notice what other people's body language is telling him. With a growing ability to direct his own body, he is more able to control his own behaviour in response to their expectations. This maturing self-control establishes the crucial neural pathway between the 'higher' orbital and medial prefrontal areas and the 'lower', more impulsive amygdala. Parents can help build synaptic connections along this pathway by gently but firmly encouraging the baby to master his own behaviour. This is achieved by offering mildly stressful but manageable challenges followed by helping the baby restore his good feelings about himself. The baby can then gradually learn how to use his higher brain to suppress his more impulsive responses to negative experience.

But when babies don't get enough good experience to build up these circuits, their ability to master their own behaviour, and to manage stress or anxiety, is weakened. Worse still, experiences of maltreatment can reduce brain volume in these regulatory areas (Van Harmelen et al. 2010; Cerqueira et al. 2005). This makes it much more difficult for the child to know how to regulate feelings, or to feel confident in turning to others for help in challenging situations. Instead, the introverted maltreated child learns to hide her feelings and may try desperately to please others to get her needs met, while the 'externaliser' tries to get his feelings noticed by making an impact on others, or takes what he wants from others regardless of their feelings. Both strategies, however, stem from the same failure in the early regulatory relationships. One curious feature is the gender difference in choice of strategy: women tend to take the depressive route, while men tend to take the aggressive route. However, this is not inevitable.

It's predictable

It is possible to predict future problems as early as the age of 6 to 10 months, but not from the baby's temperament so much as from the parent's behaviour coupled with the baby's temperament. Mothers who are not 'contingently' responsive to their baby's communications, who are not able to meet the needs of their particular baby and who impose their own goals on the baby, may unwittingly help to incubate future aggression and conduct disorder.

Left unchecked, this situation proceeds to toddlerhood, when mother and child have already become mutually rejecting and aggressive towards each other. The poorly regulated parent is irritable and prone to explode with frustration, under the stress of caring for a toddler. She tends to blame the child. She may find it unnatural to praise his good behaviour or help him to build the kind of self-control that she herself lacks. But poor regulation at this stage already predicts future externalising behaviour (Lenneke 2009). One study of 2-year-old girls found that poor emotional regulation and externalising behaviour problems go together (Hill et al. 2006).

If the parent is actively hostile, or uses physical punishment, the child may start to anticipate hostility from others and to develop a 'negativity bias' (with an overactive right brain). Repeated experiences of violence, or witnessing violence can desensitise the child, leading to the assumption that it is normal. In this sense, the children of those who use violence do *'learn'* to use it themselves.

One distressing illustration from their work with maltreated children is provided by Harvard psychologists Catherine Ayoub and Gabrielle Rappolt-Schlichtmann (2007). A little boy called Donald, aged 2 and a half, is asked to use two dolls to show how he plays nicely with his friend. Donald plunges into an aggressive dialogue: 'Guy, you wanna fight? I'll knock you down. He fight him. They fight. You wanna fight? I'm gonna fight you. Fuck my butt, fuck it.' When he's reminded that the story is supposed to be 'nice', Donald tries again, only this time he says 'Have some Playdough, guy, don't leave me, please don't leave me.' As the authors suggest, Donald has already 'come to expect aggression and loss rather than kindness and sustained care'.

Problems that exist by the age of 2 tend to be stable and to persist. Already by the age of 2, the absence of positive affection has been found to predict later problems (Belsky et al. 1998), while a mutually enjoyable and responsive early relationship leads to better behaviour and a greater willingness to comply with the parent (Kochanska 2005).

If children have not learnt self-control by the age of 3, their behaviour tends to be consistently problematic through childhood and they are more likely to demonstrate later conduct disorder (Caspi et al. 1996). One major study following a large group of children over many years found that 3 year olds with poor self-control were more likely to be convicted of a criminal offence by the age of 32 (Moffitt 2010).

Similarly, 4 year olds who are in a coercive relationship with a parent have been found to have a lack of conscience and morality. They cannot put themselves in another's shoes. They cannot think about the impact of their behaviour on others; partly because no one has done this for them, and partly because they do not have the self-control to restrain themselves in favour of another's interests.

Particularly when harsh parenting involves physical abuse and hitting, the outcome will often be aggressive behaviour at school and later on, with a greater risk of being arrested for violent offences (Lansford et al. 2007). By the age of 10 or 11, the restless, negative child has often become more overtly antisocial, displaying what is known as 'conduct disorder'. This is a serious problem which affects large numbers of children – around 6 per cent of school-age children.

A very extreme example of what can happen when children grow up lacking in self-control is serious violence or even murder. Of course, it is rare for children to go as far as Thompson and Venables, who clearly had no ability to empathise with the distress they were causing 2-year-old James Bulger, nor to imagine the pain of his family. They appear to have been radically cut off from others' feelings, preoccupied with their own need for revenge against harsh or neglectful parents and siblings. But adult murderers have similar difficulties.

Adrian Raine studied the brains of 41 murderers and compared them with the brains of 41 'controls' of similar age and sex. He found that the murderers had poorly developed prefrontal cortexes. Lacking the early experiences that would teach them the social skills of empathy and self-control, lacking the brain structure that would facilitate their practice, they were in effect invisibly handicapped people who had to rely on more primitive responses to get what they wanted. They murdered 'impulsively' rather than cold-bloodedly planning to murder, unable to control their behaviour (Raine et al. 1997a). Yet, as Raine acknowledges in his sometimes contradictory book, it is early social, emotional and nutritional deprivation which changes the brain – and with it, behaviour. As he colourfully comments, 'the social environment, far from taking a backseat in this genetic and biological voyage to violence, is driving this Wild West stagecoach' (Raine 2013: 260).

Although the social environment in the wider sense is important, it mostly has an impact on babies through its effect on their parents. Stressed parents are often harsh parents, and lack of social and financial resources is highly stressful. However, harsh parents have a variety of person-alities, educational level and life circumstances. What they all tend to share is an emotional illiteracy. In many cases, their own dependency needs have never been fully met, so they are not fully able to take on the adult role of parenting. They are still looking to others to take care of them. Many feel unsupported, lacking a family network or a social network which will cushion their difficulties. This exacerbates their difficulties in meeting their children's needs.

Billy's story

In her biography of the Scottish comedian Billy Connolly, his wife Pamela Stephenson describes a classic example of an abusive childhood (Stephenson 2002). Billy had been born to an impoverished teenage mother who felt isolated and depressed when left with her two babies while her equally young husband was away fighting in the war. She was unpre-pared for the responsibility of having children and dealt with it by ignoring their needs as much as possible. Billy and his sister Florence were neglected and left to play out on the streets from toddlerhood. By the age of 4, Billy had had pneumonia three times. Then one day their mother just 'closed the door and never came back', leaving them alone in their flat. Neighbours were alerted to the situation by the children's crying. They never saw their mother again during their childhood. After some family in-fighting, they were eventually taken in by their paternal aunts. Yet despite good intentions, these aunts could not cope with them either. Aunt Mona, in particular, took out her frustrations on Billy, as Pamela Stephenson recounts:

At first it was verbal abuse. She called him a 'lazy good-for-nothing', pronounced that he would 'come to nothing', and that it was 'a sad day' when she met him. She soon moved on to inflicting humiliation on Billy, her favourite method being grabbing him by the back of his neck and rubbing his soiled underpants in his face. She increased her repertoire to whacking his legs, hitting him with wet cloths, kicking him, and pounding him on the head with high-heeled shoes. She would usually wait until they were alone, then corner and thrash him four or five times a week for years on end.

Billy, however, had been in a few scraps in the school playground and had decided that a smack in the mouth wasn't all that painful. The more experience he had of physical pain, the more he felt he could tolerate it. 'What's the worst she could do to me?' he would ask himself. 'She could descend on me and beat the shit out of me . . . but a couple of guys have done that to me already and it wasn't that bad . . . I didn't die or anything'.

In fact, the more physical, emotional and verbal abuse he received, the more he expected it, eventually believing what they were telling him: that he was useless and worthless and stupid, a fear he keeps in a dark place even today. (p. 44)

The book describes how little adequate regulation this child had received; he had suffered stress from infancy. In response, he became defiant and devil-take-the-hindmost. As he explained to his wife, he became habituated to the physical (and inevitably emotional) pain. At a physiological level, I have suggested that this may be what is happening in the brains of such children: the body becomes habituated to high levels of cortisol and down-regulates, closes down receptors on the grounds that more isn't needed. Since stress is round every corner, there's no point revving up the body in fearful anticipation, as depressives do – it is always there. Low cortisol has been found particularly in boys who are aggressive from an early age (McBurnett et al. 2000), adding to the possibility that aggressive behaviour is the result of chronic mistreatment.

Billy Connolly got used to living on the edge. He became a risk taker. One of his childhood games was called the 'suicide leap' across buildings. He played dangerous practical jokes that risked physical injury, such as giving people electric shocks. It was as if he was actively replaying the experiences that he had had with others, that his body was of no account and could take any sort of abuse. But inevitably he also had little respect for other people's bodies, being liable to 'diving on people' and giving them a 'severe seeing to' when provoked, which was not hard to do according to Stephenson. In other words, he was reckless and violent. Billy's story is a classic precursor of an antisocial personality.

So why did Billy Connolly become a famous comedian rather than a notorious criminal? Perhaps because his alienation from other people was tempered by emotional investments. One relationship in particular, with his loving older sister Florence, provided human kindness. She had always acted as his protector. He also got involved in masculine activities that were within the law rather than outside it – particularly in activities with the Scouts, which were important to him. Through the Scouts and their 'bob-a-job' rounds, he met a middle-class man who took a warm interest in him and chatted to him as he cleaned the man's shoes; he felt valued. He had teachers he admired who were funny and smart. Later, as a teenage apprentice, he met older welders in the shipyard who had a great line in sharp patter; his own verbal facility was presumably developed through such experiences, gaining him positive attention. Combined with his warm relationship with Florence, these experiences were enough to enable Billy to build connections to other people. The early rejections which are such a potent fuel for antisocial behaviour were tempered by positive relationships.

The story of DJ Goldie has a similar ring. Abandoned by his heavy-drinking mother when he was aged 3, shuffled between foster homes and institutions, Goldie told journalist Lynn Barber how his childhood was a blank, and how he went into 'survival mode', attacking and questioning everything, while beneath the anger he was 'scared really, because you have no one else'. Unlike his brother who ended up in prison, Goldie was saved by Whispering Wheels, a skating rink, where he found 'normality', because 'normality is the thing you don't have in the social services. And just going out skating gives you enough freedom to create thought, to create the idea that there's something better out there' (*The Observer*, 27 October 2002). He played roller hockey for the English B Team, then taught himself to breakdance. Subsequently, he became a graffiti artist and met film-makers who took him to New York to meet other graffiti artists. These experiences opened up an alternative to the criminal world.

From a position of powerlessness and stress, both DJ Goldie and Billy Connolly found an alternative source of value and personal power. They built on the elements in their lives that gave them hope, that connected them back to people. Nevertheless, Billy's career as a comedian carried the antisocial element through his adult life. His jokes are designed to shock as well as amuse. He broke barriers in talking freely about 'shagging' and 'farting' long before it seeped into popular culture in general. By drawing on his formidable intelligence, he transcended coarseness, transforming his personal stories into something mythological. But his verbal violence has been a unique solution – a way of expressing the anger stored within him since childhood, without damaging others – perhaps even providing relief for the many other hurt and enraged children in his adult audience.

All the same, according to his wife Pamela Stephenson, Billy Connolly's own adult life has suffered from his early deprivation and maltreatment. For example, the early stress may have affected his capacity to retain information. Although he loved reading, he could not remember what he read and had learning difficulties at school. It is common for the hippocampus in the brain to be affected by chronic stress, affecting the laying down of memories. Stephenson also describes how jumpy and 'hypervigilant' Billy was when she first knew him. He couldn't bear to be touched and flinched at others' sudden movements, unconsciously expecting always to be hit. He overreacted to criticism. It is tragic that a man so loveable and intelligent should have had his personality shaped in this way. We think less fondly of Robert Thompson and Jon Venables, or of Ian Brady, yet they were shaped by similar forces.

What we do know is that aggression and antisocial behaviour which start in childhood are the most damaging to society. They are the most consistent through life, the most linked to adult criminality and drug abuse and marital violence. It is very costly to society (Scott et al. 2001). Yet although crime is always high on the political agenda and increasingly the behaviour of antisocial boys and young men is seen as a prime target of various initiatives, there has been little attempt to link this problem behaviour with early maltreatment. Instead of recognising its roots in infancy and early childhood, the focus is on the management of current problem behaviour. In fact, the vogue is increasingly for getting tough with offenders, training them to behave better, forcing them to take responsibility for their actions. One liberal journalist argued that the bullies needed 'bringing down a peg' and she was sick of all this 'psychobabble' about low self-esteem (Toynbee 2001). In other words, she could not find it in herself to empathise with people who cause so much harm and distress to others. Yet this is precisely the treatment that such boys are used to. Their problem is that they have never received empathy from their parents. Their feelings and needs have been ignored. They have been hit and verbally abused when they are in conflict with parents. They have had to suppress their rage with those powerful parents.

It is this rage that has nowhere to go which is the problem for society in general. When it is not expressed, managed and modulated at the appropriate time, it doesn't just go away. It remains in the body and bides its time. When fresh circumstances trigger rage, and it is safer to express it since the new instigator is less powerful than the original parent, out it comes. Disproportionate reactions to peers or weak adults are the result because the feelings have never been regulated and the child has not learned how to regulate them.

Billy Connolly struggled to regulate himself and resorted to alcohol at one time. There is a great overlap between crime and alcohol and drug use, since these can disinhibit behaviour. But the maltreated or neglected child in any case hasn't learnt to hold back feelings in order to preserve precious relationships or a self-esteem which is lacking. He does not feel valued and held in esteem by others. He holds back feelings only out of fear, and when no longer afraid he lets them out.

The infamous Moors Murderer of the 1960s, Ian Brady, killed children whom he picked up off the street. In his correspondence with the writer Colin Wilson, he revealed his need for revenge. He had been born illegitimate and was given up for adoption by his mother. This early rejection, coupled with an unhappy family life, coloured Brady's existence. Highly intelligent, he always felt second best and unable to fulfil his potential. He felt unfairly treated by the world, particularly after he was given a punitive jail sentence in his teens for helping a mate in the fruit market load up his truck with what turned out to be stolen goods. According to Wilson, this injustice turned him into 'a good hater' who stopped believing in goodness. When he killed the first of several children he abducted, he shouted at the sky 'Take that, you bastard' as if God had betrayed him and he was exacting his revenge on the whole of life (Wilson 2001).

While a child is still dependent on his parents he cannot retaliate fully because to risk losing parents might endanger his survival, but his psychological dependence is of equal importance. The dependent child cannot define himself or herself as a person. While most of us get our sense of ourselves from the people around us and how they react to us and what they tell us, the dependent child's evolving sense of self is even more acutely focused on the important adults in his or her life. Psychological survival depends on keeping in relationship to these others at all costs and accepting their version of us, however negative.

Even subtle forms of rejection can have a lasting impact on the child's developing sense of self. One of my clients was told by his mother that she loved him as mothers do, but she didn't like him. This coloured his feeling of his own worthiness throughout his youth and into middle age. Another client was told that she was not a personality that others warmed to. These people suffered from chronic depression in adulthood. But when parents hit their children and treat them with overt hostility, as in Billy Connolly's case, they are powerfully conveying the message that they are worthless and bad, as Billy testified.

Antisocial behaviour is in essence a willingness to pursue your own goals without regard for others. It suggests an alienation from other people and a lack of belief in pleasurable human contact. This cannot be specified genetically, nor can the lack of self-control. All that genes can do is to provide the raw material: genes that predispose to being an outgoing, robust type of person or a cautious, sensitive type of person, genes that help or hinder emotional regulation. But what really matters is whether the parent meets those temperamental inclinations – or neurobiological alterations caused by experiences in the womb – with the kind of response that the baby needs to establish a reliable, loving relationship with that baby.

Children who are emotionally secure and well regulated rarely become the antisocial individuals of the future. The toddler who wants to resolve a conflict with dad, or who is willing to wait for his ice cream to please mum, is the toddler who is confident of his relationships. This child is less likely to need socialisation through fear and punishment because he is beginning to grasp the effect of his own actions on other people and to be aware of their feelings. This happens only because his adult carers have been responsive to his feelings in the past and have convinced him that relationships are a source of pleasure and comfort, and therefore worth preserving.

PART 3

Too much information, not enough solutions

Where do we go from here?

'If all else fails, hug your teddybear'

Repairing the damage

Sometimes when I present the information gathered in this book to an audience, I meet with a despairing response: 'Can anything be done once these systems are in place or is it too late?' It can weigh heavily on people and also induce guilty feelings as parents in the audience cast their minds back to their own relationships with their babies.

In making the case for the importance of infancy, it is easy to lose sight of the subtleties of human development over the life span. Babyhood is an intense, concentrated moment of development that can have a disproportionate impact on our lives, but it is not the whole story by any means. Important pathways continue to be established through childhood, especially up to the age of 7. Then in early adolescence there is another intense moment of brain reorganisation, until the brain is fully fledged at 15 years old. But even after that, change and development continue because life is a process of continual adaptation. It just tends to happen at a much slower rate. Early patterns become habits which enable us to respond quickly without laboriously figuring out everything afresh each time we meet a particular experience. We tend to preserve the way that we respond unless there is a powerful challenge to established systems.

Psychoanalysts sometimes describe this tendency as 'resistance'. Even people who are unhappy enough to go into psychotherapeutic treatment find it hard to change and are often unwittingly 'resistant' to new ways of thinking and relating, even if they consciously want to change very much.

But that is no cause for despair – psychotherapies of various kinds can assist and accelerate the process of change for many people, while mindfulness meditation can help improve self-regulation (Holzel et al. 2011).

However, in my view, prevention is better than cure. There is a growing recognition that finding ways to improve the relationship between parents and their babies is a much more cost effective (and less distressing) way of improving mental health than any number of adult therapeutic treatments. For several decades now, clinicians have been providing psychotherapeutic help for parents and babies in various settings. I myself started a charity in Oxford in 1998 to provide the kind of specialised service that I believe should be the foundation of all health care. Yet despite the proven value of this kind of service (Barlow et al. 2008), there seems to be some blockage in making it universally available to all families who need it.

Although there are some impressive government policy documents out there that acknowledge the importance of the early years, there seems to be a strange disconnect between government policies and the practice on the ground. While some government departments recognise that a range of social problems have their roots in early development, this isn't a story that has found popular appeal in the press or in those government departments that deal with the hard issues of criminal justice or health care. Neither the policy makers nor the public have fully embraced the exciting possibilities of early intervention and what it could do for us all. As Graham Allen, a British member of parliament and author of the Allen Report put it, this is 'like having the cure for cancer and keeping it up your jumper' (Allen 2013).

One obstacle is that those who control budgets have yet to be convinced that it makes economic sense when financial gains are not immediately 'cashable'. As a result, resources have not shifted towards the early years. Although we have some idea of how much mental ill health costs us (at least £116 billion in Britain (Cylharova et al. 2010) and even more staggering billions of dollars in the USA), it is hard to *prove* that we can save a great deal of this future expenditure by helping babies to develop good emotional regulation through good early relationships.

The researcher who has done most to establish the social benefits of early intervention is David Olds in the USA, whose programme of home visiting during pregnancy and the first two years has produced clear evidence of financial benefit and prevention of social problems such as anti-social behaviour as well as lower rates of child abuse and neglect and child mental health problems (Olds 1998; Kitzman et al. 2010; Eckenrode et al. 2010). Nobel prize-winning economist James Heckman has estimated that for every single dollar spent on this programme, over $5 of social costs are saved further down the line (Heckman et al. 2006). This 'family nurse partnership' model is now being trialled in the UK.

There are many other good models of early intervention – such as Watch, Wait and Wonder, Video Interaction Guidance and Circle of Security which have research to back them up. But although it can be helpful to have techniques and programmes, in my view the key factor in any preventive measure is the professional helper's positive, supportive relationship with the family, and his or her encouragement to reflect on what the baby is feeling and how to support the baby's development. This can make all the difference to a parent struggling to relate to a baby or toddler.

Heckman has calculated that investing in early interventions such as these delivers a better rate of return than those targeting older children. Precisely because babies are so adaptable and in a period of accelerated mental growth, they can recover from poor care and form new emotional habits much faster than older children or adults. This can be startlingly fast. Change can occur from one week to another. In my own work with parents and babies, I have witnessed dull, lifeless babies who don't make eye contact week after week suddenly spring to life as the mother's depression lifts, or she starts to respond to them more effectively. The baby becomes more alert, starts to engage in eye contact, smiles and has a more relaxed presence. Relationships between mother and baby that were characterised by hostility or indifference can turn rapidly to passionate mutual attachment and pleasure.

As a psychotherapist used to working with adult clients who can take years to overcome depression or to develop new ways of relating to others, it has seemed shockingly easy at times to facilitate the relationship between a mother and her baby. That isn't to deny that many problems are a lot more intractable than this – they can be – but in those cases it is usually because the adult finds it so hard to change, not the baby.

What we all need, but babies even more so

The X factor, the mystery tonic that enables babies to flourish as soon as they get it, is responsiveness. If only we could bottle it and sell 'Responsiveness Cordial'. But there are certain things to note about the kind of responsiveness that babies need. Researchers have refined our knowledge to the point where we can now say that babies need not too much, not too little, but just the right amount of responsiveness – not the kind that jumps anxiously to meet their every need, nor the kind that ignores them for too long, but the kind of relaxed responsiveness that confident parents tend to have. This is one of the strange things about research in this field. After developing ingenious experiments and rigorous controls, the fruits of its labours tend to be blindingly obvious. However, at least we now 'know' in the more scientific sense of the word 'know' that there is evidence for the self-evident.

What is more, the best responsiveness for babies is the 'contingent' kind. This means that the parent needs to respond to the actual needs of their particular baby, not to their own idea of what a baby might need. A timid baby needs a different response from an outgoing baby, and a tired baby needs something different from a bored one. Each baby needs a tailor-made response, not an off-the-shelf kind, however benign. If the baby is distressed, he needs holding and rocking. If he's bored, he needs a distraction. If he's hungry, he needs food. If he has caught his foot in a blanket, it needs releasing. Each situation requires its own appropriate, contingent response, suitable for the personality of this particular baby. Clearly, it isn't much use being given a rattle when you are hungry, or being rocked in your basket if your foot is uncomfortably stuck.

If you think about your own experience as an adult, you may become aware that you too need contingent responses. General 'niceness', such as people being 'kind' when you are upset in some way, can be quite useless; it washes over you. In fact, very often such niceness is an attempt to drown your feelings and make them go away, just as much as a punitive response does. What works much better is to feel other people willing to get on your wavelength – understanding the specific way that you are feeling, helping you to express it, and thinking about solutions with you. This is the essence of emotional regulation: someone responding to what is actually happening in the moment, processing feelings with you. It involves a recognition of the psychological self, the thinking and feeling self.

This is also what babies need to develop a strong sense of self. In fact, this recognition of the baby's states is what brings the 'self' fully into being. Parents can learn to be more contingently responsive to their babies by following the baby's lead, taking their cue from the baby, observing their baby's moods and desires, and thinking about what it is like for the baby. This can be a fast track back to harmony with their baby and to the unfolding of a much more satisfying relationship through childhood. It may sound too simple, but clinicians working with the parent–baby relationship are using various techniques to achieve this basic goal. There are many obstacles in the way, however; most notably the parent's own difficulties with regulating herself, which can make it less likely that she will be able to regulate her child well. These difficulties are often much harder to resolve, and they overlap with other forms of therapy which aim to heal adults' mental distress.

The flow of feelings

Since I have suggested that many forms of adult mental dysfunction have their roots in babyhood and in the way that babies learn to regulate themselves, the question does arise of how a rickety system can be improved in later life.

As I have outlined already, when babies don't have enough contingent responsiveness to stay well regulated, they tend to try to regulate themselves as best they can. But this usually involves the setting up of patterns of emotional regulation that are defensive, either in the direction of attempts to be self-sufficient, or in the direction of being more emotionally demanding, or swinging from one to the other. The emotional plumbing is blocked either way – flooded or not operational. Inevitably, such strategies set up in early life to get our needs met by others or to protect ourselves from others tend to persist, especially because we are rarely aware of our own defensive manoeuvres.

But the opposite of defensiveness is openness. Healthy emotional life flows without blockages. Feelings come and go. They are noticed, they are responded to, they are processed as they arise. They don't get stuck. The individual with good regulation also has the ability to co-ordinate his or her states with other people, can adjust to their moods and demands, and can make his or her own demands on others. Crucially, there is a flow not only within the individual but also between the individual and others.

This is very different from the traditional psychoanalytic model which understood emotional health as the ability to control and master primitive sexual and aggressive urges. This type of Freudian thinking arose within an Enlightenment paradigm of achieving mastery over nature, and applied the same thinking to individual emotional life. But it saw the person as an isolated unit, responsible for applying willpower to face the power of (human) nature. It did not recognise the individual as the product of interactions with others, as someone shaped by the early regulation he experienced with others and emotionally maintained by others as an adult. Yet ironically the method that Freud hit upon to cure his patients was a dialectical one, the 'talking cure' which involved two people. He had inadvertently stumbled upon the most potent formula for change. Talking to others, forming a relationship with someone who listens to how you feel, is the major element in unblocking the emotional plumbing and in formulating new, more effective emotion strategies. Unfortunately, Freud defined this activity primarily in terms of controlling the biological drives – as a process of making primitive feelings conscious so that they could be better controlled. He exaggerated the role of sexuality and often failed to hear his patients' real feelings. In one of his early famous cases, the case of a young woman he named Dora, the patient was driven to leave her analysis abruptly because she did not feel that Freud had heard her feelings accurately.

There is a kernel of truth in Freud's model of the primitive self being managed by a more conscious self. This fits with our understanding of brain structure. We now know that the prefrontal cortex is a key element in advanced social behaviour. Instead of merely reacting to someone who angers you or whom you desire, behaviour that was the norm in early human societies, we now bring our social awareness into play. We use the prefrontal cortex to explore the social impact of possible behaviours and we modulate our behaviour. In fact, in the middle-class circles of the nineteenth and early twentieth centuries, there was perhaps a tendency to overuse the 'higher' brain and to deny feelings and appetites altogether, out of fear of the consequences of breaching very demanding social rules. This led to an inability to regulate feelings. Holding in feelings, unable to breathe freely or feel freely, is not conducive to good regulation. This led to many of the symptoms that Freud observed in his patients such as hysterical paralysis.

Good regulation depends on feelings flowing freely through the body, while having the mental capacity to notice and reflect on them, and to choose whether or not to act on them. The mind works with the 'primitive' feelings; it neither submits to them nor denies them. It does not try to control feelings through an act of will, but acknowledges them and uses them as a guide to action within the social context. The earthy self who is connected to others in a bodily way through sexuality, giving birth, breastfeeding, mutual protection and defence of territory is tempered by the more complex calculations of the higher social brain.

This process can go wrong in many different ways, but it is safe to say that a whole range of people who are depressed, or angrily antisocial, or anorexic, traumatised, alcoholic, or disturbed and insecure, are neither able to accept their feelings nor to manage them well in relation to other people. Their relationships with other people are frequently a source of pain, rather than a source of validation and regulation. I have suggested that the basis of these difficulties is very often the regulatory patterns that are established at the beginning of life. These patterns emerge because they are the best way to survive in relation to parents with regulatory difficulties. But they are a handicap once the child starts to relate to other people outside the family. A child who becomes very self-sufficient with a hostile parent will take that self-sufficiency into later relationships where it may not serve him or her well. A child whose pattern is to get his mother's attention through tantrums and tears will find that other people don't respond in the same way.

We all try to manage our relationships through the old strategies that are familiar to us, the ones that worked before up to a point. However, the strategies of insecure children are not very good ones. They lack flexibility because they are essentially defensive. They are designed to cope with an unresponsive partner, but they don't provide a blueprint for relating to people who are responsive. Secure children, however, expect other people to respond to them and are much more able to respond to others' different behaviours. If they experience an unresponsive, hurtful person, they are likely to turn to someone more reliable for solace.

These early patterns are persistent because they are inscribed in our brain's neuronal networks and our brain chemistry. They are learnt in an unconscious way and become assumptions about the world that the more conscious self that emerges through childhood is unlikely to be aware of. They become our emotional habits, as taken for granted as bodily habits of cleaning our teeth in the morning, blowing our noses on tissues, or going to sleep at a certain time. These emotional habits are also sustained by our inner chemistry, as the child's body itself becomes habituated to a particular level of neurotransmitters and stress hormones, which comes to feel 'normal'. The body then attempts to maintain the level, even if it is too low, too high or out of balance with other neurohormones in some way. If the stress response is affected, or the prefrontal cortex underpowered because of early experience, then the individual will have a reduced physiological capacity to meet challenging emotional situations in later life.

Can we change our brains?

This basic biological programming tends to be stable once it has been established. The way we regulate ourselves as toddlers can continue to affect our ability to manage ourselves as adults (Moutsiana et al. 2014). So can it be changed? As yet, there has been little substantial research on the process of rebuilding your emotional brain in adulthood. However, since brain plasticity is quite considerable, and connections do continue to be made, it is likely that some change is possible. One source of good news is the discovery that epigenetic changes may be reversible. Emerging evidence suggests that when social or dietary conditions change, even fully mature cells can respond to the change and modify the way DNA is expressed (Meaney 2010; Herb et al. 2012). Clearly, just as the environment is powerful enough to 'methylate' the DNA in the first place, it is also powerful enough to 'demethylate' it. (Researchers are also experimenting with drugs that may also be able to undo earlier methylation (Roth et al. 2009; Weaver et al. 2005)).

The jury is still out as to whether or not the early developing 'social' brain systems can fully recover from early stress through more positive later social experience. Those who have followed the fate of Romanian babies who spent part of their early years in the misery of a Ceausescu orphanage have found that their lives continue to be affected even after many years of adoption. Unless they were adopted before the age of 6 months, many of these teenagers still had emotional difficulties. Although in many cases their cognitive development had caught up, the amygdala was still affected (Mehta et al. 2009; Rutter et al. 2010; Tottenham 2010 et al.). (Brain volumes also tended to be up to 18 per cent smaller most likely due to the total deprivation they endured as small children (Mehta et al. 2009)). Researchers were surprised to find that emotional problems such as depression and anxiety tended to increase as they got older and a high proportion still had attachment problems (Kumsta et al. 2010).

However, in less drastic circumstances, there is increasing evidence that the effects of early stress can be repaired if good care is available quickly enough. For example, the effect of prenatal stress on a baby's hippocampus can be put right as long as he receives attentive post-natal care (Buss et al. 2012; Lemaire et al. 2006). And as we have seen, even those children with the 'risky' orchid genes with diminished access to serotonin are the most responsive and most able to change in a positive direction when social support is available. Even psychological interventions in later life have an effect on genetic expression in the brain (Yehuda et al. 2013; Feinstein and Church 2010).

But looking more specifically at particular areas of the brain involved in processing emotion, are they all equally amenable to change? For example, can the set point of various neurotransmitter systems be 'reset' later on?

Serotonin synthesis in the brain starts in the womb and increases through the first two years of life, peaking at the age of 5 (Chugani et al. 1999). During this period, stress can alter the way the serotonin system develops and can create lifelong tendencies to serotonin dysfunction and vulnerability to anxiety, depression and aggression (Whitaker-Azmitia 2010). Can this system recover in later life? It's not clear whether the brain can recover its own endogenous capacity to synthesise serotonin or whether a damaged system has to continually rely on external factors to rebalance serotonin levels. (Such external factors might include pharmaceutical treatments such as Prozac, nourishment by the right dietary factors, or loving support which reduces the stress hormones which can damage the serotonin system.)

There is emerging evidence that the HPA axis stress response itself does remain open to change and recovery. Some promising work has been done with children in foster care that suggests that it might be possible to change the brain through the right kind of care. In one study by Philip Fisher and his colleagues, foster caregivers were specially trained to see themselves as the child's 'regulatory person': the one who would provide sensitive support in managing stressful situations. This kind of 're-parenting' approach had a beneficial effect on the child's stress response; over a period of 8 or 9 months it was 'normalised' (Fisher et al. 2006). Similarly, research with depressed people has shown that after successful treatment, their cortisol levels drop down to a normal level and this itself is a sign of recovery from depression.

It is still unclear to what extent the brain *structures* affected by stress may also be able to recover. For example, there is ongoing controversy over the extent to which the stressed hippocampus can grow new neurons in adulthood, beyond the window of opportunity that exists in early life. Some scientists believe that anti-depressants can help to kickstart neurogenesis in this part of the brain. Exercise has also been found to increase the volume of the hippocampus (Carlson et al. 2009; Davidson and McEwen 2012). Others say there is no compelling evidence of any neurogenesis in the human cortex in adulthood (Costandi, 2012).

It is also unclear whether the medial prefrontal cortex can recover from the atrophy caused by early stress. Current evidence based on research with rats is hopeful; it suggests that it might be reversible by living a relatively stress-free existence for a substantial period of time (Radley et al. 2005), although the likelihood of recovery gets less possible as the individual gets older (Bloss 2010; Radley and Morrison 2005; Liston et al. 2009).

As for the amygdala, there are mixed results. Where there is severe damage, as with the Romanian orphans, there may be a limited window of opportunity in early child-hood for the amygdala to shrink back to normal. However, there may be more flexibility for those with relatively minor problems. One study with ordinary but stressed adults found that only 8 weeks of mindfulness meditation was needed to reduce their grey matter volume in the right amygdala (Holzel et al. 2010). Fascinating work by Britta Holzel has also found that mindfulness *increases* the important regula-tory connections between the amygdala and the higher brain, especially the anterior cingulate (Holzel et al. 2013).

Diet and lifestyle

The predominant model of healing is to use medication to fix our ills. Unsurprisingly, the psychiatric profession has focused on treatments that might restore brain systems from the outside with synthetic drugs. Despite their limited success with illnesses such as depression, such treatments have become ubiquitous.

More benign approaches to restoring the body's chemical balance are through encouraging the body to produce its own (endogenous) neurochemicals. It is well known that regular, mild exercise can stimulate endorphins; some evidence suggests it might also stimulate the release of serotonin (Young 2007). Exercise is increasingly seen as an effective antidepressant (NICE 2009). Likewise, body massage has a good effect on depression by reducing stress hormones and increasing serotonin (Field 2001; Field et al. 2005; Hou et al. 2010; Rapaport et al. 2012). Regular practice of mindfulness meditation can also reduce cortisol levels, and can calm anxieties by decreasing amygdala overactivation (Goldin and Gross 2010; Jacobs et al. 2013; Brand 2012; Holzel 2011). Experienced meditators tend to manage stress better (Matousek 2010).

The food we eat can have a major effect on our emotional as well as physical well-being. In particular, the essential fatty acids, which are concentrated in the central nervous system, are vital to health. Found in oily fish such as mackerel, they have a powerful anti-inflammatory effect and can decrease the production of cytokines (Calder 2006). Sulforaphane, found in broccoli and cauliflower, is another substance which defends the body against inflammatory conditions. When diets lack these constituents, the individual is less protected against inflammation, which as we have seen, is linked with depression as well as a whole range of diseases ranging from arthritis through to heart disease.

Essential fatty acids can also affect the balance of neurotransmitters. When omega-3 levels are low and inflammation is high, serotoninergic neurons can be affected, perhaps explaining the link between low levels of omega-3 and irritability and antisocial behaviour.

Once again, however, early experience may be crucial. Looking back to the mother's state of health during the perinatal period, we find that her fatty acids pass through the placenta and breast milk and may affect various systems in her offspring's brain during critical periods of development. In particular, early deficiencies of omega-3 can affect the operation of serotonin and dopamine in the frontal cortex (Hibbeln et al. 2006). Lack of omega-3 also affects levels of brain-derived neurotrophic factor (BDNF) which is needed to make synaptic connections in the frontal cortex, hypothalamus and hippocampus (Bhatia et al. 2011; Rao et al. 2007). Researchers are not yet confident in saying whether these neurodevelopmental effects which originate in infancy can be put right by taking omega-3 supplements later on. Certainly in rats, an improved diet can restore normal function during babyhood, but once the pup is weaned this opportunity has gone (Kodas et al. 2002; Bhatia et al. 2011; Hibbeln et al. 2006).

There is less strong evidence available about humans. However, research is now gathering momentum. This suggests that omega-3 in the current diet can still make a difference. Past evidence that giving omega-3 fatty acids to rats improves their ADHD behaviours is now being confirmed in humans. Omega-3 can also make a difference to children with a diagnosis of ADHD (Richardson 2006; Kine et al. 2012). It may also help children who have more general problems with self-control. For example, one controlled trial which gave omega-3 supplements to young offenders found that those who were given the supplements committed 37 per cent fewer disciplinary offences than those on dummy placebo pills (Gesch et al. 2002). Now new studies at the University of Oxford have begun to turn the spotlight on ordinary children in mainstream schools; researcher Paul Montgomery found that the level of omega-3 in the blood 'significantly predicted a child's behaviour and ability to learn' (Montgomery et al. 2013).

These natural means of rebalancing neurotransmitters, reducing stress and preventing inflammatory conditions have received little support from the medical profession to date; its reliance on pharmaceutical treatments has perhaps obstructed recognition of the impact of nutrition on health and well-being. Happily, there are signs that at least mindfulness and exercise are becoming more acceptable treatments, even though such prescriptions are still challenging for the dominant medical model. They are much more to do with lifestyle and are difficult to establish with people who are not good at taking care of themselves. However, all these methods have the same limitation: you have to keep doing it. Whether pills or vitamin supplements, the benefit often lasts only as long as they are taken.

All these approaches may improve both a person's state of mind and their capacity to regulate themselves emotionally. If they become a way of life, they may have a dramatic impact, but they will not necessarily change patterns of emotional regulation in relation to other people. The self-sufficient adult who was once an insecure child will not start to turn to others as a result of a change in diet. So how do we get to this ideal state of self-acceptance coupled with the capacity to take others' feelings seriously – to feel freely, but also to manage our feelings in response to others?

A chance to grow up again

The independent psychotherapeutic tradition offers a different kind of cure. Through establishing a personal relationship for therapeutic purposes only, the individual can explore the way that he or she regulates himself or herself in relation to other people, and can attempt to modify old emotional habits and introduce new ones. But emotional habits take time to form and time to change. First, they have to be aroused. You can only change emotional processing by *doing* it differently. When a particular feeling is aroused, neurotransmitters are released from the subcortex and old neural networks automatically become activated to manage this state of arousal in the old way. But with the help of a therapist, new forms of regulation can be practised. If your therapist accepts your feelings, they do not have to be denied by the neural network which would normally do that, or acted upon by the neural network that would normally respond in that way. The therapist's acceptance allows a mental space to reflect on the feelings and consider how to respond afresh. While the feelings are alive and active, so too are the stress hormones which will assist new (higher brain) cortical synapses to be made in response to the subcortical signals. Together with the therapist, new networks can be developed.

Some of this work may involve dealing with the unfinished business of early life, the feelings of fear that you will be abandoned or rejected which were at their most potent when you were a dependent child; feelings that were overwhelming and unmanageable without a parental regulator; feelings of rage that your parent did not help you to cope with particular feelings; many feelings that were held back because it was not safe to feel them while you were a child, so dependent on the parent to regulate you and keep you alive. These feelings often do not go away. Somehow they lie dormant, unprocessed, liable to break out at moments of stress when the adult 'flips' and releases huge rage or fear which seems incomprehensible to others since it is so disproportionate to the current event.

There is a common misconception that psychotherapy is about hating your mother. For example, John Katzenbach's thriller *The Analyst* begins with this description of the analyst's trade:

> In the year he fully expected to die, he spent the majority
> of his fifty-third birthday as he did most other days,
> listening to people complain about their mothers.
> Thoughtless mothers, cruel mothers, sexually
> provocative mothers. Dead mothers who remained
> alive in their children's minds. Living mothers,
> whom their children wanted to kill. (Katzenbach 2003)

Yet in my experience, what is much more common is a difficulty in complaining about their mothers. The majority of my clients are very protective of their mothers. They idealise them because they long for their love and approval and have never felt secure in it. They are reluctant to criticise. The progress of the therapy often depends on their ability to face their parents' human weaknesses and failings and let go of the hope that one day they will receive the loving care that they missed out on early in life. They grow up when they realise with increasing compassion that their parents are fallible human beings and perfect maternal or paternal love is unobtainable. Accepting that parents are only imperfect and struggling human beings leads to increased self-acceptance.

Missing out on acceptance of their feelings and regulation of their feelings in early childhood, clients have usually resorted to a defensive attempt to manage by themselves. They try to live up to some ideal self whom they believe would be loved by the ideal parent (often one who has no needs), and naturally keep failing over and over again; or they deny that they have any troublesome feelings, or that relationships matter that much.

The missing experience of having feelings recognised and acknowledged by another person, particularly of having strong feelings tolerated by another person, is provided by the therapist. Most important of all, when therapist and client fail to understand each other, or disagree about something important and there is a 'rupture' in the relationship, the therapist demonstrates that relationships can be 'repaired'. This cycle of rupture and repair is the key to secure relationships. Knowing that no matter what breakdowns in communication occur, they can be repaired is the source of confidence in a relationship and the knowledge that regulation will be restored. Slowly, through these types of experience with a psychotherapist, a new muscle develops, an ability to be heard and to listen, to listen and be heard. Emotional states can be shared, both verbally and non-verbally.

These are experiences that, as we saw in Chapter 2, are learnt in infancy. At the earliest stage of life, safety and acceptance are conveyed by touch. But as we mature, we increasingly use words to 'hold' each other. Depressed babies, abused babies, or neglected babies miss out on these experiences of physical and verbal holding. Their feelings and states are not well recognised, accepted and regulated. They don't learn that all states can be 'held' and that failures in acceptance or regulation can be repaired. Instead, they have to find some way to hold themselves together and this is done defensively. Then they attempt to go through life using these defensive strategies, permanently cut off from the flow of mutual regulation with others. They know there is something wrong, something missing. They are unhappy. They turn to drugs or food or other addictions to ease their inner pain.

Psychotherapy offers the chance to rework the emotional strategies, but this work takes a lot of time and a lot of money. It is not enough to organise new networks in the brain by offering new emotional experiences. For these networks to become established, the new form of regulation must happen over and over again until they are consolidated. But once they are, the individual has a portable regulation system that can be used with other people to maintain mental well-being. Some degree of real healing can be achieved.

Birth of the future

> For the first six months of Albertine's life I looked after
> her at home while my partner continued to work. This
> experience forcefully revealed to me something to which I
> had never given much thought: the fact that after a child
> is born the lives of its mother and father diverge, so that
> where before they were living in a state of some equality,
> now they exist in a sort of feudal relation to each other. A
> day spent at home caring for a child could not be more
> different from a day spent working in an office. Whatever
> their relative merits, they are days spent on opposite
> sides of the world.
>
> Rachel Cusk 2001: 5

This book might seem to suggest that a great deal hangs on
women's capacity to fulfil their mothering role. While refer-
ring to 'parents', it has conveyed the expectation that the task
of caring for young babies is one that will be almost inevitably
undertaken by women, not men. Yet in fact the capacity to
emotionally regulate others and be regulated by them is not
gender specific. We all do it. It is perfectly possible for the care
and regulation of small babies also to be done by any adult
who is attuned and available, and committed to providing
continuity of care for the infant. Increasingly, fathers are
participating in this care and even, in some cases, becoming
the primary caregiver, although recent statistics suggest that
this is less common than many would like to believe.

On the plus side, there were just over 6000 more full-
time, stay-at-home dads looking after babies and toddlers

in the UK in 2012 than there were 10 years ago, according to the Office of National Statistics. This looks like a definite shift towards gender equality in parenting. Yet, as Gideon Burrows points out, in the same period there were 44,000 fewer stay-at-home mothers. The gap is mostly filled by grandparents and paid childcare, not fathers (Burrows, 2013). In fact, many men don't even take up their entitlement to two weeks paternity leave let alone the 26 weeks of paid parental leave that is now available in the UK (if the mother does not use it). When fathers do take time off after the baby's birth, they are also more likely to be involved in the care of their toddlers later on (Tanaka and Waldfogel 2007). This choice is often made when the mother goes back to full-time work when their baby is still young (Norman et al. 2013). Perhaps these fathers instinctively recognise their baby's need for devoted personal care, or perhaps – once they have spent time on their own with their baby – they become more confident that they can have a close relationship with their own baby or toddler (Premberg et al. 2008).

The fact that this task has almost always been allocated to women is largely a result of our particular culture, as it has evolved out of earlier biological imperatives. But in the modern world, the assignment of this task to women is becoming increasingly problematic for women too. Women now rarely participate in the child-rearing process until they have their own children and often have little confidence in their capacity to tune in to a baby, mirroring the uncertainty that men have had in taking on such a role.

My own experience of caring for my children as babies was certainly one of culture shock, as Rachel Cusk describes. My busy working life was replaced by long days that seemed to pass in slow motion, trapped in the world of the baby. I orbited around my baby, focused on the baby's needs – juggling this with the attempt to keep rooms clean, to make an evening meal, to get out of the house and find other adults to speak to. Living with a baby, time took on a different rhythm from the busy, noisy life in an office that I was used to, dealing with colleagues, with paperwork, phone calls, machines. At the beginning, it was rather like being underwater in a fascinating, gloomily lit aquarium, struggling to move around and to get anything done at all.

I found that in this Baby World no one knows or cares what you think, what you have done, whom you have loved. You are simply the 'mum with the baby'. This role subsumes all other selves you have been or want to be. For many women, this is intolerable. For others, it is a pleasantly dreamy world they don't want to leave, freed from the burdens of being a striving, achieving self. But probably for most women who have a sense of identity based on their working lives, it is a very difficult adjustment. As working opportunities for women have increased, more and more women have found it hard to resist the pull of their old identity. Over the last few decades, increasing numbers of new mothers have been returning to work and leaving their babies in the care of other people, however torn they may feel about it and however much they long for their babies when they are at work.

This approach has been sanctioned by politicians. Maternity and paternity leave are very short and not guaranteed to all workers. These concessions are not based on the needs of the baby, but act as a gesture to give parents time to recover from the impact of a new baby. They still hurry parents back to work. In fact, various government policies in the UK and the USA have actively encouraged single mothers to return to work rather than to care for their babies and claim state welfare benefits. This sends women the message that mothering is not a valued activity in its own right, and that public roles are the only ones that really matter.

The arguments on each side continue to rage. Clashes between high-profile women exemplify the differences between mothers. On one side are the increasing numbers of well-paid corporate women with MBAs who have started 'opting out' to be with their babies, according to one study (Herr and Wolfram 2011); on the other side, high flyers such as the internet corporation Yahoo's chief executive Marissa Meyer, show their passionate commitment to their work by ignoring the parental leave that is available to them. Perhaps because of the implicit messages sent by politicians, the pressure to keep working is the dominant note. Certainly, many new mothers often find that they desperately want to be with their adorable babies, but feel that if they don't return to work after three months or six months they will be seen as letting the side down after the huge struggle that women have had to be taken seriously as professionals or wage earners. They may also fear that they might lose both their skills and their social networks and face the prospect of being disadvantaged in the promotion ladder.

Other women may simply be compelled by financial necessity to maintain their jobs. However, studies have shown consistently over many years that if women had a free choice most would prefer to work part time and parent part time (Pew Research Center 1997, 2007, 2012; Newell 1992). It seems ironical that after all the changes that women's status has gone through over the centuries in Western societies, at the end of the day women want what our ancestors took for granted: to be part of things, to be engaged in a social group and to take part in working life, while enjoying the care and raising of their own children.

It is also highly likely that this is what the children want, though perhaps no one has ever asked them. This book has outlined the needs of babies in particular, who cannot speak for themselves. In the past, some feminists such as Stephanie Lawler have resisted the notion of such 'needs', claiming that 'needs' talk is highly political, and that needs are socially defined, not intrinsic. Like others before her, she has objected to the way that good mothers are defined as those whose needs are 'congruent with those of the child', while 'women as mothers become invisible outside of their capacity to meet these needs' (Lawler 1999: 73). Her protests certainly ring true in the context of our present social arrangements. However, the current conditions of mothering that force women to live in isolation with their babies, largely cut off from normal social intercourse, are by no means inevitable. It is not the 'needs' that are false, but the way that we arrange our lives around those needs that turns them into a tyranny.

In this book, I have demonstrated that these needs are not imaginary, nor a propaganda tool for those who want to subjugate women, but they have a biological basis. During the 'primal period', as Michel Odent has called the time of dependent infancy (1986), babies do have very demanding needs. They are demanding because they are continuous, sometimes hard to fathom without the aid of language, and they make no concessions to adult needs. You cannot ask a baby to wait while you make a phone call or finish eating your lunch. Once the wail goes up, there is an urgency to quieten it, which takes precedence over everything. The baby cannot wait because the baby has no concept of time and therefore no capacity to anticipate needs being met in 10 minutes' time.

When parents respond to the baby's signals, they are participating in many important biological processes. They are helping the baby's nervous system to mature in such a way that it does not get overstressed. They are helping the bioamine pathways to be set at a moderate level. They are contributing to a robust immune system and a robust stress response. They are helping to build up the prefrontal cortex and the child's capacity to hold information in mind, to reflect on feelings and to restrain impulses, all of which will be a vital part of his or her future capacity to behave socially.

This sounds like a daunting task. Certainly, I wish that I had known more when I was caring for my own babies. Yet in fact parents don't have to be conscious of these processes to provide them. Any adult with reasonable sensitivity and willingness to respond is likely to be doing it without thinking about it. Babies can flourish in the strangest circumstances, given sufficient attention. Problems arise only when they don't get enough attention or when that attention is hostile and critical – experiences that can vary in intensity in a continuum that can ultimately lead to mild psychological problems or to serious disorder in adulthood. But the hostile or critical or neglectful parent (or substitute parent) is inevitably a stressed parent, and invariably someone who has had less than optimal parenting herself or himself.

This matters because the baby's nervous system is more vulnerable at this early stage than later on. Early experience can alter the biochemistry of the brain. As Joseph

LeDoux put it, 'A few extra connections here, a little more or a little less neurotransmitter there, and animals begin to act differently' (LeDoux 2002). What may look to the observer like very small differences in behaviour – between a parent who goes to her baby when he cries, or one who finishes her cup of coffee first, between a parent who talks positively about her baby or one who talks about him being 'a pain in the neck' – may cumulatively have significant consequences. Parents who are reluctant, stressed, hostile, absent or indifferent to their children won't be able to provide the kind of environment a baby needs for optimum development of his underlying emotional equipment. Their babies may be well fed and meet all their developmental milestones, they may even be cognitively 'bright' if they receive other kinds of stimulation, but they may nevertheless develop poorly in an emotional sense.

I have described how the quality of the relationship between parent and child influences both the biochemistry and the structure of the brain. The most frequent behaviours of the parental figures, both mother and father, will be etched in the baby's neural pathways as guides to relating. These repeated experiences turn into learning, and in terms of the pathways involved in emotion, this consists primarily of learning what to expect from others in close relationships. Are other people responsive to feelings and needs, or do they need to be hidden? Will they help to regulate them and help me to feel better or will they hurt me or disappoint me? Our basic psychological organisation is learnt from our generalised experiences in the earliest months and years.

Another reason that this social learning is so crucial is that it provides the means to recover from distress. Having confidence that important others will respond when you need them makes it possible to get through difficult situations. Knowing how to distract yourself from uncomfortable feelings when you can't do anything about them helps to survive them. Having ways of soothing yourself through words or music can restore equilibrium. These regulatory abilities are the foundation of emotional well-being, and psychopathology arises when there is a problem with these recovery mechanisms.

People who are not well equipped with these tools find it hard to maintain equilibrium. Their arousal gets stuck in the 'on' or the 'off' position. In the 'on' position, they are easily upset and stay upset; their thoughts aggravate their distress; they make inappropriate demands on others, and fail to get the support they need. In the 'off' position, they suppress feelings, avoid other people, don't talk about their distress, and remain distressed while less conscious of it. These two tendencies are very close to the attachment categories of insecure 'resistant' and 'avoidant'; the 'disorganised' might flip from one to the other. In effect, the recent work on the stress response and early brain development has expanded our understanding of the biological underpinnings of these attachment terms, and has confirmed that attachment psychology is scientifically credible.

When parents struggle to meet the needs of their babies, because they are depressed, lonely, poorly equipped to regulate themselves, with partners who fail to provide adequate support, and so on, then the delicate processes of early development can become skewed and the same difficulties in regulating arousal can be passed on. Babies then develop the same kinds of insecure strategies for dealing with emotional ups and downs and are in danger of going down a variety of pathways towards psychopathology when they meet emotional challenges in later life. I have described some of these pathways in this book. The depressed person is constantly aroused, with thoughts churning, unable to soothe himself. The traumatised person is even more aroused and helpless to turn off his stress response. Emotional pain in the personality disorders also involves similar arousal that cannot be modulated. At the other end of the continuum, those who suffer from psychosomatic illness tend to suppress their feelings. Those who suppress angry feelings within their families may become unpredictably violent elsewhere, and so on. The origins of many emotional disturbances are in essence regulatory. They have never been easy to define as specific 'diseases' because there is so much overlap between them or 'comorbidity'. What seems most likely is that emotional disturbances are the result of a complex chain of events, rooted in early regulatory pathways, influenced by later circumstances and subsequent learning. Specific combinations such as anxiety with depression or panic with anxiety may arise in particular circumstances.

Although the psychiatric profession responds with interest to the steady output of research on the stress response, it still does not seem to have taken fully on board the significance of early infant experience in particular in shaping the stress response and the bioamine pathways. The past president of the American Psychiatric Association, Nancy Andreasen, recognises that the stress response is probably implicated in a variety of mental health issues, commenting that cortisol may play some causative role in many types of mental illness (Andreasen 2001: 107), yet she does not acknowledge that the stress response itself can be conditioned and altered by early experience in the womb and in the primal period.

At the same time she reports that depression is massively increasing (and recent statistics confirm that it has risen 400 per cent in the USA since the late 1980s (Pratt et al. 2011)). Others also claim that antisocial behaviour in children is massively increasing. Andreasen puts all this down to a more stressful way of life, one that is more intensely competitive than before, with less certain values to guide people, an age of cynicism and materialism (Andreasen 2001: 239). Whether or not this is the case, she fails to note that women's lives have certainly changed in this period. Women's greater participation in the economy, increasingly while their children are very young, has made it much harder for them to juggle the demands of a career with the demands of motherhood. During this period, when depression has apparently surged dramatically, more and more babies have been cared for by strangers during daylight hours, and by their parents at the end of a busy working day.

In the process, I believe that we have swung from one unworkable situation to another, where either mothers pay or children pay the price. Betty Friedan first described the oppression of young mothers in the 1960s, suffocating in the suburbs, unable to play any social role except that of 'mom' or wife. But our current situation may be equally oppressive to babies and toddlers who are increasingly being shunted to and from nurseries or childminding groups, plonked in front of DVDs, fitting around their parents' busy lives which are elsewhere. How are such children learning to regulate their emotions?

The implicit message of such practices is that relationships are not a priority; work is the priority. Relationships have become a kind of 'treat', encapsulated in the concept of 'quality time'. The regulatory aspect of close relationships is all but lost in this approach. While adults may be able to get by with a conversation at the end of the day, or a phone call when regulation is needed from their partner (or often end up being regulated by their colleagues at work), children need much more continuous regulation. This is usually only available in expensive childcare arrangements, where there is the possibility of good-quality attention from a familiar adult. Substitute care on a more economic scale is less likely to provide this kind of attention and will be depriving the child of the essential emotional learning that characterises this period of early life.

The qualities of good parenting (and of close relationships in general) are essentially regulatory qualities: the capacity to listen, to notice, to shape behaviour and to be able to restore good feelings through some kind of physical, emotional or mental contact, through a touch, a smile, a way of putting feelings and thoughts into words. These capacities are personal ones, but they cannot be expressed fully in a culture which relegates children to the margins. To be able to notice and respond to others' feelings, takes up time. It requires a kind of mental space to be allocated to feelings, and a willingness to prioritise relationships. This is a challenge to a goal-oriented society.

In a restaurant recently, I noticed a tall, good-looking man with grey hair who was giving the waiters a hard time. He complained about the speed of the service and then he questioned whether they had brought the right drinks. Then he asked why he had not been offered Parmesan cheese. He was so agitated about getting his physical needs met that he did not seem to be aware of the emotional state of the other diners at his table, who were looking increasingly uncomfortable and embarrassed. The conversation, which had been animated as they sat down, petered out as the atmosphere became more and more tense. This little scene is in some ways typical of the mentality which is so focused on getting things done, getting things, achieving goals, that it loses track of relationships. This man was not taking others' feelings into account. He was not thinking about how the waiter felt, nor the people with whom he was eating. His goal was to get the right meal at the right time. He lost touch with the pleasure of company, of conversation, of relaxing together with other people – the process of eating together, rather than the goal of achieving a successful meal.

The goal-oriented mentality is the same mentality which writes columns in newspapers deriding the need for self-esteem, the same mentality which talks about 'wallowing' in feelings. It encompasses the 'stiff upper lip', the Protestant work ethic, and the 'hurry sickness' aspects of our culture. Will-power and exertion are prized over responsiveness and a willingness to take time. Life is tough, they will say, just get on with it. In this way the splits between mind and body, thought and feeling, personal and public, are perpetuated. Listening to feelings, your own or someone else's, can slow you down. It can delay the achievement of goals.

For the last 200 years or more, our Western culture has pursued its material goals through an explosion of science and technology. We live so well materially that almost everyone in these societies has light and heat whenever needed, has entertainment at the flick of a switch, long-distance communication across the world without any effort, and an array of easily prepared foods available in every supermarket. We are saturated with goods and services, to the point where it has been argued that there is a ceiling of wealth beyond which there is no increase in well-being. Perhaps this is why we now have the luxury of asking the question of how we might improve our lives in non-material ways.

Many of the scientific discoveries in the field of emotion look like reinventing the wheel. They affirm the importance of touch, of responsiveness, of giving time to people. How can we legislate for such things? Perhaps it is a pipe dream to imagine that policy makers could have any effect on the quality of early parenting. Isn't this a very private affair that takes place in private homes? What more could be done than is already being done in terms of promoting more maternity and paternity leave, and encouraging employers to embrace more flexibility in working hours? This book is not the place to supply the answers to such questions, but it can ask the question of whether we can afford to leave early parenting in the realm of the private and personal.

Underlying the privacy of early child rearing lies an assumption, I think, that mothering is something innate. It is true that giving birth and suckling a baby are intensely physical, biological processes like making love. There is an innate biological 'preparedness' to have such experiences. Yet, like sexual activity, it is also highly cultural. In societies that live more simply, babies and children are ever present. The opportunities to hold babies, soothe them, discipline them and learn about them are ample. In other words, there is psychological preparation for becoming a parent through social learning and observation. But in Western societies where people are cut off from each other physically by their elaborate houses and apartments, and work is rigidly separated from domestic life, these opportunities do not arise. There is little chance to observe how an experienced mother deals with a baby or a toddler, and less chance of practising with other people's children. In these circumstances, the only sources of information are books and television programmes. More often, the new parent simply relies on their own unconscious learning based on their own experience of being a baby and toddler. These 'instincts' will direct them. This is partly why maladaptive patterns repeat down the generations.

If we continue to insist on the primacy of production, drawing all adults including the parents of young children relentlessly into the pursuit of material goals and careers, then we may have to bear the emotional fall-out. Without attentive adults to protect their developing nervous systems, enabling children to develop into emotionally robust adults capable of meeting challenges and sustaining relationships, there is a price to pay. These problems have huge social impact and generate huge costs. The bill for antidepressants alone is over $10 billion dollars a year in the USA (Insel 2011). But politicians, like doctors, tend to respond to symptoms. When faced with the antisocial activities of young men or the depression of young women, it is understandable to look for ways of stopping these behaviours and alleviating distress. However, we have the information to go further than this.

The new information that science has offered in recent decades makes it clear that something can be done to alleviate many social and mental health problems. To turn the situation around, to provide more children with the optimal start for being emotionally equipped to deal with life, we need to invest in early parenting. This investment will be costly. To bring about conditions where every baby has the kind of responsive care that he or she needs to develop well means that the adults who do this work must be valued and supported in their task. This in itself would involve a sea change in our cultural attitudes. Instead of hiding breast-feeding away, we would accept and value it. Instead of isolating women in their homes with a baby, parenting – whoever takes on the role – would be much more based in a local community of adults.

Considering how to reduce the twin stresses of isolation and inexperience that plague parenting in advanced economies will involve some radical rethinking of the conditions in which it takes place. It implies the need to provide much greater flexibility in working practices, shared parenting options, as well as community facilities. Equally, if parents prefer to work and delegate their child rearing to others, those substitute carers must be well educated and trained in the needs of babies, and given incentives (including better pay) to have a highly developed commitment to their job – all of which requires financial backing.

As well as looking to the future, we must also consider the legacy of inadequate care that tends to repeat itself down the generations. It is not enough to alleviate external stress, while failing to address the internal world of parents. We need to do both. Those who have grown up with difficulties in managing stress because of their own early experiences are not necessarily going to treat their own children very differently even if they do feel more supported by the wider community. This backlog of emotional problems must also be dealt with if we are going to stop the cycle of poor regulation from unwittingly being handed on.

There are many ways forward; they all cost money. Fully paid, longer and more flexible parental leave is a priority. But parents 'being there' for their babies is only the first step. We also need to train more parent–infant psychotherapists to help parents who want to stop damaging emotional patterns from repeating themselves. We need more health visitors or home visitors to provide direct guidance and encouragement with parenting, to every parent who is in need of support. Parenting programmes should be available to all new parents. Solutions such as these would not be hard to establish and are proving effective where they have been tried (Stewart-Brown and Macmillan 2010; Lieberman et al. 1991; Olds et al. 1998). At an earlier stage, schools could do more to educate children about parenting and to encourage boys to think of themselves as future parents (for example, using the Roots of Empathy programme (Gordon 2012)). All these solutions already exist in piecemeal fashion; what we need now is the will to create universally available provision that could be the basis for a 'National Emotional Well-being Service' (NEWS). Although the financial calculations are challenging and complex, the evidence points towards massive long-term savings in the social costs of crime, of putting children into care, and managing the consequences of poor emotional regulation (Conti and Heckman 2012).

The evidence I have presented in this book makes it imperative, I believe, that we do something. The babies who are born now and in the years to come will be the adults who nurse us in old age, who manage our industry, who entertain us, who live next door. What kind of adults will they be? Will they be emotionally balanced enough to contribute their talents, or will they be disabled by hidden sensitivities? Their early start, and the degree to which they felt loved and valued, will surely play an important part in determining that.

Bibliography

Abraham, S. and Llewellyn-Jones, D. (2001) *Eating Disorders – The Facts*, Oxford: Oxford University Press.

Ader, R. and Cohen, N. (1981) 'Conditioned immunopharmacologic responses', in R. Ader (ed.) *Psychoneuroimmunology*, New York: Academic Press.

Agrawal, H., Gunderson, J., Holmes, B. and Lyons-Ruth, K. (2004) 'Attachment studies with borderline patients: a review', *Harvard Review of Psychiatry* 12 (2): 94–104.

Ainsworth, M., Blehar, M., Waters, E. and Wall, S. (1978) *Patterns of Attachment: A Psychological Study of the Strange Situation*, Hillsdale, NJ: Lawrence Erlbaum Associates, Inc.

Allen, G. (2011) 'Early intervention: the next steps. An independent report to Her Majesty's Government', London: HM Government.

Allen, G. (2013) Comment made at Westminster Social Policy Forum July 2013.

Allen, J. (2001) *Traumatic Relationships and Serious Mental Disorders*, Chichester: Wiley.

Alpern, L. and Lyons-Ruth, K. (1993) 'Preschool children at social risk', *Development and Psychopathology* 5: 371–87.

American Psychiatric Association. (2013) *Diagnostic and Statistical Manual of Mental Disorders*, 5th edn, Washington, DC: APA.

Anda, R., Felitti, V., Bremner, D., Walker, J., Whitfield, C., Perry, B. et al. (2006) 'The enduring effects of abuse and related adverse experiences in childhood', *European Archives of Psychiatry and Clinical Neuroscience* 256 (3): 174–86.

Anderson, S., Tomada, A., Vincow, E., Valente, E., Polcari, A. and Teicher, M. (2008) 'Preliminary evidence for sensitive periods in the effect of childhood sexual abuse on regional brain development', *The Journal of Neuropsychiatry and Clinical Neurosciences* 20 (3).

Andreasen, N. (2001) *Brave New Brain: Conquering Mental Illness in the Era of the Genome*, Oxford: Oxford University Press.

Ansorge, M., Morelli, E. and Gingrich, J. (2008) 'Inhibition of serotonin but not norepinephrine transport during development produces delayed, persistent perturbations of emotional behaviors in mice', *The Journal of Neuroscience* 28 (1): 199–207.

Antoni, M., Lutgendorf, S., Cole, S., Dhabhar, F., Sephton, S., McDonald, P. et al. (2006) 'The influence of bio-behavioural factors on tumour biology: pathways and mechanisms', *Nature Reviews Cancer* 6 (3): 240–8.

Appleyard, B. (1992) *Understanding the Present*, London: Picador.

Arnsten, A. (2009) 'Stress signaling pathways that impair prefrontal structure and function', *Nature Reviews Neuroscience* 10: 410–22.

Ashman, S., Dawson, G., Panagiotides, H., Yamada, E. and Wilkins, C. (2002) 'Stress hormone levels of children of depressed mothers', *Development and Psychopathology* 14 (2): 333–49.

Ayoub, C. and Rappolt-Schlichtmann, G. (2007) 'Child maltreatment and the development of alternate pathways in biology and behavior', in D. Coch et al. (eds), *Human Behavior, Learning and the Developing Brain*, New York: Guilford Press.

Badanes, L., Dmitrieva, J. and Watamura, S. (2012) 'Understanding cortisol reactivity across the day at child care', *Early Child Research Questions* 27 (1): 156–65.

Baibazarova, E., van de Beek, C., Cohen-Kettenis, P., Buitelaar, J., Shelton, K. and van Goozen, S. (2013) 'Influence of prenatal maternal stress, maternal plasma cortisol and cortisol in the amniotic fluid on birth outcomes and child temperament at 3 months', *Psychoneuroendocrinology* 38 (6): 907–15.

Bakermans-Kranenburg, M., van Ijzendoorn, M., Pijlman, F., Mesman, J. and Juffer, F. (2008) 'Experimental evidence for differential susceptibility: DRD4 VNTR moderates intervention effects on toddlers' externalizing behaviour in a randomized controlled trial', *Developmental Psychology* 44: 293–300.

Bakermans-Kranenburg, M. and van Ijzendoorn, M. (2011) 'Differential susceptibility to rearing environment depending on dopamine-related genes: new evidence and a meta-analysis', *Development and Psychopathology* 23: 39–52.

Barbas, H. (2007) 'Flow of information for emotions through temporal and orbitofrontal pathways', *Journal of Anatomy* 211: 237–49.

Barker, D. (1992) *Fetal and Infant Origins of Adult Disease*, London: British Medical Journal.

Barlow, J., McMillan, A., Kirkpatrick, S.B., Ghate, D., Smith, M. and Barnes, J. (2008) 'Health-led parenting interventions in pregnancy and early years', Rearch Report No. DCSF-RW070.

Bates, J., Pettit, G., Dodge, K. and Ridge, B. (1998) 'Interaction of temperamental resistance to control and restrictive parenting in the development of externalising behaviour, *Developmental Psychology* 34: 982.

Beals, J. (2010), 'PTSD linked to epigenetic changes in immune function genes', Medscape, 4 May.

Beebe, B. (2002) Unpublished talk at Bowlby Memorial Lecture.

Beebe, B. and Lachmann, F. (2002) *Infant Research and Adult Treatment*, Hillsdale, NJ: Analytic Press.

Bellis, M., Hughes, K., Jones, A., Perkins, C. and McHale, P. (2013) 'Childhood happiness and violence: a retrospective study of their impacts on adult well-being', BMJ Open 3:e003427.

Belsky, J. (1995) 'The origins of attachment security', in S. Goldberg, R. Muir and J. Kerr (eds) *Attachment Theory: Social, Developmental and Clinical Perspectives*, Hillsdale, NJ: Analytic Press.

Belsky, J. and Fearon, R. (2002) 'Infant–mother attachment security, contextual risk, and early development: a moderational analysis', *Development and Psychopathology* 14: 293–310.

Belsky, J. and Pluess, M. (2009) 'Beyond diathesis stress: differential susceptibility to environmental influences', *Psychological Bulletin* 135 (6): 885–908.

Belsky, J., Fearon, P. and Bell, B. (2007) 'Parenting, attention and externalizing problems', *Journal of Child Psychology and Psychiatry* 48 (12): 1233–42.

Belsky, J., Hsieh, K. and Crnic, K. (1998) 'Mothering, fathering and infant negativity as antecedents of boys' externalising problems and inhibition at age 3 years: differential susceptibility to rearing experience?', *Development and Psychopathology* 10: 301–19.

Bench, C., Friston, K., Brown, R. and Dolan, R. (1993) 'Regional cerebral blood flow in depression measured by positon emission tomography: the relationship with clinical dimensions', *Psychological Medicine* 23: 579–90.

Bennett, C. (2013) 'Pregnant women deserve more than this infantile advice', *Observer*, 9 June.

Bergman, K., Sarkar, P., Glover, V. and O'Connor, T. (2008) 'Quality of child-parent attachment moderates the impact of antenatal stress on child fearfulness', *Journal of Child Psychology and Psychiatry* 49 (10): 1089–98.

Bergman, K., Sarkar, P., Glover, V. and O'Connor, T.G. (2010) 'Maternal prenatal cortisol and infant cognitive development: moderation by infant–mother attachment', *Biological Psychiatry* 67:1026–32.

Berk, M., Williams, L., Jacka, F., O'Neil, A., Pasco, J., Moylan, S. et al. (2013) 'So depression is an inflammatory disease, but where does the inflammation come from?', *BMC Medicine* 11: 200.

Bernard, K. and Dozier, M. (2010) 'Examining infants' cortisol responses to lab tasks among children varying in attachment disorganization: stress reactivity or return to baseline?', *Developmental Psychology* 46 (6): 1771–8.

Bernier, A., Carlson, S. and Whipple, N. (2010) 'From external regulation to self-regulation: early parenting precursors of young children's executive functioning', *Child Development* 81 (1): 326–39.

Bhatia, H., Agrawal, R., Sharma, S., Huo, Y-X., Ying, Z. and Gomez-Pinilla, F. (2011), 'Omega-3 fatty acid deficiency during brain maturation reduces neuronal and behavioral plasticity in adulthood', *Plos One* 6 (12): e28451.

Bilbo, S. and Schwartz, J. (2009) 'Early-life programming of later-life brain and behavior: a critical role for the immune system', *Frontiers in Behavioral Neuroscience* 3 (14).

Blalock, E. (1984) 'The immune system as a sensory organ', *Journal of Immunology* 132: 1067.

Blass, E., Fitzgerald, E. and Kehoe, P. (1986) 'Interactions between sucrose, pain, and isolation distress', *Pharmacology, Biochemistry and Behaviour* 26: 483–89.

Bloss, E., Janssen, W., McEwen, B. and Morrison, J. (2010) 'Interactive effects of stress and ageing on structural plasticity in the prefrontal cortex', *Journal of Neuroscience* 30 (19): 3726–31.

Blum, D. (2003) *Love at Goon Park: Harry Harlow and the Science of Affection*, Chichester: Wiley.

Bohman, M. (1996) 'Predisposition to criminality: Swedish adoption studies in retrospect', in M. Rutter (ed.) *Genetics of Criminal and Antisocial Behaviour*, Chichester: Wiley.

Bonne, O., Brandes, D., Gilboa, M., Gomori, J., Shenton, M., Pitman, R. and Shater, M. (2001) 'Longitudinal study of hippocampal volume in trauma survivors with PTSD', *American Journal of Psychiatry* 158: 1248–51.

Bowlby, J. (1969) *Attachment*, London: Pelican.

Bradley, S. (2000) *Affect Regulation and the Development of Psychopathology*, New York: Guilford Press.

Bradley, R. and Westen, D. (2005) 'The psychodynamics of borderline personality disorder', *Development and Psychopathology* 17: 927–57.

Bradshaw, J. (2001) *Developmental Disorders of the Frontostriatal System*, Hove: Psychology Press.

Branchi, I., Curley, J., D'Andrea, I., Cirulli, F., Champagne, F. and Alleva, E. (2012) 'Early interactions with mother and peers independently build adult social skills and shape BDNF and oxytocin receptor brain levels', *Psychoneuroimmunology* http://dx.doi, org/10.1016/j.psyneuen.2012.07.010.

Brand, S., Holsboer-Trachsler, E., Naranjo, J. and Schmidt, S., (2012) 'Influence of mindfulness practice on cortisol and sleep in long-term and short-term meditators', *Neuropsychobiology* 65 (3): 109–18.

Braun, J., Kahn, R., Forelich, T., Auinger, P. and Lanphear, B. (2006) 'Exposures to environmental toxicants and ADHD in US children', *Environmental Health Perspectives* 114: 1904–9

Bremner, J.D. (2002) *Does Stress Damage the Brain? Understanding Trauma Related Disorders from a Mind–Body Perspective*, New York: Norton.

Bremner, J.D. (2006) 'Traumatic stress: effects on the brain', *Dialogues in Clinical Neuroscience* 8 (4): 445–61.

Bremner, J.D., Southwick, S., Johnson, D., Yehuda, R. and Charney, D. (1993) 'Childhood physical abuse and combat-related PTSD in Vietnam veterans', *American Journal of Psychiatry* 150: 235–39.

Bremner, J.D., Staib, L., Kaloupek, D., Southwick, S., Soufer, R. and Charney, D. (1999) 'Neural correlates of exposure to traumatic pictures and sound in Vietnam combat veterans with and without post-traumatic stress disorder: a PET study', *Biological Psychiatry* 45 (7): 806–16.

Bremner, J.D., Innis, R., Southwick, S., Staib, L., Zoghbi, S. and Charney, D. (2000a) 'Decreased benzodiazepine receptor binding in prefrontal cortex in combat-related post-traumatic stress disorder, *American Journal of Psychiatry* 157 (7): 1120–26.

Bremner, J.D., Narayan, M., Staib, L., Anderson, E., Miller, H. and Charney, D. (2000b) 'Hippocampal volume reduction in major depression', *American Journal of Psychiatry* 157 (1): 115–17.

Bremner, J.D., Randall, P., Scott, T., Bronen, R., Seibyl, J., Southwick, S. et al. (1995) 'MRI-based measurement of hippocampal volume in PTSD', *American Journal of Psychiatry* 152: 973–81.

Bremner, J.D., Randall, P., Vermetten, E., Staib, L., Bronen, R., Capelli, S. et al. (1997) 'Magnetic resonance image-based measurement of hippocampal volume in PTSD related to childhood physical and sexual abuse: a preliminary report', *Biological Psychiatry* 41: 23–32.

Brendel, G., Stern, E. and Silbersweig, D. (2005) 'Neuroimaging of borderline personality disorder', *Development and Psychopathology* 17: 1197–206.

Brennan, P., Grekin, E. and Mortensen, E. (2002) 'Relationship of maternal smoking during pregnancy with criminal arrest and hospitalisation for substance abuse in male and female adult offspring', *American Journal of Psychiatry* 159 (1): 48–54.

Brier, A., Albus, M. and Pickar, D. (1987) 'Controllable and uncontrollable stress in humans: alterations in mood, neuroendocrine and psychophysiological function', *American Journal of Psychiatry* 144: 1419–25.

Brion, M-J., Victora, C., Matijasevich, A., Horta, B., Anselmi, L., Steer, C. et al. (2010) 'Maternal smoking and child psychological problems: disentangling causal and non-causal effects', Pediatrics 126 (1): e57–e65.

Brown, G. and Harris, T. (1978) *Social Origins of Depression*, London: Tavistock.

Bruinsma, K. and Taren, D. (2000) 'Dieting, essential fatty acid intake, and depression', *Nutrition Review* 58 (4): 98–108.

Bucci, W. (1997) *Psychoanalysis and Cognitive Science*, New York: Guilford Press.

Buckholtz, J. and Meyer Lindenberg, A. (2008) 'MAOA and the neurogenetic architecture of human aggression', *Trends in Neuroscience* 31 (3): 120–9.

Buckingham, J., Gillies, G. and Cowell, A.-M. (eds) (1997) *Stress, Stress Hormones and the Immune System*, Chichester: Wiley.

Buehler, C. and O'Brien, M. (2011), 'Mothers' part-time employment: associations with mother and family well-being', *Journal of Family Psychology* 25 (6): 895–906.

Burrows, G. (2013) 'Childcare – why don't men pull their weight?', *Guardian* 5 July.

Buss, C., Davis, E., Shahbaba, B., Pruessner, J., Head, K. and Sandman, C. (2012) 'Maternal cortisol over the course of pregnancy and subsequent child amygdala and hippocampus volumes and affective problems', *PNAS* 109 (2): e1312–e1319.

Butik, C., Thornton, L., Pinheiro, A., Kaye, W. et al. (2008) 'Suicide attempts in anorexia nervosa', *Psychosomatic Medicine* 70: 378–83.

Buydens-Branchey, L., Branchey, M. and Hibbeln, J. (2008) 'Associations between increases in plasma N-3 polyunsaturated fatty acids following supplementation and decreases in anger and anxiety in substance abusers', *Progress in Neuropsychopharmacology and Biological Psychiatry* 32(2): 568–75.

Cadoret, R., Yates, W., Troughton, E., Woodworth, G. and Stewart, M. (1995) 'Genetic–environmental interaction in the genesis of aggressivity and conduct disorders', *Archives of General Psychiatry* 52: 916.

Calder, P. (2006) 'n-3 polyunsaturated fatty acids, inflammation and inflammatory diseases', *American Journal of Clinical Nutrition* 83: 1505s–19s.

Caldji, C., Diorio, J. and Meaney, M. (2000) 'Variations in maternal care in infancy regulate the development of stress reactivity', *Biological Psychiatry* 48: 1164–74.

Caldji, C., Tannenbaum, B., Sharma, S., Francis, D., Plotsky, P. and Meaney, M. (1998) 'Maternal care during infancy regulates the development of neural systems mediating the expression of fearfulness in the rat', *Proceedings of the National Academy of Sciences USA* 95 (9): 5335–40.

Calkins, S. and Fox, N. (2002) 'Self regulatory processes in early personality development: a multilevel approach to the study of childhood social withdrawal and aggression', *Development and Psychopathology* 14: 477–98.

Campbell, P. and Cohen, J. (1985) 'Effects of stress on the immune response', in T. Field, P. McCabe and N. Schneiderman (eds) *Stress and Coping*, Hillsdale, NJ: Lawrence Erlbaum Associates, Inc.

Capitanio, J., Mendoza, S., Lerche, N. and Mason, W. (1998) 'Social stress results in altered glucocorticoid regulation and shorter survival in simian acquired immune deficiency syndrome', *Proceedings of the National Academy of Sciences of the USA* 95 (8).

Cardinal, M. (1984) *The Words To Say It*, London: Picador.

Carlson, E., Egeland, B. and Sroufe, A. (2009) 'A prospective investigation of development of borderline personality symptoms', *Development and Psychopathology* 21 (4): 1311–34.

Carlson, V., Ciccetti, D., Barnett, D. and Braunwald, K. (1989) 'Finding order in disorganisation: lessons from research on maltreated infants' attachments to their caregivers', in D. Ciccetti and V. Carlson (eds) *Child Maltreatment: Theory and Research on the Causes and Consequences of Child Abuse and Neglect*, Cambridge: Cambridge University Press.

Carpenter, H. (1999) *Dennis Potter: A Biography*, London: Faber and Faber.

Carr, D., House, J., Kessler, R., Sonnega, J. and Wartman, C. (2000) 'Marital quality and psychological adjustment to widowhood among older aldults: a longditudinal analysis', *Journals of Gerontology Series B: Psychological Sciences and Social Sciences* 55.

Carroll, J., Gruenewald, T., Taylor, S., Janicki-Deverts, D., Matthews, K. and Seeman, T. (2013) 'Childhood abuse, parental warmth and adult multisystem biological risk in the coronary artery risk development in young adults study', *PNAS* 110 (42): 17149–53.

Carroll, R. (2001) 'The autonomic nervous system: barometer of emotional intensity and internal conflict', unpublished lecture.

Carver, C. and Scheier, M. (1998) *On the Self-Regulation of Behaviour*, Cambridge: Cambridge University Press.

Caspi, A., Moffit, T., Newman, D. and Silva, P. (1996) 'Behavioural observations at age 3 predict adult psychiatric disorders: longitudinal evidence from a birth cohort', *Archives of General Psychiatry* 53: 1033–9.

Caspi, A., Henry, B., McFee, R., Moffit, T. and Silva, P. (1995) 'Temperamental origins of child and adolescent behaviour problems: from age three to age fifteen', *Child Development* 66: 55–68.

Caspi, A., McClay, J., Moffitt, T., Mill, J., Martin, J., Craig, I., Taylor, A. and Poulton, R. (2002) 'Role of genotype in the cycle of violence in maltreated children', *Science* 297 (5582): 851–4.

Cerqueira, J., Pego, J., Taipa, R., Bessa, J., Almeida, O. and Sousa, N. (2005) 'Morphological correlates of corticosteroid-induced changes in prefrontal cortex-dependent behaviors', *The Journal of Neuroscience* 25 (34): 7792–800.

Chalmers, D., Kwak, S., Mansour, A. and Watson, S. (1993) 'Cortisosteroids regulate brain hippocampal 5HT–1A receptor mRNA expression', *Journal of Neuroscience* 13: 914–23.

Chalon, S. (2006) 'Omega-3 fatty acids and monoamine neurotransmission', *Prostaglandins, Leukotrienes and Essential Fatty Acids* 75 (4): 259–69.

Chambers, R.A., Bremner, J., Moghaddam, B., Southwick, S., Charney, D. and Krystal, J. (1999) 'Glutamate and PTSD', *Seminars in Clinical Neuropsychiatry* 4 (4): 274–81.

Charuvastra, A and Cloitre, M. (2008) 'Social bonds and PTSD', *Annual Review Psychology* 59: 301–28.

Chen, E., Miller, G., Kobor, M. and Cole, S. (2010) 'Maternal warmth buffers the effects of low early-life socioeconomic status on proinflammatory signaling in adulthood', *Molecular Psychiatry* 16(7): 729–37.

Chida, Y., Hamer, M., Wardle, J. and Steptoe, A (2008) 'Do stress-related psychosocial factors contribute to cancer incidence and survival?', *Nature Reviews Clinical Oncology* 5: 466–75.

Chisholm, K., Carter, M., Ames, E. and Morison, S. (1995) 'Attachment security and indiscriminately friendly behaviour in children adopted from Romanian orphanages', *Development and Psychopathology* 7: 283–94.

Chopra, D. (1989) *Quantum Healing*, New York: Bantam.

Chu, J. (1998) *Rebuilding Shattered Lives*, Chichester: Wiley.

Chugani, H. (1997) 'Neuroimaging of developmental nonlinearity and developmental pathologies', in R. Thatcher et al. (eds) *Developmental Neuroimaging*, New York: Academic Press.

Chugani, H., Behen, M., Muzik, O., Juhasz, C., Nagy, F. and Chugani, D. (2001) 'Local brain functional activity following early deprivation: a study of post-institutionalised Romanian orphans', *Neuroimage* 14: 1290–301.

Chugani, D.C., Muzik, O., Behen, M., Rothermel, R., Janisse, J.J., Lee, J. and Chugani, H.T. (1999) 'Developmental changes in brain serotonin synthesis capacity in autistic and nonautistic children', *Annals of Neurology* 45 (3): 287–95.

Ciccetti, D. (1994) 'Development and self-regulatory structures of the mind', *Development and Psychopathology* 6: 533–49.

Ciccetti, D. and Rogosch, F. (2001) 'Diverse patterns of neuroendocrine activity in maltreated children', *Development and Psychopathology* 13 (3): 759–82.

Cima, M., Smeets, T. and Jelicic, M. (2008) 'Self-reported trauma, cortisol levels and aggression in psychopathic and non-psychopathic prison inmates', *Biological Psychology* 78: 75–86

Clyman, R. (1991) 'The procedural organisation of emotions', in T. Shapiro and R. Emde (eds) *Affect, Psychoanalytic Perspectives*, New York: International Universities Press.

Coan, J., Schaefer, H. and Davidson, R. (2006) 'Lending a hand: social regulation of neural response to threat', *Psychological Science* 17 (12): 1032–9.

Cockburn, F. (2013) 'Alcohol and health: a paediatrician's perspective', *Fetal Alcohol Forum*, 9.

Cohen, J. and Crnic, L. (1982) 'Glucocorticoids, stress and the immune response', in D. Webb (ed.) *Immunopharmacology and the Regulation of Leucocyte Function*, New York: Marcel Dekker.

Cohen, R., Grieve, S., Hoth, K., Paul, R. Sweet, L., Tate, D. et al. (2006), 'Early life stress and morphometry of the adult ACC and caudate nuclie', *Biological Psychiatry* 59 (10): 975–82.

Cohn, J., Campbell, S., Matias, R. and Hopkins, J. (1990) 'Face-to-face interactions of postpartum depressed and nondepressed mother–infant pairs at 2 months', *Developmental Psychology* 26 (1): 15–23.

Cole, J., Costafreda, S. and McGuffin, P. (2011), 'Hippocampal atrophy in first episode depression: a metaanalysis of MRI studies' *Journal of Affective Disorders* 134 (1–3): 483–7.

Collins, A., Maccoby, E., Steinberg, L., Hetherington, M. and Bornstein, M. (2000) 'Contemporary research on parenting: the case for nature and nurture', *American Psychologist* 55 (2): 218–32.

Collins, P. and Depue, R. (1992) 'A neurobehavioural systems approach to developmental psychopathology: implications for disorders of affect', in D. Ciccetti and S. Toth (eds) *Rochester Symposium on Developmental Psychopathology*, vol. 4, Rochester: University of Rochester Press.

Collins, W., Maccoby, E., Steinberg, L., Hethenrigten, E. and Bornstein, M. (2000) 'Contemporary research on parenting', *American Psychologist* 55: 218.

Colombo, J., Kannass, K., Shaddy, D., Kundurthi, S., Maikranz, J. and Anderson, C. (2004) 'Maternal DHA and the development of attention in infancy and toddlerhood', *Child Development* 75: 1254–67.

Connan, F. and Treasure, J. (1998) 'Stress, eating and neurobiology', in H. Hoek, J. Treasure and M. Katzman (eds) *Neurobiology in the Treatment of Eating Disorders*, Chichester: Wiley.

Conti, G. and Heckman, J. (2012), 'The economics of child well-being', Discussion Paper 6930.

Cooper, P. and Murray, L. (1998) 'Post-natal depression', *British Medical Journal* 316: 1884–6.

Cornelius, M., Goldschmidt, L. and Day, N. (2012), 'Prenatal cigarette smoking: long-term effects on young adult behavior problems and smoking behavior', *Neurotoxicology Teratology* 34 (6): 554–9.

Cornelius, M., De Genna, N., Leech, S., Willford, J., Goldschmidt, L. and Day, N. (2011) 'Effects of prenatal cigarette smoke exposure on neurobehavioral outcomes in 10 year old children of teenage mothers', *Neurotoxiology Teratology* 33 (1): 137–44.

Costandi, M. (2012) 'Does your brain produce new cells? A skeptical view of human adult neurogenesis', *Guardian*, 23 February.

Crow, S., Peterson, C., Swanson, S. et al (2009) 'Increased mortality in bulimia nervosa and other eating disorders', *American Journal of Psychiatry* 166: 1342–6.

Cusk, R. (2001) *A Life's Work: On Becoming a Mother*, London: Fourth Estate.

Cyhlarova, E., McCulloch, A., McGuffin, P. and Wykes, T. (2010) *Economic Burden of Mental Illness Cannot be Tackled Without Research Investment*, London: Mental Health Foundation.

Cyr, C., Euser, E., Bakermans-Kranenburg, M. and Van Ijzendoorn, M. (2010), 'Attachment security and disorganization in maltreating and high risk families: a series of meta-analyses', *Development and Psychopathology* 22: 87–108.

Damasio, A. (1994) *Descartes' Error*, London: Pan Macmillan.

Danese, A., Pariante, C., Caspi, A., Gaylor, A and Poulton, R. (2007) 'Childhood maltreatment predicts adult inflammation in a life-course study', *PNAS* 104 (4): 1319–24.

Danese, A., Moffitt, T., Pariante, C., Ambler, A., Poulton, R. and Caspi, A. (2008) 'Elevated inflammation levels in depressed adults with a history of childhood maltreatment', *Arch Gen Psychiatry* 65 (4): 409–15.

Daniels, L., Mallan, K., Nicholson, J., Battistutta, D. and Magarey, A. (2013) 'Outcomes of an early feeding practices intervention to prevent childhood obesity', *Pediatrics* 132 (1): e109.

Dannlowski, U., Ohrmann, P., Konrad, C., Domschke, K., Bauer, J., Kugel, H. et al. (2009) 'Reduced amygdala-prefrontal coupling in major depression: association with MAOA genotype and illness severity', *International Journal of Neuropsychopharmacology*, 12: 11–22.

Dantzer, R., O'Connor, J., Freund, G., Johnson, R. and Kelley, K., (2008) 'From inflammation to sickness and depression: when the immune system subjugates the brain', *Nature Reviews Neuroscience* 9 (1): 46–56.

Das, U. (2001) 'Is obesity an inflammatory condition?', *Nutrition* 17: 953–66.

Das, U. (2008) 'Can essential fatty acids reduce the burden of disease?', *Lipids in Health and Disease* 7: 9.

Davidson, R. (1992) 'Anterior cerebral asymmetry and the nature of emotion', *Brain and Cognition* 20 (1): 125–51.

Davidson, R. (1994) 'Asymmetric brain function, affective style, and psychopathology: the role of early experience and plasticity', *Development and Psychopathology* 6: 741–58.

Davidson, R. and Fox, N. (1992) 'Asymmetrical brain activity discriminates between positive v. negative affective stimuli in human infants', *Science* 218: 1235–7.

Davidson, R. and McEwen, B. (2012) 'Social influences on neuro-plasticity: stress and interventions to promote well-being', *Nature Neuroscience* 15 (5): 689–95.

Davidson, R., Putnam, K. and Larson, C. (2000) 'Dysfunction in the neural circuitry of emotion regulation – a possible prelude to violence', *Science* 289: 591–4.

Davies, J. (2013) *Cracked: Why Psychiatry is Doing More Harm Than Good*, London: Icon Books.

Davis, E. and Sandman, C. (2007) 'The timing of prenatal exposure to maternal cortisol and psychosocial stress is associated with human infant cognitive development', *Child Development* 81 (1): 131–48.

Dawson, G., Groter-Klinger, L., Panagiotides, H., Hill, D. and Spieker, S. (1992) 'Frontal lobe activity and affective behaviour in infants of mothers with depressive symptoms', *Child Development* 63: 725–37.

Dawson, G., Ashman, S. and Carver, L. (2000) 'The role of early experience in shaping behavioural and brain development and its implications for social policy', *Development and Psychopathology* 12: 695–712.

Dayan, J., Creveuil, C., Dreyfus, M., Herlicoviez, M., Baleyte, J-M. et al. (2010) 'Developmental model of depression applied to prenatal depression: role of present and past life events, past emotional disorders and pregnancy stress', *PLoS ONE* 5 (9): e12942.

De Bellis, M., Keshavan, M., Shifflett, H., Iyengar, S., Beers, S., Hall, J. and Moritz, G. (2002) 'Brain structures in pediatric maltreatment-related PTSD: a sociodemographically matched study', *Biological Psychiatry* 52: 1066–78.

De Brito, S., Viding, E., Sebastian, C., Kelly, P., Mechelli, A., Maris, H. and McCrory, E. (2013) 'Reduced orbitofrontal and temporal grey matter in a community sample of maltreated children', *Journal of Child Psychology and Psychiatry* 54 (1).

De Kloet, E., Oilzl, M. and Joels, M. (1993) 'Functional implications of brain corticosteroid receptor diversity', *Cellular and Molecular Neurobiology* 13: 433–55.

Denham, S., Workman, E., Cole, P., Weissbrod, C., Kendziora, K. and Zahn-Wexler, C. (2000) 'Prediction of externalising behaviour problems from early to middle childhood: the role of parental socialisation and emotion expression', *Development and Psychopathology* 12: 23–45.

Depue, R. and Collins, P. (1999) 'Neurobiology of the structure of personality: dopamine, facilitation of incentive motivation, and extraversion', *Behavioural and Brain Sciences* 22: 491–569.

Depue, R., Luciana, M., Arbisi, P., Collins, P. and Leon, A. (1994) 'Dopamine and the structure of personality: relation of agonistin-duced dopamine activity to positive emotionality', *Journal of Personality and Social Psychology* 67: 485–98.

Derryberry, D. and Rothbart, M. (1997) 'Reactive and effortful processes in the organisation of temperament', *Development and Psychopathology* 9: 633.

Dettling, A., Gunnar, M. and Donzella, B. (1999) 'Cortisol levels of young children in full-day childcare centres', *Psychoneuroendocrinology* 24: 519–36.

Dettling, A., Feldon, J. and Pryce, C. (2002) 'Repeated parental deprivation in the infant common marmoset', *Biological Psychiatry* 52: 1037–46.

Dettling, A., Parker, S., Lane, S., Sebanc, A. and Gunnar, M. (2000) 'Quality of care and temperament determine changes in cortisol concentrations over the day for young children in childcare', *Psychoneuroendocrinology* 25: 819–36.

Di Pietro, J., Novak, M., Costigan, K., Atella, L. and Reusing, S. (2006) 'Maternal psychological distress during pregnancy in relation to child development aged 2', *Child Development* 77 (3): 573–8.

Di Santis, K., Hodges, E., Johnson, S. and Fisher, J. (2011) 'The role of responsive feeding in overweight during infancy and toddler-hood: a systematic review', *International Journal of Obesity* 35: 480–92.

Dickerson, S. and Kemeny, M. (2004) 'Acute stressors and cortisol responses: a theoretical integration and synthesis of laboratory research', *Psychological Bulletin* 130 (3): 355–91.

Dodge, K. (2009), 'Mechanisms of gene-environment interaction effects in the development of conduct disorder', *Perspectives in Psychological Science* 4 (4): 408–14.

Dodge, K. and Somberg, D. (1987) 'Hostile attributional biases among aggressive boys are exacerbated under conditions of threats to the self', *Child Development* 58: 213–24.

Dodic, M., Peers, A., Coghlan, J. and Wintour, M. (1999) 'Can excess glucocorticoid in utero predispose to cardiovascular and metabolic disorder in middle age', *Trends in Endocrinology and Metabolism* 10: 86–910.

Dokoupil, T. (2012) 'A new theory of PTSD and veterans: moral injury', www.thedailybeast.com/newsweek/2012/12/02.

D'Onofrio, B., van Hulle, C., Waldman, I., Rodgers, J., Harden, K.,

Rathouz, P and Lahey, B. (2008) 'Smoking during pregnancy and offspring externalizing problems: an exploration of genetic and environmental confounds', *Development and Psychopathology* 20: 139–64.

Douglas, K., Chan, G., Gelernter, J., Arias, A.J., Anton, R.F., Poling, J. et al. (2011) '5-HTTLPR as a potential moderator of the effects of adverse childhood experiences on risk of antisocial personality disorder', *Psychiatric Genetics* 21 (5): 240–8.

Drevets, W., Gadde, K. and Krishnan, K. (1999) 'Neuroimaging studies of mood disorders', in D. Charney, E. Nestler and B. Bunney (eds) *Neurobiology of Mental Illness*, Oxford: Oxford University Press.

Drevets, W., Price, J., Simpson, J., Todd, R., Reich, T., Vannier, M. and Raichle, M. (1997) 'Subgenual prefrontal cortex abnormalities in mood disorders', *Nature* 386: 824–7.

Duman, R., Heninger, G. and Nestler, E. (1997) 'A molecular and cellular theory of depression', *Archives of General Psychiatry* 54: 597–606.

Eckenrode, J., Campa, M., Luckey, D., Henderson, C., Cole, R., Kitzman et al. (2010) 'Long-term effects of prenatal and infancy nurse home visitation on the life course of youths', *Archives of Pediatric and Adolescent Medicine* 164 (1): 9–15.

Egeland, B. and Sroufe, A. (1981) 'Attachment and early maltreatment', *Child Development* 52: 44–52.

Eiden, R., Edwards, E. and Leonard, K. (2007) 'A conceptual model for the development of externalizing behavior problems among kindergarten children of alcoholic families', *Developmental Psychology* 43(5): 1187–201.

Eiden, R., Colder, C., Edwards, E. and Leonard, K. (2009) 'A longitudinal study of social competence among children of alcoholic and non-alcoholic parents: role of parental psychopathology, parental warmth and self-regulation', *Psychology of Addictive Behavior* 23 (1): 36–46.

Eisenberg, N., Spinrad, T. and Eggum, N. (2010) 'Emotion-related self-regulation and its relation to children's maladjustment', *Annual Review of Clinical Psychology* 6: 495–525.

Ellingson, J., Rickert, M. and D'Onofrio, B. (2012) 'Disentangling the relationships between maternal smoking during pregnancy and co-occurring risk factors', *Psychological Medicine* 42 (7): 1547–57.

Ellis, B. and Boyce, T. (2008), 'Biological sensitivity to context', *Current Directions in Psychological Science* 17 (3): 183–7.

Elovainio, M., Ferrie, J., Singh-Manoux, A., Gimeno, D., De Vogli, R., Shipley, M. et al. (2010) 'Organisational justice and markers of inflammation: the Whitehall II study', *Occupational and Environmental Medicine* 67: 78–83.

Eluvathingal, T., Chugani, H., Behen, M., Juhasz, C., Muzik, O., Maqbool, M. et al. (2006) 'Abnormal brain connectivity in children after early severe socioemotional deprivation: a diffusion tensor imaging study', *Pediatrics* 117 (6): 2093–100.

Emde, R. (1988) 'Development terminable and interminable', *International Journal of Psycho-Analysis* 69: 23–42.

Emde, R. et al. (1992) 'Temperament, emotion and cognition at 14 months', *Child Development* 63: 1437–55.

Entringer, S., Buss, C., Swanson, J., Cooper, D., Wing, D., Waffarn, F. and Wadhwa, P. (2012) 'Fetal programming of body composition, obesity, and metabolic function: the role of intrauterine stress and stress biology', *Journal of Nutrition and Metabolism* volume 2012: article 632548.

Essex, M., Klein, M., Cho, E. and Kalin, N. (2002) 'Maternal stress beginning in infancy may sensitise children to later stress exposure: effects on cortisol and behaviour', *Biological Psychiatry* 52: 776–84.

Etkin, A. and Wager, T. (2007) 'Functional neuroimaging of anxiety', *American Journal Psychiatry* 164 (10): 1376–488.

Etkin, A. and Wager, T. (2010) 'Brain systems underlying anxiety disorders: a view from neuroimaging', in Simpson, H et al. (eds), *Anxiety Disorders*, Cambridge: Cambridge University Press.

Fairbairn, R. (1952) *Psychoanalytic Study of the Personality*, London: Routledge and Kegan Paul.

Fearon, P., Bakermans-Kranenburg, M., Van Ijzendoorn, M., Lapsley, A-M. and Roisman, G. (2010) 'The significance of insecure attachment and disorganization in the development of children's externalizing behavior: a meta-analytic study', *Child Development* 81 (2): 435–56.

Feilhauer, J., Cima, M., Korebrits, A. and Nicolson, N. (2013) 'Salivary cortisol and psychopathy dimensions in detained antisocial adolescents', *Psychoneuroendocrinology* 38 (9): 1586–95.

Feldman, R., Gordon, I., Influs, M., Gutbir, T. and Ebstein, R. (2013) 'Parental oxytocin and early caregiving jointly shape children's oxytocin response and social reciprocity', *Neuropsychopharmacology* 38: 1154–62.

Felitti, V., Anda, R., Nordenberg, D., Williamson, D., Spitz, A., Edwards, V. et al. (1998) 'Relationship of childhood abuse and household dysfunction to many of the leading causes of death in adults: the Adverse Childhood Experiences (ACE) Study', *American Journal of Preventive Medicine* 14: 245–58.

Feinman, S. (ed.) (1992) *Social Referencing and the Social Construction of Reality in Infancy*, New York: Plenum Press.

Feinstein, D. and Church, D. (2010), 'Modulating gene expression through psychotherapy: the contribution of noninvasive somatic interventions', *Review of General Psychology* 14 (4): 283–95.

Field, T. (1985) 'Attachment as psychological attunement', in T.

Field and M. Reite (eds) *The Psychobiology of Attachment and Separation*, New York: Academic Press.

Field, T. (1995) 'Infants of depressed mothers', *Infant Behavior and Development* 18: 1–13.

Field, T. (2001) *Touch*, Cambridge, MA: MIT Press.

Field, T., Diego, M. and Hernandez-Reif, M. (2006) 'Prenatal depression effects on the fetus and newborn: a review', *Infant Behavior and Development* 29: 445–55.

Field, T., Hernandez-Reif, M. and Diego, M. (2005) 'Cortisol decreases and serotonin and dopamine increase following massage therapy', *International Journal of Neuroscience* 115: 1397–413.

Field, T., Healy, B., Goldstein, S., Perry, S. and Bendell, D. (1988) 'Infants of depressed mothers show "depressed" behaviour even with non-depressed adults', *Child Development* 59: 1569–79.

Fisher, P., Gunnar, M.D., Sozier, M., Bruce, J. and Pears, K. (2006) 'Effects of therapeutic interventions for foster children on behavioral problems, caregiver attachment and stress regulatory neural systems', *Annals of New York Academy of Science* 1094: 215–25.

Flack, W., Litz, B., Hsieh, F., Kaloupek, D. and Keane, T. (2000) 'Predictors of emotional numbing, revisited: a replication and extension', *Journal of Trauma and Stress* 13 (4): 611–18.

Flandera, V. and Novakova, V. (1974) 'Effect of mother on the development of aggressive behaviour in rats', *Developmental Psychobiology* 8 (1): 49–54.

Fleshner, M. (2013), 'Stress-evoked sterile inflammation, DAMPS, MAMPS and the inflammasome', *Brain Behavior and Immunity* 27 (1): 1–7.

Fonagy, P. (2003) 'The development of psychopathology from infancy to adulthood: the mysterious unfolding of disturbance in time', *Infant Mental Health Journal* 24 (3): 212–39.

Fonagy, P., Target, M., Steele, M., Steele, H., Leigh, T., Levinson, A. and Kennedy, R. (1997) 'Morality, disruptive behaviour, borderline personality disorder, crime and their relationships to security of attachment', in L. Atkinson and K. Zucker (eds) *Attachment and Psychopathology*, New York: Guilford Press.

Fox, N. (ed.) (1994) *The Development of Emotion Regulation*, monograph of the Society for Research in Child Development.

Fox, N., Rubin, K., Calkins, S., Marshall, T., Coplan, R., Porges, S. et al. (1995) 'Frontal activation asymmetry and social competence at four years of age', *Child Development* 66 (6): 1770–84.

Francis, D., Champagne, F., Liu, D. and Meaney, M. (1997) 'Maternal care, gene expression and the development of individual differences in stress reactivity', *Annals of the New York Academy of Sciences* 896: 66–81.

Frankl, V. (1973) *The Doctor and the Soul*, Harmondsworth: Penguin.

Fries, E., Hesse, J., Hellhammer, J. and Hellhammer, D. (2005), 'A new view on hypocortisolism', *Psychoneuroendocrinology* xx: 1–7

Frodi, A. and Lamb, M. (1980) 'Child abusers' responses to infant smiles and cries', *Child Development* 51: 238–41.

Frodl, T., Reinhold, E., Koutsouleris, N, Reiser, M, Meisenzahl, E, (2010) 'Interaction of childhood stress with hippocampus and frefrontal cortex volume reduction in major depression', *Journal Psychiatric Research* 44 (13): 799–807.

Furman, E. (1992) *Toddlers and their Mothers*, New York: International Universities Press.

Gapp, K., Jawaid, A., Sarkies, P. Mansuy, I. et al. (2014) 'Implication of sperm RNAs in transgenerational inheritance of the effects of early trauma in mice', *Nature Neuroscience* 17: 667–9.

Garber, J. and Dodge, K. (1991) *The Development of Emotion Regulation and Dysregulation*, Cambridge: Cambridge University Press.

Garcia-Segura, L. (2009), *Hormones and Brain Plasticity*, Oxford University Press.

Garland, C. (2001) *Woman and Home*, April.

Gendlin, E. (1978) *Focusing*, New York: Bantam.

Gergely, G. and Watson, J. (1996) 'The social biofeedback theory of parental affect-mirroring', *International Journal of Psychoanalysis* 77: 1181–212.

Gesch, B., Hammond, S., Hampson, S., Eves, A. and Crowder, M. (2002) 'Influence of supplementary vitamins, minerals and essential fatty acids on the antisocial behaviour of young adult prisoners', *British Journal of Psychiatry* 181: 22–8.

Gilbertson, M., Shenton, M., Ciszewski, A., Kasai, K., Lasko, N., Orr, S. and Pitman, R. (2002) 'Smaller hippocampal volume predicts pathologic vulnerability to psychological trauma', *Nature Neuroscience* 5 (11): 1242–6.

Gilliom, M., Shaw, D., Beck, J., Schonberg, M. and Lukon, J. (2002) 'Anger regulation in disadvantaged pre-school boys', *Developmental Psychology* 38 (2): 222.

Gillman, M., Rich-Edwards, J., Huh, S., Majzoub, J., Oken, E., Taveras, E. and Rifas-Shiman, S (2006) 'Maternal CRH levels during pregnancy and offspring adiposity', *Obesity* 14 (9): 1647–53.

Gimeno, D., Kivimaki, M, Brunner, E., Elovainio, M., De Vogli, R., Steptoe, A. et al. (2009) 'Associations of C-reactive protein and interleukin–6 with cognitive symptoms of depression: 12 year follow-up of the Whitehall II study', *Psychological Medicine* 39 (3): 413–23.

Gitau, R., Fisk, N., Teixeira, J., Cameron, A. and Glover, V. (2001a) 'Fetal hypothalamic-pituitary-adrenal stress responses to invasive procedures are independent of maternal responses', *Journal of Clinical Endocrinology and Metabolism* 86 (1): 104.

Gitau, R., Menson, E., Pickles, V., Fisk, N., Glover, V. and Maclachlan, N. (2001b) 'Umbilical cortisol levels as an indicator of the fetal stress response to assisted vaginal delivery', *European Journal of Obstetrics and Gynecology and Reproductive Biology* 98 (1): 14–17.

Glaser, D. (2000) 'Child abuse and neglect and the brain – a review', *Journal of Child Psychology and Psychiatry* 41 (1): 97–116.

Glover, V. (2011) 'Annual research review: prenatal stress and the origins of psychopathology: an evolutionary perspective', *Journal of Child Psychology and Psychiatry* 52 (4): 356–67.

Glover, V., O'Connor, T. and O'Donnell, K. (2010) 'Prenatal stress and the programming of the HPA axis', *Neuroscience and Biobehavioral Reviews* 35: 17–22.

Glover, V., Bergman, K., Sarkar, P. and O'Connor, T. (2009) 'Association between maternal and amniotic fluid cortisol is moderated by maternal anxiety', *Psychoneuroendocrinology* 34 (3): 430–5.

Gluckman, P. and Hanson, M. (2004) *The Fetal Matrix: Evolution, Development and Disease*, Cambridge: Cambridge University Press.

Goeden, N., Velasquez, J. and Bonnin, A. (2013), 'Placental tryptophan metabolism as a potential novel pathway for the developmental origins of mental diseases', *Translational Developmental Psychiatry* 1: 20593.

Gold, P., Drevets, W. and Charney, D. (2002) 'New insights into the role of cortisol and the glucocorticoid receptor in severe depression', *Biological Psychiatry* 52: 381–5.

Goldberg, S., Muir, R. and Kerr, J. (eds) (1995) *Attachment Theory: Social, Developmental and Clinical Perspectives*, Hillsdale, NJ: Analytic Press.

Goldin, P. and Gross, J. (2010) 'Effects of mindfulness-based stress reduction on emotion regulation in social anxiety disorder', *Emotion* 10: 83–91.

Golding, J., Steer, C., Emmett, P., Davis, J. and Hibbeln, J. (2009) 'High levels of depressive symptoms in pregnancy with low omega-3 fatty acid intake from fish', *Epidemiology* 20(4): 598–603.

Goleman, D. (1996) *Emotional Intelligence*, London: Bloomsbury.

Gonzalez-Pardo, H. and Alvarez, M. (2013). 'Epigenetics and its implications for psychology', *Psicothema* 25(1): 3–12.

Goosens, K. and Sapolsky, R. (2007) 'Stress and glucocorticoid contributions to normal and pathological aging', in Riddle, D. (ed.) *Brain Aging*, Boca Raton: CRC Press.

Gordon, M. (2012), *The Roots of Empathy: Changing the World Child by Child*, New York: The Experiment.

Gouin, J-P., Glaser, R., Malarkey, W., Beversdorf, D. and Kiecolt-Glaser, J. (2012, 'Childhood abuse and inflammatory responses to daily stressors', *Annals of Behavioral Medicine* 44 (2): 287–92.

Green, B. (2003) 'PTSD symptom profiles in men and women', *Currents in Medical Research and Opinion* 19 (3): 200–4.

Greenough, W. and Black, J. (1992) 'Induction of brain structure by experience', *Developmental Behavioural Neuroscience*, Hillsdale, NJ: Lawrence Erlbaum Associates, Inc.

Gross, J. and Levenson, R. (1993) 'Emotional suppression: physiology, self-report and expressive behaviour', *Journal of Personality and Social Psychology* 64: 970–86.

Gross, J. and Levenson, R. (1997) 'Hiding feelings: the acute effects of inhibiting negative and positive emotion', *Journal of Abnormal Psychology*, 106 (1): 95–103.

Grove, W., Eckert, E., Hesten, L., Bouchard, T., Segal, N. and Lykken, D. (1990) 'Heritability of substance abuse and antisocial behaviour', *Biological Psychiatry* 27.

Gunnar, M. and Donzella, B. (2002) 'Social regulation of the cortisol levels in early human development', *Psychoneuroendocrinology* 27: 199–220.

Gunnar, M. and Nelson, C. (1994) 'Event related potentials in year old infants: relations with emotionality and cortisol', *Child Development* 65: 80.

Gunnar, M. and Vazquez, D. (2001) 'Low cortisol and a flattening of expected daytime rhythm: potential indices of risk in human development', *Development and Psychopathology* 13 (3): 515–38.

Gunnar, M., Malone, S. and Fisch, R. (1985b) 'The psychobiology of stress and coping in the human neonate: studies of adrenocortical activity in response to aversive stimulation', in T. Field, P. McCabe and N. Schneiderman (eds) *Stress and Coping*, Hillsdale, NJ: Lawrence Erlbaum Associates Inc.

Gunnar, M., Kryzer, E., Van Ryzin, M and Phillips, D. (2010) 'The rise in cortisol in family daycare: associations with aspects of care quality, child behavior and child sex', *Child Development* 81(3): 851–69.

Gunnar, M., Malone, S., Vance, G. and Fisch, R. (1985a) 'Coping with aversive stimulation in the neonatal period: quiet sleep and plasma cortisol levels during recovery from circumcision', *Child Development* 56: 824–34.

Gunnar, M., Morison, S., Chisholm, K. and Schuder, M. (2001) 'Salivary cortisol levels in children adopted from Romanian orphanages', *Development and Psychopathology* 13 (3): 611–28.

Gunnar, M., Brodersen, L., Nachmias, M., Buss, K. and Rigatuso, J. (1996) 'Stress reactivity and attachment security', *Developmental Psychobiology* 29: 191–204.

Gutman, D. (n.d.) 'Remission in depression and the mind–body link', www.medscape.com.

Hackman, D., Betancourt, L. Brodsky, N, Kobrin, L. Hurt, H, Farah, M (2013) 'Selective impact of early parental responsivity on adolescent stress reactivity', *PLoS ONE* 8 (3): e58250.

Hakim, C., Bradley, K, Price, E. and Mitchell, L (2008) *Little Britons: Financing Childcare Choice*, London: Policy Exchange.

Hammen, C., Burge, D., Burney, E. and Adrian, C. (1990) 'Longitudinal study of diagnoses in children of women with unipolar and bipolar affective disorder', *Archives of General Psychiatry* 47: 1112–17.

Hansel, A. and Kanel, R. (2008) 'The ventromedial prefrontal cortex: a major link between the autonomic nervous system, regulation of emotion, and stress reactivity?', *BioPsychoSocial Medicine* 2: 21.

Hanson, J., Chung, M., Pollak, S. et al. (2010) 'Early stress is associated with alterations in the orbitofrontal cortex: a tensor-based morphometry investigation of brain structure and behavioral risk', *Journal of Neuroscience* 30 (22): 7466–72.

Harburg, E., Gleiberman, L., Russell, M. and Cooper, M. (1991) 'Anger-coping styles and blood pressure in black and white males: Buffalo, New York', *Psychosomatic Medicine* 53 (2): 153–64.

Hay, D., Pawlby, S., Angold, A., Harold, G. and Sharp, D. (2003) 'Pathways to violence in the children of mothers who were depressed postpartum', *Developmental Psychology* 39 (6): 1083–94.

Heckman, J., Grunewald, G. and Reynolds, A. (2006) 'The dollars and cents of investing early: cost-benefit analysis in early care and education', *Zero To Three* 26 (6): 10–17.

Heim, C. and Nemeroff, C. (2001) 'The role of childhood trauma in the neurobiology of mood and anxiety disorders: preclinical and clinical studies', *Biological Psychiatry* 49 (112): 1023–39.

Heim, C., Ehlert, U. and Hellhammer, D. (2000a) 'The potential role of hypocortisolism in the pathophysiology of stress-related bodily disorders', *Psychoneuroendocrinology* 25: 1–35.

Heim, C., Newport, D., Bonsall, R., Miller, A. and Nemeroff, C. (2001) 'Altered pituitary adrenal axis responses to provocative challenge tests in adult survivors of childhood abuse', *American Journal of Psychiatry* 158 (4): 575–81.

Heim, C., Newport, J., Wagner, D., Wilcox, M., Miller, A. and Nemeroff, C. (2002) 'The role of early adverse experience and adulthood stress in the prediction of neuroendocrine stress reactivity in women: a multiple regression analysis', *Depression and Anxiety* 15: 117–25.

Heim, C., Newport, J., Heit, S., Graham, Y., Wilcox, M., Bondall, R., Miller, A. and Nemeroff, C. (2000b) 'Pituitary-adrenal and autonomic responses to stress in women after sexual and physical abuse in childhood', *Journal of the American Medical Association* 284 (5): 592–7.

Hennebelle, M., Balasse, L., Latour, A., Champeil-Potokar, G., Denis, S., Lavialle, M. et al. (2012) 'Influence of Omega-3 fatty acid status on the way rats adapt to chronic restraint stress', *PLoS ONE* 7 (7): e42142

Hennessy, M. (1997) 'HPA responses to brief social separation', *Neuroscience and Biobehavioural Reviews* 21 (1): 11–29.

Henry, J. (1993) 'Psychological and physiological responses to stress, the right hemisphere and the HPA axis', *Integrative Physiological and Behavioural Science*, 28: 368–87.

Henry, J., Haviland, M., Cummings, M., Anderson, D., Nelson, J., MacMurray, J. et al. (1992) 'Shared neuroendocrine patterns of post-traumatic stress disorder and alexithymia', *Psychosomatic Medicine* 54 (4): 407–15.

Herb, B., Wolschin, F., Hansen, K., Aryee, M., Langmead, B., Irizarry, R. et al. (2012) 'Reversible switching between epigenetic states in honeybee behavioral subcastes', *Nature Neuroscience* 15 (10): 1371–3.

Herr, J. and Wolfram, C. (2011) 'Work environment and "opt-out" rates at motherhood across high-education career paths', National Bureau of Economic Research Working Paper no.14717.

Hertsgaard, L., Gunnar, M., Erickson, M. and Nachmias, M. (1995) 'Adrenocortical responses to the strange situation in infants with disorganised/disoriented attachment relationships', *Child Development* 66: 1100–06.

Hertzman, C. (1997) 'The biological embedding of early experience and its effects on health in adulthood', *Annals of the New York Academy of Sciences*: 85–95.

Herzman, C. and Boyce, T. (2010) 'How experience gets under the skin to create gradients in developmental health', *Annual Review of Public Health* 31: 329–47.

Herzog, A., Edelheit, P., Jacobs, A. and McBurnett, K. (2001) 'Low salivary cortisol and persistent aggression in boys referred for disruptive behaviour', *Archives of General Psychiatry* 58 (5): 513–15.

Hessler, D. and Katz, L. (2007), 'Children's emotion regulation: self report and physiological response to peer provocation', *Developmental Psychology* 43 (1): 27–38.

Hibbeln, J., Ferguson, T. and Blasbalg, T. (2006) 'Omega-3 fatty acid deficiencies in neurodevelopment, aggression and autonomic dysregulation: opportunities for intervention', *International Review of Psychiatry* 18(2): 107–18.

Hill, A., Degnan, K., Calkins, S. and Keane, S. (2006), 'Profiles of externalizing behavior problems for boys and girls across pre-school', *Developmental Psychology* 42 (5): 913–28.

Hilz, M., Devinsky, O., Szczepanska, H., Borod, J., Marthol, H. and Tutaj, M. (2006) 'Right ventromedial prefrontal lesions result in paradoxical cardiovascular activation with emotional stimuli', *Brain* 129: 3343–55.

Hoek, H., Treasure, J. and Katzman, M. (1998) *Neurobiology in the Treatment of Eating Disorders*, Chichester: Wiley.

Hofer, M. (1995) 'Hidden regulators: implications for a new understanding of attachment, separation and loss', in S. Goldberg, R. Muir and J. Kerr (eds) *Attachment Theory: Social, Developmental and Clinical Perspectives*, Hillside, NJ: Analytic Press.

Holmes, J. (2002) Unpublished talk at John Bowlby Memorial Conference.

Holsboer, F. (2000) 'The corticosteroid receptor hypothesis of depression', *Neuropsychopharmacology* 23 (5): 477–507.

Holzel, B., Lazar, S., Gard, T., Schuman-Olivier, Z., Vago, D., and Ott, U. (2011) 'How does mindfulness meditation work? Proposing mechanisms of action from a conceptual and neural perspective', *Perpectives in Psychological Science* 6 (6): 537–59.

Holzel, B., Carmody, J., Evans, K., Hoge, E., Dusek, J., Morgan, L. et al. (2010) 'Stress reduction correlates with structural changes in the amygdala', *Social Cognitive and Affective Neuroscience* 5 (1): 11–17.

Holzel, B., Hoge, E., Greve, D., Gard, T. Creswell, D., Brown, K. et al. (2013), 'Neural mechanisms of symptom improvements in generalized anxiety disorder following mindfulness training', *NeuroImage: Clinical*, 2, 448–58.

Horowitz, M. (1992) 'Formulation of states of mind in psychotherapy', in N. G. Hamilton (ed.) *From Inner Sources: New Directions in Object Relations Psychotherapy*, New York: Jason Aronson.

Hou, W., Chiang, P., Hsu, T., Chiu, S., Yen, Y. (2010) 'Treatment effects of massage therapy in depressed people: a meta-analysis', *Journal of Clinical Psychiatry* 71 (7): 894–901.

Huijbregts, S., Seguin, J., Zoccolillo, M, Boivin, M and Tremblay, R. (2012) 'Maternal prenatal smoking, parental antisocial behaviour and early childhood physical aggression', *Development and Psychopathology* 20 (2): 437–53.

Hyun Rhee, S. and Waldman, I. (2002) 'Genetic and environmental influences on antisocial behaviour: a meta-analysis of twin and adoption studies', *Psychological Bulletin* 128 (3): 490–529.

Iacoboni, M. (2009) *Mirroring People: The Science of Empathy and How we Connect with Others*, 1st edition, London: Picador.

Iacoboni, M., Molnar-Szakacs, I., Gallese, V., Buccino, G., Mazziotta, J., Rizzolatti, G. (2005) 'Grasping the intentions of others with one's own mirror neurons', *PLoS Biology* 3 (3): e79.

Ichise, M., Vines, D., Gura, T., Anderson, G., Suomi, S., Higley, D. and Innis, R. (2006) 'Effects of early life stress on (C)DASB positron emission tomography imaging of serotonin transporters in adolescent peer- and mother-reared monkeys', *The Journal of Neuroscience* 26 (17): 4638–43.

Insel, T. (2011) National Institute of Mental Health Director's blog. www.nimh.nih.gov/about/director/2011/antidepressants-a-complicated-picture.shtml.

Jacobs, T.L., Shaver, P.R., Epel, E.S., Zanesco, A.P., Aichele, S.R., Bridwell, D.A. et al. (2013) 'Self-reported mindfulness and cortisol during a shamatha meditation retreat', *Health Psychology*. Advance online publication.

Jacobson, S., Bihun, J. and Chiodo, L. (1999) 'Effects of prenatal alcohol and cocaine exposure on infant cortisol levels', *Development and Psychopathology* 11: 195–208.

Jaffee, S., Strait, L. and Odgers, C. (2012), 'From correlates to causes: can quasi-experimental studies and statistical innovations bring us closer to identifying the causes of antisocial behavior?', *Psychological Bulletin* 138 (2): 272–95.

Jevning, R. Wilson, A. and Davidson, J. (1978) 'Adrenocortical activity during meditation', *Hormones and Behaviour* 10 (1): 54–60.

Jones, N. and Field, T. (1999) 'Massage and music therapies attenuate frontal EEG asymmetry in depressed adolescents', *Adolescence* 34 (135): 529–34.

Jones, N., Field, T., Fox, N., Davalos, M., Malphus, J. et al. (1997) 'Infants of intrusive and withdrawn mothers', *Infant Behaviour and Development* 20: 175–86.

Kagan, J. (1999) 'The concept of behavioral inhibition', in L. Schmidt and J. Schulkin (eds) *Extreme Fear, Shyness and Social Phobia*, New York: Oxford University Press.

Kalin, N., Shelton, S. and Davidson, R. (2000) 'Cerebrospinal fluid corticotropin-releasing hormone levels are elevated in monkeys with patterns of brain activity associated with fearful temperament', *Biological Psychiatry* 47 (7): 579–85.

Kalin, N., Larson, C., Shelton, S. and Davidson, R. (1998a) 'Individual differences in freezing and cortisol in infant and mother rhesus monkeys', *Behavioural Neuroscience* 112 (1): 251–4.

Kalin, N., Larson, C., Shelton, S. and Davidson, R. (1998b) 'Asymmetric frontal brain activity, cortisol and behaviour associated with fearful temperament in rhesus monkeys', *Behavioural Neuroscience* 112 (2): 286–92.

Kang, D., Davidson, R., Coe, C., Wheeler, R., Tomaraken, A. and Ershler, W. (1991) 'Frontal brain asymmetry and immune function', *Behavioural Neuroscience* 105 (6): 860–9.

Kanter, E., Wilkinson, C., Radant, A., Petrie, E., Dobie, D., Peskin, E. and Raskind, M. (2001) 'Glucocorticoid feedback sensitivity and adrenocortical responsiveness in PTSD', *Biological Psychiatry* 50 (4): 238–45.

Kaplan, L., Evans, L. and Monk, C. (2008) 'Effects of mothers' prenatal psychiatric status and post-natal caregiving on infant biobehavioural regulation: can prenatal programming be modified?', *Early Human Development* 83 (4): 249–56.

Karr-Morse, R. and Wiley, M. (1997) *Ghosts from the Nursery*, New York: Atlantic Monthly Press.

Karatsoreos, I. and McEwen, B. (2011) 'Psychobiological allostasis: resistance, resilience and vulnerability', *Trends in Cognitive Sciences* 15 (12): 576–82.

Kasai, K., Yamasue, H., Gilbertson, M., Shenton, M., Rauch, S. and Pitman, R. (2008) 'Evidence for acquired pregenual anterior cingulate gray matter loss from a twin study of combat-related PTSD', *Biological Psychiatry* 63 (6): 550–6.

Katz, I., Corlyon, J., LaPlaca, V. and Hunter, S. (2007) *The Relationship Between Parenting and Poverty*, York: Joseph Rowntree Foundation.

Katzenbach, J. (2003) *The Analyst*, London: Corgi.

Kaufman, J., Plotsky, P., Nemeroff, C. and Charney, D. (2000) 'Effects of early adverse experiences on brain structure and function: clinical implications', *Biological Psychiatry* 48: 778–90.

Kelmanson, I., Erman, L. and Litvana, S. (2002) 'Maternal smoking during pregnancy and behavioural characteristics in 2–4 month olds', *Klinische Padiatrie* 214 (6): 359–64.

Kendell-Tackett, K., Williams, L. and Finkelhor, D. (1993) 'Impact of sexual abuse on children: a review and synthesis of recent empirical studies', *Psychological Bulletin* 113: 164–80.

Kern, S., Oakes, T., Stone, C., McAuliff, E. Kirschbaum, C. and Davidson, R. (2008) 'Glucose metabolic changes in the prefrontal cortex are associated with HPA axis response to a psychosocial stressor', *Psychoneuroendocrinology* 33 (4): 517–29.

Kessler, R. and Ustun, T. (2011) *WHO World Mental Health Survey*, Cambridge: Cambridge University Press.

Kiecolt-Glaser, J., Gouin, J-P., Weng, N., Malarkey, W., Beversdorf, M. and Glaser, R (2011), 'Childhood adversity heightens the impact of later life caregiving stress on telomere length and inflammation', *Psychosomatic Medicine* 73 (1): 16–22.

Kim, M. and Whalen, P. (2009) 'The structural integrity of an amygdala-prefrontal pathway predicts trait anxiety', *J Neurosci*, 29: 11614–8.

Kine, S., Roberg, B., Woien, G, Bogen, I., Sandvik, T., Sagvolden, T. et al. (2012) 'Marine omega-3 polyunsaturated fatty acids induce sex-specific changes in reinforcer-controlled behaviour and neurotransmitter metabolism in a spontaneously hypertensive rat model of ADHD', *Behavioural and Brain Functions* 8 (1): 56.

King, J., Mandansky, D., King, S., Fletcher, K. and Brewer, J. (2001) 'Early sexual abuse and low cortisol', *Psychiatry and Clinical Neuroscience* 55 (1): 71–4.

Kirsch, I. (2008), 'Challenging received wisdom: antidepressants and the placebo effect', *McGill Journal of Medicine* 11 (2): 219–22.

Kitzman, H., Olds, D., Cole, R., Hanks, C., Anson, E., Arcoleo, K. et al. (2010), 'Enduring effects of prenatal and infancy home visiting by nurses on children', *Archives of Pediatric and Adolescent Medicine* 164(5): 412–18.

Klein, M. (1988) *Envy and Gratitude*, London: Virago Press.

Kochanska, G. (2001) 'Emotional development in children with different attachment histories: the first three years', *Child Development* 72 (2): 474–90.

Kochanska, G., Philibert, R. and Barry, R. (2009) 'Interplay of genes and early mother child relationship in the development of self-regulation from toddler to pre-school age', *Journal of Child Psychology and Psychiatry* 50 (11): 1331–8.

Kochanska, G., Forman, D. Aksan, N. and Dunbar, S. (2005) 'Pathways to conscience: early mother-child mutually responsive orientation and children's moral emotion, conduct and cognition', *Journal of Child Psychology and Psychiatry* 46 (1): 19–34.

Kodas, E., Vancassel, S., Lejeune, B., Guilloteau, D. and Chalon, S. (2002) 'Reversibility of n-3 fatty acid deficiency-induced changes in dopaminergic neurotransmission in rats: critical role of developmental stage', *Journal of Lipid Research* 43 (8): 1209–19.

Koenigs, M. and Grafman, J. (2009) 'Post-traumatic stress disorder: the role of medial prefrontal cortex and amygdala', *Neuroscientist* 15 (5): 540–8.

Kohler, E., Keysers, C., Umilta, M., Fogassi, L. Gallese, V. and Rizzolatti, G. (2002) 'Hearing sounds, understanding actions: action representation in mirror neurons', *Science* 297 (5582): 846–8.

Kolb, B., Mychasiuk, R., Muhammad, A., Li, Y., Frost, D. and Gibb, R. (2012) 'Experience and the developing prefrontal cortex', *PNAS*, www.pnas.org/cgi/doi/10.1073/pnas.1121251109.

Konyecsni, W. and Rogeness, G. (1998) 'The effects of early social relationships on neurotransmitter development and the vulnerability to affective disorders', *Seminars in Clinical Neuropsychiatry* 3 (4): 285–301.

Krystal, H. (1988) *Integration and Self-Healing: Affect, Trauma, Alexithymia*, Hillsdale, NJ: Analytic Press.

Krystal, J. and Neumeister, A. (2009) 'Noradrenergic and serotonergic mechanisms in the neurobiology of posttraumatic stress disorder and resilience', *Brain Research* 1293: 13–23.

Kumsta, R., Kreppner, J., Rutter, M., Beckett, C., Castle, J., Stevens, S. and Sonuga-Barke, E., (2010) 'Deprivation specific psychological patterns', *Monographs of the Society for Research in Child Development* 75 (1): 48–78.

Lagercrantz, H. and Herlenius, E. (2001) 'Neurotransmitters and neuromodulators', *Early Human Development* 65 (1): 139–59.

Lansford, J., Miller-Johnson, S., Berlin, L., Dodge, K., Bates, J. and Pettit, G., (2007) 'Early physical abuse and later violent delinquency: a prospective longitudinal study', *Child Maltreatment* 12 (3): 233–45.

Larque, E., Demmelmair, H. and Koletzko, B. (2002) 'Perinatal supply and metabolism of long-chain polyunsaturated fatty acids: importance for the early development of the nervous system', *Annals of the New York Academy of Sciences* 967: 299–310.

Laudenslager, M., Capitanio, J. and Reite, M. (1985) 'Possible effects of early separation experiences on subsequent immune function in adult macaque monkeys', *American Journal of Psychiatry* 142: 7.

Laurent, H. and Ablow, J. (2012) 'A cry in the dark: depressed mothers show reduced neural activation to their own infant's cry', *Social Cognitive and Affective Neuroscience* 7: 125–34.

Lawler, S. (1999) 'Children need but mothers only want: the power of "needs talk" in the constitution of childhood', in J. Seymour and P. Bagguley (eds) *Relating Intimacies: Power and Resistance*, London: Macmillan.

LeDoux, J. (1998) *The Emotional Brain*, London: Weidenfeld and Nicholson.

LeDoux, J. (2002) *The Synaptic Self: How Our Brains Become Who We Are*, London: Macmillan.

Lee, D., Brooks-Gunn, J., McLanahan, S., Notterman, D. and Garfinkel, I. (2013) 'The great recession, genetic sensitivity and maternal harsh parenting', *PNAS* 110 (34): 13780–4.

Lemaire, V., Lamarque, S., Le Moal, M., Piazza, P-V. and Abrous, D. (2006) 'Postnatal stimulation of the pups counteracts prenatal stress-induced deficits in hippocampal neurogenesis', *Biological Psychiatry* 59 (9): 786–92.

Lenneke, R., Cicchetti, D., Kim, J. and Rogosch, F. (2009) 'Mediating and moderating processes in the relation between maltreatment and psychopathology: mother-child relationship quality and emotion regulation', *Journal of Abnormal Child Psychology* 37: 831–43.

LeShan, L. (1977) *You Can Fight for Your Life*, New York: Evans.

Levine, S. (1994) 'The ontogeny of the hypothalamic-pituitary-adrenal axis', *Annals of the New York Academy of Sciences* 746: 275–88.

Levine, S. (2001) 'Primary social relationships influence the development of the HPA axis in the rat', *Physiology and Behaviour* 73 (3): 255–60.

Lewis, M. and Ramsay, D. (1995) 'Stability and change in cortisol and behavioural response to stress during the first 18 months of life', *Developmental Psychobiology* 28 (8): 419–28.

Liberzon, I., Taylor, S., Amdur, R., Jung, T., Chamberlain, K., Minoshima, S. et al. (1999) 'Brain activation in PTSD in response to trauma-related stimuli', *Biological Psychiatry* 45 (7): 817–26.

Lichter, D. and Cummings, J. (eds) (2001) *Frontal-Subcortical Circuits in Psychiatric and Neurological Disorders*, New York: Guilford Press.

Lieberman, A., Weston, D. and Pawl, J. (1991) 'Preventive intervention and outcome with anxiously attached dyads', *Child Development* 62: 199–209.

Lin, P and Su, K (2007), 'A meta-analytic review of double-blind, placebo-controlled trials of antidepressant efficacy of omega-3 fatty acids', Journal Clinical Psychiatry 68 (7): 1056–61.

Linehan, M. (1993) *Cognitive-Behavioural Treatment of Borderline Personality Disorder*, New York: Guilford Press.

Liston, C., McEwen, B., and Casey, B. (2009) 'Psychosocial stress reversibly disrupts prefrontal processing and attentional control', PNAS 106 (3).

Liston, C., Miller, M., Goldwater, D., McEwen, B. et al. (2006) 'Stress induced alterations in prefrontal cortex dendritic morphology', *Journal of Neuroscience* 26 (30): 7870–4.

Liu, D., Diorio, J., Tannenbaum, B., Caldji, C., Francis, D. and Freedman, A. (1997) 'Maternal care, hippocampal glucocorticoid receptors and HPA responses to stress', *Science* 277: 1659–62.

Luby, J, Barch, D, Belden, A, Gaffrey, M, Tillman, R., Babb, C. et al. (2012), 'Maternal support in early childhood predicts larger hippocampal volumes at school age', Proceedings of the National Academy of Sciences vol, 109 (8): 2854–2859,

Luby, J., Belden, A., Botteron, K., Marrus, N., Harms, M., Babb, C. et al. (2013), 'The effects of poverty on childhood brain development: the mediating effect of caregiving and stressful life events', *JAMA Pediatrics* 167 (11): 1135–42.

Lupien, S., Parent, S., Evans, A., Tremblay, R. Zelazo, P. Corbo, V. et al. (2011) 'Larger amygdala but no change in hippocampal volume in 10 year old children exposed to maternal depressive symptomatology since birth', *PNAS* 108 (34): 14324–9.

Lutgendorf, S., De Geest, K., Bender, D., Ahmed, A. et al. (2012) 'Social influences on clinical outcomes of patients with ovarian cancer', *Journal of Clinical Oncology* 30 (23): 2885–90.

Luu, P. and Tucker, D. (1997) 'Self-regulation and cortical development: implications for functional studies of the brain', in R. Thatcher et al. (eds) *Developmental Neuroimaging*, Oxford: Academic Press.

Lyons, D., Lopez, J., Yang, C. and Schatzberg, A. (2000a) 'Stress level cortisol treatment impairs inhibitory control of behaviour in monkeys', *Journal of Neuroscience* 20 (20).

Lyons, D., Yang, C., Mobley, B., Nickerson, J. and Schatzburg, A. (2000b) 'Early environmental regulation of glucocorticoid feedback sensitivity in young adult monkeys', *Journal of Neuroendocrinology* 12: 723–8.

Lyons-Ruth, K. (1992) 'Maternal depressive symptoms, disorganised infant–mother attachments and hostile–aggressive behaviour in the preschool classroom: a prospective longitudinal view from infancy to age five', *Rochester Symposium on Developmental Psychopathology* 4: 131–71.

Lyons-Ruth, K. (1996) 'Attachment relationships among children with aggressive behaviour problems: the role of disorganised early attachment patterns', *Journal of Consulting and Clinical Psychology* 64 (1): 64–73.

Lyons-Ruth, K. and Jacobovitz, D. (1999) 'Attachment disorganisation: unresolved loss, relational violence, and lapses in behavioural and attentional strategies', in J. Cassidy and P. Shaver (eds) *Handbook of Attachment*, London: Guilford Press.

Lyons-Ruth, K., Connel, D. and Zoll, D. (1991) 'Patterns of maternal behaviour among infants at risk for abuse', in D. Ciccetti and V. Carlson (eds) *Child Maltreatment*, Cambridge: Cambridge University Press.

Lyons-Ruth, K., Choi-Kain, L., Pechtel, P. and Gunderson, J. (2011) 'Perceived parental protection and cortisol responses among young females with borderline personality disorder and controls', *Psychiatry Research* 189 (3): 426–32.

Lyons-Ruth, K., Bureau, J., Holmes, B., Easterbrooks, A. and Brooks, N. (2013) 'Borderline symptoms and suicidality and self-injury in adolescence: prospectively observed correlates in infancy and childhood', *Psychiatry Research* 206 (2): 273–81.

MacLean, F. (1970) 'The triune brain emotion and scientific bias', in F. Schmitt (ed.) *The Neurosciences Second Study Program*, New York: Rockefeller University Press.

McBurnett, K., Lahey, B., Rathouz, P. and Loeber, R. (2000) 'Low salivary cortisol and persistent aggression in boys referred for disruptive behaviour', *Archives of General Psychiatry* 57 (1): 38–43.

McCarthy, M. (1963) *The Group*, London: Weidenfeld and Nicholson.

McEwen, B. and Margarinos, A. (1997) 'Stress effects on morphology and function of the hippocampus', *Annals of the NewYork Academy of Sciences* 821: 271–84.

McEwen, B. (1999) 'Lifelong effects of hormones on brain development', in L. Schmidt and J. Schulkin (eds) *Extreme Fear, Shyness and Social Phobia*, Oxford: Oxford University Press.

McEwen, B. (2000) 'Effects of adverse experiences for brain structure and function', *Biological Psychiatry* 48: 721–31.

McEwen, B. (2001) 'Plasticity of the hippocampus', *Annals of the New York Academy of Sciences* 933: 265–77.

McEwen, B., Eiland, L., Hunter, R. and Miller, M. (2012) 'Stress and anxiety: structural plasticity and epigenetic regulation as a consequence of stress', *Neuropharmacology* 62 (1): 3–12.

McGowan, P., Meaney, M. and Szyf, M. (2011) 'Epigenetics, phenotype, diet and behavior', in V Preedy et al. (eds) *Handbook of Behavior, Food and Nutrition*, New York: Springer Science.

McKee, L., Colletti, C., Rakow, A., Jones, D. and Forehand, R. (2008) 'Parenting and child externalizing behaviors: are the associations specific or diffuse?', *Aggression and Violent Behavior* 13 (3): 201–15.

McNamara, R. and Carlson, S. (2006), 'Role of omega-3 fatty acids in brain development and function: potential implications for the pathogenesis and prevention of psychopathology', *Prostaglandins, Leukotrienes and Essential Fatty Acids* 75 (4–5): 329–49.

Madigan, S., Bakermans-Kranenburg, M., Van Ijzendoorn, M., Moran, G., Pederson, D. and Benoit, D. (2006) 'Unresolved states of mind, anomalous parental behavior, and disorganized attachment: a review and meta-analysis of a transmission gap', *Attachment and Human Development* 8 (2): 89–111.

Maes, M., Christophe, A., Delanghe, J., Altamura, C., Neels, H. and Meltzer, H. (1999) 'Lowered omega3 polyunsaturated fatty acids in serum phospholipids and cholesteryl esters of depressed patients', *Psychiatry Research* 85 (3): 275–91.

Magai, C. and Hunziker, J. (1998) ' "To Bedlam and part way back": discrete emotions theory and borderline symptoms', in W. Flack and J. Laird (eds) *Emotions in Psychopathology*, Oxford: Oxford University Press.

Maguen, S., Metyzler, T., Litz, B., Seal, K., Knight, S. and Marmar, C. (2009). 'The impact of killing in war on mental health symptoms and related functioning', *Journal of Trauma and Stress* 22 (5): 435–43.

Mah, L., Arnold, M. and Grafman, J. (2005), 'Deficits in social knowledge following damage to ventromedial prefrontal cortex', *Journal of Neuropsychiatry and Clinical Neuroscience* 17: 66–74.

Maier, S. and West, J. (2001) 'Drinking patterns and alcohol related birth defects', *Alcohol Research and Health* 25 (3): 168–74.

Main, M. and Goldwyn, R. (1985) 'Adult attachment classification system', unpublished manuscript, Berkeley: University of California.

Maiorana, A., Del Bianco, C. and Cianfarani, S. (2007) 'Adipose tissue: a metabolic regulator', *The Review of Diabetic Studies* 4 (3): 134–46.

Main, M. and Solomon, J. (1990) 'Procedures for identifying infants as disorganised–disoriented during the strange situation', in M. Greenberg et al. (eds) *Attachment in the Pre-School Years: Theory, Research and Intervention*, Chicago: University of Chicago Press.

Makino, S., Gold, P. and Schulkin, J. (1994) 'Effects of corticosterone on CRHmRNA and content in the bed nucleus of the stria terminalis: comparison with the effects in the central nucleus of the amygdala and the paraventricular nucleus of the hypothalamus', *Brain Research* 657: 141–9.

Martin, B. and Hoffman, J. (1990) 'Conduct disorders', in M. Lewis and S. Miller (eds) *Handbook of Developmental Psychopathology*, London: Plenum.

Martin, P. (1997) *The Sickening Mind*, London: HarperCollins.

Mason, J., Wang, S., Yehuda, R., Riney, S., Charney, D. and Southwick, S. (2001) 'Psychogenic lowering of urinary cortisol levels linked to increased emotional numbing and a shame-depressive syndrome in combat-related posttraumatic stress disorder', *Psychosomatic Medicine* 63: 387–401.

Mathers, C. and Loncar, D. (2005), 'Updated projections of global mortality and burden of disease 2002–2030', World Health Organisation.

Matousek, R. H., Dobkin, P. L. and Pruessner, J. (2010) 'Cortisol as a marker for improvement in mindfulness-based stress reduction', *Complementary Therapies in Clinical Practice* 16: 13–19.

Matthews, S. and Phillips, D. (2010) 'Minireview: transgenerational inheritance of the stress response: a new frontier in stress research', *Endocrinology* 151 (1): 7–13.

McEwen, B. (2012, 'Brain on stress: how the social environment gets under the skin', *PNAS* 109 (2).

Mealey, L. (1995) 'The sociobiology of sociopathy: an integrated evolutionary model', *Behavioural and Brain Sciences* 18: 523–99.

Meaney, M. (2010) 'Epigenetics and the biological definition of gene x environment interactions', *Child Development* 81, 41–79.

Mednick, S., Gabrielli, W. and Hutchings, B. (1984) 'Genetic influences in criminal convictions: evidence from an adoption cohort', *Science* 224: 891–4.

Mehedint, M., Craciunescu, C. and Zeisel, S. (2010) 'Maternal dietary choline deficiency alters angiogenesis in fetal mouse hippocampus', *PNAS* 107 (29): 12840–5.

Mehta, M., Golembo, N., Nosarti, C., Colvert, E., Mota, A., Williams, S. et al. (2009) 'Amygdala, hippocampal and corpus callosum size following severe early institutional deprivation: the English and Romanian adoptees study pilot', *Journal of Child Psychology and Psychiatry* 50 (8): 943–51.

Middlebrook, D.W. (1991) *Anne Sexton: A Biography*, London: Virago Press.

Milad, M., Quinn, B., Pitman, R., Orr, S., Fischl, B. and Rauch, S. (2005) 'Thickness of ventromedial prefrontal cortex in humans is associated with extinction memory', PNAS 102 (30): 10706–11.

Mileva-Seitz, V., Steiner, M., Atkinson, L., Meaney, M., Levitan, R., Kennedy, J. et al. (2013) 'Interaction between oxytocin genotypes and early experience predicts quality of mothering and post-partum mood', *PLoS ONE* 8 (4): e61443.

Miller, E. and Cohen, J. (2001) 'An integrative theory of prefrontal cortex function', *Annual Review Neuroscience* 24: 167–202.

Miller, G and Chen, E. (2010), 'Harsh family climate in early life presages the emergence of a proinflammatory phenotype in adolescence', *Psychological Science* 21 (6): 848–56.

Miller, G., Chen, E. and Parker, K. (2011), 'Psychological stress in childhood and susceptibility to the chronic diseases of ageing', *Psychological Bulletin* 137 (6): 959–97.

Miller, S. and Seligman, M. (1980) 'The reformulated model of helplessness and depression: evidence and theory', in R. Neufeld (ed.) *Psychological Stress and Psychopathology*, New York: McGraw-Hill.

Miluk-Kolasa, B., Obiminski, Z., Stupnicki, R. and Golec, L. (1994) 'Effects of music treatment on salivary cortisol', *Experimental and Clinical Endocrinology* 102 (2): 118–20.

Minagawa-Kawai, Y., Matsuoka, S., Dan, I., Naoi, N., Nakamura, K. and Kojima, S. (2009) 'Prefrontal activation associated with social attachment: facial-emotion recognition in mothers and infants', *Cerebral Cortex* 19: 284–92.

Mizoguchi, K., Yuzurihara, M., Ishige, A., Sasaki, H., Chui, D. and Tabira, T. (2001) 'Chronic stress differentially regulates glucocorticoid negative feedback response in rats', *Psychoneuroendocrinology* 26 (5): 443–59.

Moberg, K. (2011), *The Oxytocin Factor*, London: Pinter and Martin.

Moffitt, T., Arseneault, L., Belsky, D., Dickson, N., Hancox, R., Harrington, H. et al. (2010) 'A gradient of childhood self-control predicts health, wealth, and public safety', *PNAS* www.pnas.org/cgi/doi/10.1073.

Moghaddam, B., Bolinao, M., Stein-Behrens, B. and Sapolsky, R. (1994) 'Glucocorticoids mediate the stress-induced accumulation of glutamate', *Brain Research* 655 (1–2): 251–4.

Mollon, P. (1993) *The Fragile Self*, London: Whurr.

Montgomery, P., Burton, J., Sewell, R., Spreckelsen, T. and Richardson, A. (2013) 'Low blood long chain omega-3 fatty acids in UK children are associated with poor cognitive performance and behaviour: a cross-sectional analysis from the DOLAB Study', *Plos One* 8 (6): e66697.

Moriguchi, Y., Ohnishi, T., Lane, R., Maeda, M., Mori, T., Nemoto, K. et al. (2006) 'Impaired self-awareness and theory of mind: an fMRI study of mentalising in alexythymia', *Neuroimage* 32 (3): 1472–82.

Moriguchi, Y. and Komaki, G. (2013) 'Neuroimaging studies of alexithymia: physical, affective and social perspectives', *BioPsychoSocial Medicine* 7 (8).

Morrell, J. and Murray, L. (2003) 'Parenting and the development of conduct disorder and hyperactive symptoms in childhood: a prospective longitudinal study from 2 months to 8 years', *Journal of Child Psychology and Psychiatry* 44 (4): 489–508.

Morrison, B. (1997) *As If*, London: Granta Books.

Morrison, R. (1999) *The Spirit in the Gene*, Ithaca, NY: Cornell University Press.

Moutsiana, C., Fearon, P., Murray, L., Cooper, P., Goodyer, I., Johnstone, T. and Halligan, S. (2014) 'Making an effort to feel positive: insecure attachment in infancy predicts the nural underpinnings of emotion regulation in adulthood', *Journal of Child Psychology and Psychiatry*.

Murgatroyd, C. and Spengler, D. (2011) 'Epigenetics of child development', *Frontiers in Psychiatry* 2 (16).

Murmu, M., Salomon, S., Biala, Y., Weinstock, M., Braun, K. and Bock, J. (2006) 'Changes of spine density and dendritic complexity in the prefrontal cortex in offspring of mothers exposed to stress during pregnancy', *European Journal of Neuroscience* 24 (5): 1477–87.

Murray, L. (1992) 'The impact of post-natal depression on infant development', *Journal of Child Psychology and Psychiatry* 33 (3): 543–61.

Murray, L. and Cooper, P. (eds) (1997) *Postpartum Depression and Child Development*, London: Guilford Press.

Murray, L., Halligan, S., Goodyer, I. and Herbert, J. (2010) 'Disturbances in early parenting of depressed mothers and cortisol secretion in offspring: a preliminary study', *Journal of Affective Disorders* 122 (3): 218–23.

Murray, L., Arteche, A., Fearon, P., Halligan, S., Goodyer, I. and Cooper, P. (2011) 'Maternal post-natal depression and the development of depression in offspring up to 16 years of age', *Journal of the American Academy of Child and Adolescent Psychiatry* 50 (5): 431–4.

Murrough, J., Czermak, C., Neumeister, A. et al. (2011) 'The effect of early trauma exposure on serotonin type 1B receptor expression', *Archives of General Psychiatry* 68 (9): 892–900.

Nachmias, M., Gunnar, M., Mangelsdorf, S., Parritz, R. and Buss, K. (1996) 'Behavioural inhibition and stress reactivity: the moderating role of attachment security', *Child Development* 67 (2): 508–22.

National Institute for Health and Clinical Excellence (NICE) (2009) 'Depression in adults', NICE clinical guideline 90.

Nemiah, J. and Sifneos, P. (1970) 'Affect and fantasy in patients with psychosomatic disorders', in O. Hill (ed.) *Modern Trends in Psychosomatic Medicine*, vol. 2, Oxford: Butterworths.

Neugebauer, R., Hoek, H. and Susser, E. (1999) 'Prenatal exposure to wartime famine and development of antisocial personality disorder in early adulthood', *Journal of the American Medical Association* 282 (5): 455–62.

New, A., Hazlitt, E., Buchsbaum, M., Goodman, M., Mitelman, S., Newmark, R. et al. (2007) 'Amygdala prefrontal disconnection in borderline personality disorder', *Neuropsychopharmacology* 32: 1629–40.

Newell, S. (1992) 'The myth and destructiveness of equal opportunities: the continued dominance of the mothering role', *Personnel Review* 21 (9): 37–47.

Norman, H., Elliot, M. and Fagan, C. (2013) 'An investigation of the predictors of paternal involvement', CCSR Paper 2013–04.

Oberlander, T. (2012) 'Fetal serotonin signaling: setting pathways for early childhood development and behavior', *Journal of Adolescent Health* 51 (2 supplement): s9–s16.

Oberlander, T., Weinberg, J., Papsdorf, M., Grunau, R., Misri, S. and Devlin, A. (2008a) 'Prenatal exposure to maternal depression, neonatal methylation of human glucocorticoid receptor gene and infant cortisol stress responses', *Epigenetics* 3 (2): 97–106.

Oberlander, T., Grunau, R., Mayes, L., Riggs, W., Rurak, D., Papsdorf, M. et al. (2008b) 'HPA axis function in 3 month old infants with prenatal SSRI antidepressant exposure', *Early Human Development* 83 (10): 689–97.

Odent, M. (1986) *Primal Health*, London: Century Hutchinson.

O'Connor, T., Heron, J., Golding, J., Beveridge, M., Glover, V., (2002) 'Maternal antenatal anxiety and children's behavioural/ emotional problems at 4 years', Report from the Avon Longitudinal Study of Parents and Children. *British Journal of Psychiatry* 180: 502–8.

O'Connor, T., Heron, J., Golding, J., Glover, V. and ALSPAC Study Team (2003) 'Maternal antenatal anxiety and behavioural/ emotional problems in children: a test of a programming hypothesis', *Journal of Child Psychology and Psychiatry* 44 (7): 1025–36.

O'Doherty, J., Critchley, H., Deichmann, R. and Dolan, R. (2003) 'Dissociating valence of outcome from behavioural control in human orbital and ventral prefrontal cortices', *Journal of Neuroscience* 23 (21): 7931–9.

O'Donnell, K., O'Connor, T. and Glover, V. (2009) 'Prenatal stress and neurodevelopment of the child: focus on the HPA axis and role of the placenta', *Developmental Neuroscience* 31 (4): 285–92.

Olds, D., Henderson, C., Cole, R., Eckenrode, J., Kitzman, H., Luckey, D. et al. (1998) 'Long term effects of nurse home visitation on children's criminal and antisocial behaviour: 15 year follow-up of a randomised controlled trial', *Journal of the American Medical Association* 280: 1238–44.

Ouellet-Morin, I., Odgers, C., Danese, A., Bowes, L., Shakoor, S, Papadopoulos, A. et al. (2011) 'Blunted cortisol responses to stress signal social and behavioural problems among maltreated/ bullied 12 year old children', *Biological Psychiatry* 70(11): 1016–23.

Out, D., Bakermans-Kranenburg, M. and van Ijzendoorn, M. (2009) 'The role of disconnected and extremely insensitive parenting in the development of disorganized attachment: the validation of a new measure', *Attachment and Human Development* 11 (5): 419–43.

Pace, T., Mletzko, T., Alagbe, O., Musselman, D., Nemeroff, C., Miller, A. and Heim, C. (2006) 'Increased stress-induced inflammatory responses in male patients with major depression and increased early life stress', *American Journal of Psychiatry* 163 (9): 1630–3.

Panksepp, J. (1998) *Affective Neuroscience*, Oxford: Oxford University Press.

Paternain, L., Garza, A. Batlle, M., Milagro, F, Martinez, J. and Campion, J. (2013) 'Prenatal stress increases the obesogenic effects of a high fat sucrose diet in adult rats in a sex-specific manner', *Stress* 16 (2): 220–32.

Paul, A.M. (2010) *Origins: how the nine months before birth shape the rest of our lives*, London: Hay House.

Pawlby, S., Hay, D., Sharp, D., Waters, C. and O'Keane, V. (2009) 'Antenatal depression predicts depression in adolescent offspring: a prospective longitudinal community-based study', *Journal of Affective Disorders* 113: 236–43.

Pawlby, S., Hay, D., Sharp, D., Waters, C. and Pariante, C. (2011) 'Antenatal depression and offspring psychopathology: the influence of childhood maltreatment', *British Journal of Psychiatry* 199: 106–12.

Pearson, R., Evans, J., Kounali, D., Lewis, G., Heron, J., Ramchandani, P., O'Connor, T. and Stein, A. (2013) 'Maternal depression during pregnancy and the post-natal period, risks and possible mechanisms for offspring depression at age 18 years', *JAMA Psychiatry* 70 (12): 1312–19.

Peet, M. and Horrobin, D. (2002) 'A close-ranging study of the effects of ethyl-eicosapentaenoate in patients with ongoing depression despite apparently adequate treatment with standard drugs', *Archives of General Psychiatry* 59 (10): 913–19

Peet, M., Murphy, B., Shay, J. and Horrobin, D. (1998) 'Depletion of omega 3 fatty acid levels in red blood cell membranes of depressed patients', *Biological Psychiatry* 43 (5): 315–19.

Pennebaker, J. (1993) 'Putting stress into words', *Behaviour Research and Therapy* 31 (6): 539–48.

Perry, B. (1997) 'Incubated in terror: neurodevelopmental factors in the "cycle of violence" ', in J. Osofsky (ed.) *Children in a Violent Society*, New York: Guilford Press.

Pert, C. (1998) *Molecules of Emotion*, New York: Simon and Schuster.

Phan, K., Fitzgerald, D., Nathan, P., Moore, G., Uhde, T. and Tancer, M. (2005) 'Neural substrates for voluntary suppression of negative affect: a fmri study', *Biological Psychiatry* 57: 210–19.

Pilgaard, K., Mosbech, T., Grunnet, L., Eiberg, H., Hall, G., Fallentin, E. et al. (2011) 'Differential nongenetic impact of birth weight vs third trimester growth velocity on glucose metabolism and MRI abdominal obesity in young healthy twins', *Journal of Clinical Endocrinology and Metabolism* 96 (9): 2835.

Pilowsky, D., Wickramaratne, P., Talati, A., Tang, M., Hughes, C., Garber, J. et al. (2008) 'Children of depressed mothers 1 year after the initiation of maternal treatment', *American Journal of Psychiatry* 165 (9): 1136–47.

Pinker, S. (2002) *The Blank Slate*, Harmondsworth: Penguin Allen Lane.

Pitchot, W., Herrera, C. and Ansseau, M. (2001) 'HPA axis dysfunction in major depression: relationship to 5HT(1A) receptor activity', *Neuropsychobiology* 44 (2): 74–7.

Plant, D., Barker, E., Waters, C., Pawlby, S. and Pariante, C. (2013) 'Intergenerational transmission of maltreatment and psychopathology: the role of antenatal depression', *Psychological Medicine* 43: 519–28.

Plomin, R. (ed.) (1993) *Nature, Nurture and Psychology*, Washington, DC: APA.

Plotsky, P. and Meaney, M. (1993) 'Early post-natal experience alters hypothalamic CRF mRNA', *Brain Research* 18 (3): 195–200.

Pluess, M. and Belsky, J. (2013), 'Vantage sensitivity: individual differences in response to positive experiences', *Psychological Bulletin* 139 (4): 901–16.

Poeggel, G., Nowicki, L. and Braun, K. (2003) 'Early social deprivation alters monoaminergic afferents in the orbital prefrontal cortex of octodon degus', *Neuroscience* 116: 617.

Posner, M. and Rothbart, M. (2000) 'Developing mechanisms of self-regulation', *Development and Psychopathology* 12: 427–41.

Posner, M., Rothbart, M., Sheese, B. and Tang, Y. (2007) 'The anterior cingulated gyrus and the mechanism of self-regulation', *Cognitive, Affective & Behavioural Neuroscience* 7 (4): 391–5.

Post, R. and Weiss, S. (1997) 'Emergent properties of neural systems: how focal molecular neurobiological alterations can affect behaviour', *Development and Psychopathology* 9: 907–29.

Powell, J., Lewis, P., Roberts, N., Garcia-Finana, M. and Dunbar, R. (2012) 'Orbital prefrontal cortex volume predicts social network size: an imaging study of individual differences in humans', *Proceedings of the Royal Society*, 279 (1736): 2157–62.

Pratt, L., Brody, D. and Gu, Q. (2011) 'Antidepressant use in persons aged 12 and over: United States, 2005–2008', National Center for Health Statistics Number 76.

Premberg, A., Hellstrom, A-L. and Berg, M. (2008) 'Experiences of the first year as father', *Scandinavian Journal of Caring Sciences* 22: 56–63.

Pulkkinen, L. and Pitkanen, T. (1993) 'Continuities in aggresive behaviour from childhood to adulthood', *Aggressive Behaviour* 19: 263.

Radley, J. and Morrison, J. (2005) 'Repeated stress and structural plasticity in the brain', *Ageing Research Reviews* 4 (2): 271–87.

Radley, J., Rocher, A., Janssen, W., Hof, P., McEwen, B. and Morrison, J. (2005) 'Reversibility of apical dendritic retraction in the rat medial prefrontal cortex following repeated stress', *Experimental Neurology* 196 (1): 199–203.

Raine, A. (2002) 'Annotation: the role of prefrontal deficits, low autonomic arousal, and early health factors in the development of antisocial and aggressive behaviour in children', *Journal of Child Psychology and Psychiatry* 43 (4): 417–34.

Raine, A. (2013) *The Anatomy of Violence*, London: Allen Lane.

Raine, A., Brennan, P. and Mednick, S. (1994) 'Birth complications combined with early maternal rejection at age 1 year predispose to violent crime at age 18', *Archives of General Psychiatry* 51: 984.

Raine, A., Brennan, P. and Mednick, S. (1997c) 'Interaction between birth complications and early maternal rejection in predisposing individuals to adult violence', *American Journal of Psychiatry* 154 (9): 1265–71.

Raine, A., Buchsbaum, M. and LaCasse, L. (1997a) 'Brain abnormalities in murderers indicated by PET', *Biological Psychiatry* 42: 495–508.

Raine, A., Brennan, P., Farrington, D. and Mednick, S. (eds) (1997b) *Biosocial Bases of Violence*, London: Plenum.

Raison, C. and Miller, A. (2013) 'The evolutionary significance of depression', *Molecular Psychiatry* 18: 15–37.

Ramchandani, P., Stein, A., Evans, J., O'Connor, T. and ALSPAC study team (2005) 'Paternal depression in the post-natal period and child development: a prospective population study', *The Lancet* 365 (9478): 2201–5.

Ramchandani, P., Domoney, J., Sethna, V., Psychogiou, L., Vlachos, H. and Murray, L. (2013) 'Do early father-infant interactions predict the onset of externalizing behavours in young children? Findings from a longitudinal cohort study', *Journal of Child Psychology and Psychiatry* 54 (1): 56–64.

Rao, J., Ertley, R., Lee, H-J., Demar, J., Arnold, J., Rapoport, S. and Bazinet, R. (2007) 'n-3 Polyunsaturated fatty acid deprivation in rats decreases frontal cortex BDNF via a p38 MAPK-dependent mechanism', *Molecular Psychiatry* 12: 36–46.

Rao, H., Betancourt, L., Giannetta, J., Brodsky, N., Korczykowski, M., Avants, B. et al. (2010) 'Early parental care is important for hippocampal maturation', *Neuroimage* 49 (1): 1144–50.

Rapaport, M., Schettler, P. and Bresee, C. (2012) 'A preliminary study of the effects of repeated massage on HPA and immune function in healthy individuals', *Journal of Alternative and Complementary Medicine* 18 (8): 789–97.

Rauch, S., Van der Kolk, B., Fisler, R., Alpert, N., Orr, S., Savage, C. et al. (1996) 'A symptom provocation study using PET and script driven imagery', *Archives of General Psychiatry* 53: 380–7.

Renken, B., Egeland, B., Marvinney, D., Mangelsdorf, S. and Sroufe, A. (1989) 'Early childhood antecedents of aggression and passive-withdrawal in early elementary school', *Journal of Personality* 57: 2.

Reuters (1998) Column 412.

Rice, F., Harold, G., Boivin, J., van den Bree, M., Hay, D. and Thapar, A. (2010) 'The links between prenatal stress and offspring development and psychopathology: disentangling environmental and inherited influences', *Psychological Medicine* 40 (2): 335–45.

Rich, A. (1977) *Of Woman Born*, London: Virago Press.

Richardson, A. (2006) 'Omega-3 fatty acids in ADHD and related neurodevelopmental disorders', *International Review of Psychiatry* 18 (2): 155–72.

Rifkin-Graboi, A., Bai, J., Chen, H., Hameed, W., Sim, L., Tint, M. et al. (2013) 'Prenatal maternal depression associates with microstructure of right amygdala in neonates at birth', *Biological Psychiatry* 74 (11): 837–44.

Riley, E. and McGee, C. (2005) 'Fetal alcohol spectrum disorders: an overview with emphasis on changes in brain and behavior', *Experimental Biology and Medicine* 230 (6): 357–65.

Riley, V. (1975) 'Mouse mammary tumours: alteration of incidence as apparent function of stress', *Science* 189: 465–7.

Rinne, T., de Kloet, E.R., Wouters, L., Goekoop, J., DeRijk, R. and van den Brink, W. (2002) 'Hyperresponsiveness of HPA axis to combined dexamethasone/CRH challenge in female borderline personality disorder subjects with a history of sustained childhood abuse', *Biological Psychiatry* 52: 1102–12.

Rodrigues, A., Leao, P., Carvalho, M., Almeida, O. and Sousa, N. (2011) 'Potential programming of dopaminergic circuits by early life stress', *Psychopharmacology* 214 (1): 107–20.

Rogeness, G., Javors, M. and Pliszka, S. (1992) 'Neurochemistry and child and adolescent psychiatry', *Journal of the American Academy of Child and Adolescent Psychiatry* 31: 765–81.

Rolls, E. (1999) *The Brain and Emotion*, Oxford: Oxford University Press.

Rolls, E. and Grabenhorst, F. (2008) 'The orbitofrontal cortex and beyond', *Progress in Neurobiology* 86: 216–44.

Roseboom, T., de Rooij, S. and Painter, R. (2006) 'The Dutch famine and its long-term consequences for adult health', *Early Human Development* 82: 485–91.

Rosen, J. and Schulkin, J. (1998) 'From normal fear to pathological anxiety', *Psychological Review* 105 (2): 325–50.

Rosenblum, L., Coplan, J., Friedman, S., Bassoff, T., Gorman, J. and Andrews, M. (1994) 'Adverse early experiences affect noradrenergic and serotonergic functioning in adult primates', *Biological Psychiatry* 35 (4): 221–7.

Roth, T., Lubin, F., Funk, A. and Sweatt, D. (2009) 'Lasting epigenetic influence of early life adversity on the BDNF gene', *Biological Psychiatry* 65 (9): 760–9.

Rothbart, M. (1994) 'Temperament and social behaviour in childhood', *Merill-Palmer Quarterly* 40: 221–39.

Rothbart, M., Evans, D. and Ahadi, S. (2000) 'Temperament and personality: origins and outcomes', *Journal of Personality and Social Psychology* 78 (1): 122–35.

Rothschild, B. (2000) *The Body Remembers*, New York: Norton.

Royal College of Obstetricians and Gynaecologists (2006) 'Alcohol consumption and the outcomes of pregnancy', RCOG Statement No. 5.

Rubin, K., Hastings, P., Sheu, X., Stewart, S. and McNichol, K. (1998) 'Intrapersonal and maternal correlates of aggression, conflict and externalising problems in toddlers', *Child Development* 69 (6): 1614–29.

Rushworth, M. and Behrens, T. (2008), 'Choice, uncertainty and value in prefrontal and cingulate cortex', *Nature Neuroscience* 11 (4): 389–97.

Rutter, M. (ed.) (1996) *Genetics of Criminal and Antisocial Behaviour*, Chichester: Wiley.

Rutter, M., Sonuga-Barke, E., Beckett, C., Castle, J., Kreppner, J., Kumsta, R. et al. (2010) 'Deprivation-specific psychological patterns: effects of institutional deprivation: 75–1', Monographs of the Society for Research in Child Development.

Ruttle, P., Shirtcliff, E., Serbin, L., Fisher, D., Stack, D. and Schwartzman, A. (2011) 'Disentangling psychobiological mechanisms underlying internalizing and externalizing behaviors in youth: longitudinal and concurrent associations with cortisol', *Hormones and* Behavior 59 (1): 123–32.

Russo, R., Murrough, J., Han, M-H., Charney, D. and Nestler, E. (2012) 'Neurobiology of resilience', *Nature Neuroscience* 15 (11): 1475–84.

Rymer, R. (1994) *Genie: A Scientific Tragedy*, London: Penguin.

Sanchez, M., Ladd, C. and Plotsky, M. (2001) 'Early adverse experience as a developmental risk factor for later psychopathology: evidence from rodent and primate models, *Development and Psychopathology* 13 (3): 419–49.

Sandman, C., Davis, E., Buss, C. and Glynn, L. (2011) 'Prenatal programming of human neurological function', *International Journal of Peptides* Article ID 837596.

Sandman, C. and Davis, E. (2012) 'Neurobehavioral risk is associated with gestational exposure to stress hormones', expert review of endocrinology and metabolism, 7 (4): 445–59.

Sapolsky, R. (1992) *Stress: The Aging Brain and the Mechanisms of Neuron Death*, Cambridge, MA: MIT Press.

Sapolsky, R. (1995) 'Social subordinance as a marker of hypercortisolism: some unexpected subtleties', *Annals of the New York Academy of Sciences* 771: 626–39.

Sapolsky, R. (2002) 'Chickens, eggs and hippocampal atrophy', *Nature Neuroscience* 5 (11): 1111–13.

Sapolsky, R. (2004) *Why Zebras Don't Get Ulcers*, New York: W.H. Freeman, St. Martin's Griffin.

Schieche, M. and Spangler, G. (2005) 'Individual differences in biobehavioral organization during problem-solving in toddlers: the influence of maternal behavior, infant–mother attachment, and behavioral inhibition on the attachment-exploration balance', *Developmental Psychobiology* 46 (4): 293–306.

Schmidt, U, Holsboer, F. and Rein, T. (2011) 'Epigenetic aspects of post-traumatic stress', *Disease Markers* 30: 77–87.

Schore, A. (1994) *Affect Regulation and the Origin of the Self*, Hillsdale, NJ: Lawrence Erlbaum Associates Inc.

Schore, A. (2003) *Affect Dysregulation and Disorders of the Self*, New York: Norton.

Schulkin, J. (1999) *Neuroendocrine Regulation of Behaviour*, Cambridge: Cambridge University Press.

Scott, S., Knapp, M., Henderson, J. and Maugham, B. (2001) 'Financial cost of social exclusion: follow up study of antisocial children into adulthood', *British Medical Journal*, 323: 191–4.

Seckl, J. (2008) 'Glucocorticoids, developmental "programming" and the risk of affective dysfunction', *Progress in Brain Research* 167: 17–34.

Seckl, J. and Meaney, M. (2006) 'Glucocorticoid "programming" and PTSD risk', *Annals of New York Academy of Science* 1071: 351–78.

Segerstrom, S. and Miller, G. (2004) 'Psychological stress and the human immune system: A meta-analytic study of 30 years of inquiry', *Psychological Bulletin* 130 (4): 601–30.

Segman, R., Cooper-Kazazz, R., Macciardi, F., Goltser, T., Halfon, Y., Dobroborski, T. and Shalev, A. (2002) 'Identification of the first gene in posttraumatic stress disorder', *Molecular Psychiatry* 7 (8): 903–7.

Seligman, M. and Beagley, G. (1975) 'Learned helplessness in the rat', *Journal of Comparative and Physiological Psychology* 88: 534–41.

Sellers, R., Harold, G., Elam, K., Rhoades, K., Potter, R., Mars, B. et al. (2013) 'Maternal depression and co-occurring antisocial behaviour: testing maternal hostility and warmth as mediators of risk for offspring psychopathology', *Journal of Child Psychology and Psychiatry* 22: 108–14.

Seo, D. and Patrick, C. (2008) 'Role of serotonin and dopamine system interactions in the neurobiology of impulsive aggression', *Aggression and Violent Behavior* 13 (5): 383–95.

Sexton, A. (2000) *Selected Poems of Anne Sexton*, New York: First Mariner Books.

Shair, H., Barr, G. and Hofer, M. (eds) (1991) *Developmental Psychobiology*, Oxford: Oxford University Press.

Shin, L. (2009) 'The amygdala in PTSD', in P. Shiromani, T. Keane and J. LeDoux (eds) *Neurobiology of PTSD*, Totowa, NJ: Humana Press.

Shin, L., McNally, R. and Kosslyn, S. (1999) 'Regional cerebral blood flow during script-driven imagery in childhood sexual abuse-related PTSD', *American Journal of Psychiatry* 156: 575–84.

Shin, L., Whalen, P., Pitman, R. et al. (2001) 'An fMRI study of anterior cingulate function in PTSD', *Biological Psychiatry* 50: 932–42.

Shipman, K. and Zeman, J. (2001) 'Socialisation of children's emotion regulation in mother–child dyads', *Development and Psychopathology* 13: 317–36.

Shirtcliff, E., Granger, D, Booth, A and Johnson, D. (2005) 'Low salivary cortisol levels and externalizing behavior problems in youth', *Development and Psychopathology* 17: 167–84.

Shoda, Y., Mischel, W. and Peake, P. (1990) 'Predicting adolescent cognitive and self-regulatory competencies from pre-school delay of gratification', *Developmental Psychology* 26 (6).

Siegel, D. (1999) *The Developing Mind*, New York: Guilford Press.

Silbersweig, D., Clarkin, J., Goldstein, M. and Kernberg, O. (2007) 'Failure of frontolimbic inhibitory function in the context of negative emotion in borderline personality disorder', *American Journal of Psychiatry* 164: 1832–41.

Slavich, G., Way, B., Eisenberger, N. and Taylor, S. (2010) 'Neural sensitivity to social rejection is associated with inflammatory responses to social stress', *PNAS* 107 (33): 14817–22.

Slotkin, T. (1998) 'Fetal nicotine or cocaine exposure: which one is worse?', *Journal of Pharmacology and Experimental Therapy* 285 (3): 931–45.

Solomon, A. (2001) *The Noonday Demon*, London: Chatto and Windus.

Solomon, J. and George, C. (eds) (1999) *Attachment Disorganisation*, New York: Guilford Press.

Sompayrac, L. (2012) *How the Immune System Works*, Wiley-Blackwell.

Speltz, M. et al. (1999) 'Attachment in boys with early onset conduct problems', *Development and Psychopathology* 11: 269.

Sroufe, A. (1995) *Emotional Development*, Cambridge: Cambridge University Press.

Sroufe, A. (1997) 'Psychopathology as an outcome of development', *Development and Psychopathology* 9: 251–68.

Steele, H., Steele, M. and Fonagy, P. (1996), 'Associations among attachment classifications of mothers, fathers, and their infants', *Child Development* 67: 541–55.

Steingard, R., Renshaw, P., Hennen, J., Lenox, M., Cintron, C., Young, A. et al. (2002) 'Smaller frontal lobe white matter volumes in depressed adolescents', *Biological Psychiatry* 52: 413–17.

Stephenson, P. (2002) *Billy*, London: HarperCollins.

Stern, D. (1985) *The Interpersonal World of the Infant*, New York: Basic Books.

Sternberg, E. (2000) *The Balance Within: The Science Connecting Health and Emotions*, New York: Freeman.

Sternberg, E. (2001) 'Neuroendocrine regulation of autoimmune/inflammatory disease', *Journal of Endocrinology* 169 (3): 429–35.

Stewart-Brown, S. and McMillan, A. (2010), 'Home and community based parenting support programmes and interventions', www2. warwick.ac.uk/fac'med/staff/stewartbrown.

Stoll, A., Severus, W., Freeman, M., Reuter, S., Zboyan, H., Diamond, E., Cress, K. and Marangell, L. (1999) 'Omega 3 fatty acids in bipolar disorder: a preliminary double-bind, placebocontrolled trial', *Archives of General Psychiatry* 56 (5): 407–12.

Styron, W. (1991) *Darkness Visible: A Memoir of Madness*, London: Cape.

Sublette, E., Milak, M., Hibbeln, J., Freed, P., Oguendo, M., Malone, K. et al. (2009) 'Plasma polyunsaturated fatty acids and regional cerebral glucose metabolism in major depression', *Prostaglandins Leukot Essent Fatty Acids* 80 (1): 57–64.

Sullivan, R. and Gratton, A. (2002) 'Prefrontal cortical regulation of hypothalamic-pituitary-adrenal function in the rat and implications for psychopathology: side matters', *Psychoneuroendocrinology* 27: 99–114.

Suomi, S. (1997) 'Early determinants of behaviour: evidence from primate studies', *British Medical Bulletin* 53: 170–84.

Suomi, S. (1999) 'Developmental trajectories, early experiences and community consequences: lessons from studies with rhesus monkeys', in D. Keating and C. Hertzman (eds) *Children of the Information Age: Developmental Health as the Wealth of Nations*, Perth: Australian Research Alliance for Children and Youth.

Suttie, I. (1935) *The Origins of Love and Hate*, Harmondsworth: Penguin.

Swann, W. (1987) 'Identity negotiation: where two roads meet', *Journal of Personality and Social Psychology* 53 (6): 1038–51.

Symington, N. (1993) *Narcissism*, London: Karnac.

Tanaka, S. (2005) 'Parental leave and child health across OECD countries', *Economic Journal* 115.

Tanaka, S. and Waldfogel, J. (2007) 'Effects of parental leave and work hours on fathers' involvement with their babies', *Community, Work and Family* 10 (4): 409–26.

Tarullo, A. and Gunnar, M. (2006) 'Child maltreatment and the developing HPA axis', *Hormones and Behavior* 50: 632–9.

Taylor, A., Fisk, N.M. and Glover, V. (2000) Mode of delivery and subsequent stress response. *Lancet* 355: 120.

Taylor, G. (1987) *Psychosomatic Medicine and Contemporary Psychoanalysis*, New York: International Universities Press.

Taylor, G. (1992) 'Psychosomatics and self-regulation', in J. Barron, M. Eagle and D. Wolitzky (eds) *Interface of Psychoanalysis and Psychology*, Washington DC: American Psychological Association.

Taylor, G., Bagby, M. and Parker, J. (1997) *Disorders of Affect Regulation: Alexithymia in Medical and Psychiatric Illness*, Cambridge: Cambridge University Press.

Teicher, M., Anderson, C. and Polcan, A. (2012) 'Childhood maltreatment is associated with reduced volume in hippocampal subfields CA3, dentate gyrus and subiculum', *PNAS* 109 (9).

Teisl, M. and Ciccetti, D. (2008), 'Physical abuse, cognitive and meotional processes and aggressive/disruptive behavior problems', *Social Development* 17: 1–23.

Temoshok, L. (1992) *The Type C Connection*, New York: Random House.

Temoshok, L., Wald, R. and Synowski, S. (2008) 'Coping as a multi-system construct associated with pathways mediating HIV relevant immune function and disease progression', *Psychosomatic Medicine* 70: 555–61.

Tielbeek, J., Medland, S., Benyamin, B., Byrne, E, Heath, A., Madden, P., Martin, N., Wray, N. and Verweij, K. (2012) 'Unraveling the genetic etiology of adult antisocial behavior: a genome-wide association study', *PLoS ONE* 7 (10): e45086.

Tiihonen, J., Virkkunen, M., Räsänen, P., Pennanen, S., Saino, E., Calloway, J. et al. (2001) 'Free L-tryptophan plasma levels in antisocial violent offenders', *Psychopharmacology* 157 (4): 395–400.

Tolstoy, L. (1877/1995) *Anna Karenina*, Ware: Wordsworth.

Tomarken, A., Davidson, R. and Henriques, J. (1990) 'Resting frontal brain asymmetry predicts affective responses to films', *Journal of Personality and Social Psychology* 59: 791–801.

Tomarken, A., Davidson, R., Wheeler, R. and Doss, R. (1992) 'Individual differences in anterior brain asymmetry and fundamental dimensions of emotion', *Journal of Personality and Social Psychology* 62: 676–87.

Toro, R., Leonard, G., Lerner, J., Lerner, R., Perron, M., Pike, G. et al. (2008) 'Prenatal exposure to maternal cigarette smoking and the adolescent cerebral cortex', *Neuropsychopharmacology* 33: 1019–27.

Tottenham, N. (2012), 'Human amygdala development in the absence of species-expected caregiving', *Developmental Psychobiology* 54 (6): 598–611.

Tottenham, N. and Sheridan, M. (2010) 'A review of adversity, the amygdala and the hippocampus: a consideration of developmental timing', *Frontiers in Human Neuroscience* 3: 68.

Toynbee, P. (2001) *Guardian*, 28 December.

Tranter, R., O'Donovan, C., Chandarana, P. and Kennedy, S. (2002) 'Prevalence and outcome of partial remission in depression', *Journal of Psychiatry and Neuroscience* 27 (4): 241–7.

Tronick, E. and Weinberg, M. (1997) 'Depressed mothers and infants: failure to form dyadic states of consciousness', in L. Murray and P. Cooper (eds) *Postpartum Depression and Child Development*, New York: Guilford Press.

Tucker, D. (1992) 'Developing emotions and cortical networks', in M. Gunnar and C. Nelson (eds) *Developmental Behavioural Neuroscience*, Hillsdale, NJ: Lawrence Erlbaum Associates, Inc.

Turner, E. et al. (2007) 'Selective publication of antidepressant trials and its influence on apparent efficacy', *New England Journal of Medicine* 358: 252–60.

Turner, J. (2000) *On the Origin of Human Emotions*, Palo Alto: Stanford University Press.

Uhart, M., Oswald, L., McCaul, M. Chong, R. and Wand, G. (2006) 'Hormonal responses to stress and family history of alcoholism', *Neuropsychopharmacology* 31 (10): 2255–63.

Valzelli, L. (1981) *The Psychobiology of Aggression and Violence*, New York: Raven Press.

Van den Boom, D. (1994) 'The influence of temperament and mothering in attachment and exploration: an experimental manipulation of sensitive responses among lower-class mothers with irritable infants', *Child Development* 65: 1449.

Van der Kolk, B. and McFarlane, A. (1996) 'The black hole of trauma', in Van der Kolk, B., McFarlane, A. and Weisaeth, L. (eds) *Traumatic Stress: the Effects of Overwhelming Experience on Mind, Body and Society*, New York: Guilford Press.

Van der Kolk, B., Burbridge, J. and Suzuki, J. (1997) 'The psychobiology of traumatic memory: clinical implications of neuroimaging studies', in R. Yehuda and A. McFarlane (eds) *Psychobiology of PTSD*, New York: Annals of the New York Academy of Science.

Van der Wal, M., van Eijsden, M. and Bonsel, G. (2007) 'Stress and emotional problems during pregnancy and excessive infant crying', *Journal of Developmental and Behavioral Pediatrics*, 28 (6): 431–7.

Van Goozen, S. and Fairchild, G. (2006) 'Neuroendocrine and neurotransmitter correlates in children with antisocial behavior', *Hormone Behaviour* 50(4): 647–54.

Van Harmelen, A-L., van Tol, M-J., van der Wee, N., Verltman, D., Aleman, A., Spinhoven, P. et al. (2010) 'Reduced medial prefrontal cortex volume in adults reporting childhood emotional maltreatment', *Biological Psychiatry* 68: 832–8.

Van Ijzendoorn, M. and Bakermans-Kranenburg, M. (2009) 'Attachment security and disorganization in maltreating families and orphanages', *Encyclopedia on Early Childhood Development*, CEECD.

Van Ijzendoorn, M., Bakermans-Kranenburg, M. and Ebstein, R. (2011) 'Methylation matters in child development: toward developmental behavioral epigenetics', *Child Development Perspectives* 5 (4): 305–10.

Van Ijzendoorn, M., Schuengel, C. and Bakermans-Kranenburg, M. (1999) 'Disorganized attachment in early childhood: meta-analysis of precursors, concomitants, and sequelae', *Development and Psychopathology* 11 (2): 225–49.

Varela, F., Thompson, E. and Rosch, E. (1996) *The Embodied Mind*, Cambridge, MA: MIT Press.

Villareal, G. and King, C. (2001) 'Brain imaging in PTSD', *Seminars in Clinical Neuropsychiatry* 6: 131–45.

Viltart, O. and Vanbesien-Maillot, C. (2007) 'Impact of prenatal stress on neuroendocrine programming', *Scientific World Journal* 7: 1493–537.

Virkkunen, M., Goldman, D. and Linnoila, M. (1996) 'Serotonin in alcoholic violent offenders', in G.R. Bock and J.A. Goode (eds) *Genetics of Criminal and Antisocial Behaviour*, Chichester: Wiley.

Visintainer, M., Volpicelli, J. and Seligman, M. (1982) 'Tumour rejection in rats after inescapable or escapable shock', *Science* 216: 437–9.

Vrijkotte, TR., van der Wal, M., van Eijsden, M., Bonsel, G. (2009) 'First trimester working conditions and birthweight: a prospective cohort study, *American Journal of Public Health* 99 (8): 1409–16.

Vyas, A., Pillai, A., Chattarji, S. (2004) 'Recovery after chronic stress fails to reverse amygdaloid neuronal hypertrophy and enhanced anxiety-like behavior', *Neuroscience* 128 (4): 667–73.

Vyas, A., Mitra, R., Shankaranarayana Rao, B. and Chattarji, S. (2002) 'Chronic stress induces contrasting patterns of dendrites remodelling in hippocampal and amygdaloid neurons', *Journal of Neuroscience* 22 (15): 6810–18.

Vythilingan, M. et al. (2002) 'Childhood trauma associated with smaller hippocampal volume in women with major depressive disorder', *American Journal of Psychiatry* 159: 2072–80.

Wainwright, P. (2002) 'Dietary essential fatty acids and brain function: a developmental perspective on mechanisms', *Proceedings of the Nutrition Society* 61 (1): 61–9.

Wakshlak, A. and Weinstock, M. (1989) 'Neonatal handling reverses behavioural abnormalities induced in rats by prenatal stress', *Physiology and Behaviour* 48: 289–92.

Wakschlag, L., Lahey, B., Loeber, R., Green, S., Gordon, R. and Leventhal, B. (1997) 'Maternal smoking during pregnancy and the risk of conduct disorder in boys', *Archives of General Psychiatry* 54: 670–6.

Wakschlag, L., Henry, D., Blair, J., Dukic, V., Burns, J. and Pickett, K. (2011) 'Unpacking the association: individual differences in the relation of prenatal exposure to cigarettes and disruptive behaviour phenotypes', *Neurotoxicology Teratology* 33 (1): 145–54.

Wall, P. and Messier, C. (2001) 'The hippocampal formationorbito-medial pre-frontal cortex circuit in the attentional control of meaning', *Behaviour and Brain Research* 127 (1–2): 99–117.

Walter, M., Bureau, J-F., Holmes, B., Bertha, E., Hollander, M., Wheelis, J. et al. (2008) 'Cortisol response to interpersonal stress in young adults with borderline personality disorder: a pilot study', *European Psychiatry* 23 (3): 201–4.

Wand, G., McCaul, M., Gotjen, D., Reynolds, J. and Lee, S. (2001) 'Confirmation that offspring from families with alcohol dependent individuals have greater HPA axis activation', *Alcohol Clinical and Experimental Research* 25 (8): 1134–9.

Wang, W. (2013) 'Mothers and work: what's "ideal?" ', Fact Tank, Pew Research Center. www.pewresearch.org/fact-tank/2013/08/19/mothers-and-work-whats-ideal/.

Watt, D. (2001) 'Emotion and consciousness: implications of affective neuroscience for extended reticular thalamic activating system theories of consciousness'. www.phil.vt.edu/ASSC/watt/default.html.

Weaver, I. (2007) 'Epigenetic programming by maternal behavior and pharmacological intervention', *Epigenetics* 2 (1): 22–8.

Weaver, I., Champagne, F., Brown, S., Dymov, S., Sharma, S., Meaney, M. and Szyf, M. (2005) 'Reversal of maternal programming of stress responses in adult offspring through methyl supplementation: altering epigenetic marking later in life', *The Journal of Neuroscience* 25 (47): 11045–54.

Weissman, M., Pilowsky, D., Wickramaratne, P. et al. (2006) 'Remissions in maternal depression and child psychopathology', *JAMA* 295 (12): 1389–98.

Welburn, V. (1980) *Post-natal Depression*, London: Fontana.

Westen, D. (2000) 'Integrative psychotherapy: integrating psychodynamic and cognitive-behavioural theory and technique', in C. Snyder and R. Ingram (eds) *Handbook of Psychological Change: Psychotherapy Processes and Practices for the 21st Century*, Chichester: Wiley.

Westen, D. and Harnden-Fischer, J. (2001) 'Personality profiles in eating disorders', *American Journal of Psychiatry* 158 (4): 547–62.

Wheeler, R., Davidson, R. and Tomarken, A. (1993) 'Frontal brain asymmetry and emotional reactivity: a biological substrate of affective style', *Psychophysiology* 30 (1): 82–9.

Whitaker-Azmitia, P. (2010), 'Serotonin and development', in Muller, C. and Jacobs, B. (eds) *Handbook of the Behavioral Neurobiology of Serotonin*, San Diego, CA: Elsevier Academic Press.

Widom, C., Czaja, S. and Paris, J, (2009), 'A prospective investigation of personality disorder in abused and neglected children followed up into adulthood', *Journal of Personality Disorders* 23 (5): 433–46.

Wiener, H. (1989) 'The dynamics of the organism: implications of recent biological thought for psychosomatic theory and research', *Psychosomatic Medicine* 51: 608–35.

Willner, P. (1985) *Depression: A Psychobiological Synthesis*, Chichester: Wiley.

Wilson, C. (2001) 'My friend Ian Brady has something to tell you', *Sunday Times*, 25 November.

Winnicott, D. (1992) 'Primary maternal preoccupation', in D. Winnicott (ed.) *Collected Papers: Through Paediatrics to Psychoanalysis*, London: Karnac.

Wolff, P. (1987) *The Development of Behavioural States and the Eexpression of Emotions in Early Infancy*, Chicago: University of Chicago Press.

Wolke, D. and St. James-Robert, I. (1987) 'Multi-method measurement of the early parent–infant system with easy and difficult newborns', in H. Rauh and H.-C. Steinhausen (eds) *Psychobiology and Early Development*, Oxford: Elsevier.

Woodside, D., Bulik, C. and Halmi, K. et al. (2002) 'Personality, perfectionism, and attitudes toward eating in parents of individuals with eating disorders', *International Journal of Eating Disorders* 31: 290–9.

Woodward, S., Kuo, J., Schaer, M., Kaloupek, D. and Eliez, S. (2013) 'Early adversity and combat exposure interact to influence anterior cingulated cortex volume in combat veterans', *NeuroImage: Clinical* 2: 670–4.

Wurmser, H., Rieger, M., Domogalla, C., Kahnt, A., Buchwald, J., Kowatsch, M. et al. (2005) 'Association between life stress during pregnancy and infant crying in the first 6 months postpartum: a prospective longitudinal study', *Early Human Development* 82: 341–9.

Xu, Y., Farver, J-A., and Zhang, Z. (2009) 'Temperament, harsh and indulgent parenting and Chinese children's pro-active and reactive aggression', *Child Development* 80 (1): 244–58.

Yajnik, C. (2004) 'Early life origins of insulin resistance and type 2 diabetes in India and other Asian countries', *The American Society for Nutritional Sciences* 134: 205–10.

Yan, J., Jiang, X., West, A., Perry, C. Malysheva, O., Brenna, J. et al. (2013) 'Pregnancy alters choline dynamics: results of a randomized trial using stable isotope methodology in pregnant and nonpregnant women', *American Journal of Clinical Nutrition* 98 (6): 1459–67.

Yehuda, R. (1999) 'Linking the neuroendocrinology of PTSD with recent neuroanatomic findings', *Seminars in Clinical Neuropsychiatry* 4: 256–65.

Yehuda, R. (2001) 'Biology of PTSD', *Journal of Clinical Psychiatry* 62: 41–6.

Yehuda, R. and Bierer, L. (2009), 'The relevance of epigenetics to PTSD', *Journal of Trauma and Stress* 22 (5): 427–34.

Yehuda, R. and LeDoux, J. (2007) 'Response variation following trauma: a translational neuroscience approach to understanding PTSD', *Neuron* 56: 19–32.

Yehuda, R. and Mcfarlane, A. (1995) 'Conflict between current knowledge of PTSD and its original conceptual base', *American Journal of Psychiatry* 152: 1705–13.

Yehuda, R., Engel, S., Brand, S. (2005) 'Transgenerational effects of PTSD in babies of mothers exposed to the World Trade Centre attacks', *Biological Psychiatry* 66: 708–11.

Yehuda, R., Kahana, N.B., Schmeidler, J., Southwick, S., Skyewilson, B. and Giller, E. (1995) 'Impact of cumulative lifetime trauma and recent stress on current PTSD symptoms in Holocaust survivors', *American Journal of Psychiatry* 152: 1815–18.

Yehuda, R., Bierer, L., Schmeidler, J., Aferiat, D., Breslau, I. and Dolan, S. (2000) 'Low cortisol and risk for PTSD in adult offspring of holocaust survivors', *American Journal of Psychiatry* 157: 1252–9.

Yehuda, R., Engel, S., Brand, S., Seckl, J., Marcus, S. and Berkowitz, G. (2005) 'Transgenerational effects of PTSD in babies of mothers exposed to the World Trade Center attacks during pregnancy', *Journal of Clinical Endocrinology and Metabolism* 90 (7): 4115–18.

Yehuda, R., Daskalakis, N., Desarnaud, F., Makotkine, I. Lehrnher, A., Koch, E. et al. (2013) 'Epigenetic biomarkers as predictors and correlates of symptom improvement following psychotherapy in combat veterans with PTSD', *Frontiers in Psychiatry* 4: 118.

Yovell, Y. (2000) 'From hysteria to PTSD: psychoanalysis and the neurobiology of traumatic memories', *Neuropsychoanalysis* 2 (1): 171–81.

Young, S. (2007) 'How to increase serotonin in the human brain without drugs', *Journal of Psychiatry and Neuroscience* 32 (6): 394–9.

Zanarini, M., Williams, A., Lewis, R., Reich, R., Soledad, C., Marino, M. et al. (1997) 'Reported pathological childhood experiences associated with the development of borderline personality disorder', *American Journal of Psychiatry* 154: 1101–6.

Ziol-Guest, K., Duncan, G., Kalil, A. and Boyce, T. (2012) 'Early childhood poverty, immune-mediated disease processes, and adult productivity', *Proceedings of the National Academy of Sciences* 109, Supplement 2.

Zulueta, F. de (1993) *From Pain to Violence: The Traumatic Roots of Destructiveness*, London: Whurr.

Zulueta, F. de (1997) 'The treatment of trauma from the psychobiological perspective of attachment theory', Proceedings of conference on PTSD, St. George's Hospital, London.

Index

abuse 36; and right brain 203; and brain volume 209; and anti-social behaviour 202 *see also* sexual abuse, Pinker and 'abuse excuse' 204; and parental arousal 177

Ader, R. and Cohen, N. 122

ADHD 233

adrenaline 76, 159

Adverse Childhood Experiences (ACE) study 118–19; and cytokines 119; and immune system 118–19

aggression 193; and low cortisol 100, 213; and low serotonin 199; and smoking 198, 199, 200; and harsh parenting 201, 202, 211; and insecure attachment 201; and genetic predisposition 194–7; and MAOA-L gene 199, 200, 201

Ainsworth, M. 5

alcohol 216–17; and addiction 128; and parenting 93; and pregnancy 16, 198; Foetal Alcohol Syndrome 16

alexythymia 101, 114, 126

Allen, G. 222

Allen, J. 172

amygdala (diagram 52), xi, 20, 50, 52, 54, 171,183; and abuse 187; and anterior cingulate 81, 231; and cortisol 26, 84 ; and fear 63, 70; and oxytocin 163; and prefrontal cortex 56; and pre-natal stress 20; and PTSD 162; and serotonin 198; and stress response 75, 79, 231; and mindfulness meditation 231

Andreasen, N. 245

anorexia and cortisol 128; cut off from emotion 131

anterior cingulate cortex (diagram 52); 49,52,53,61; and amygdala 81; and conscious self 64; and communication 68; and serotonin 163, 198; and social rejection 117; and trauma 163

anti-depressants 135, 230, 232, 249

Appleyard, B. 9

attachment, insecure attachment 91, 108; avoidant attachment 41, 42, 113,132; resistant attachment 42; disorganised attachment 42, 43, 170, 178, 179, 188, 203; and approach/avoid dilemma 170; and immune system

124; and narrative self 71; and high cortisol 171; secure attachment and cortisol 90; and intervention 87; and maltreatment 170, 203; and self-regulation 112; and unborn baby 25

Auden, W.H. 15

Ayoub, C. and Rappolt-Schlichtmann, G. 210

baby, difficult baby 35; interactive development 33; leaving to cry 84, 111; low birth weight 19; sleep patterns 83

baby of depressed mother, and left brain 145; and risk of depression 145; and insecure attachment 145; and larger amygdala 145; and high cortisol 145

Barber, L. 214

Bateson, G. 9

BDNF 154, 164, 233; and omega 3, 233

Beebe, B. 47

Belsky, J. 37, 35, 210

Bennett, C. 22

Bergman, I. 169

beta-endorphin 60; and alcohol 128; and sugar addiction 127, 128

Blalock, E. 123

borderline personality disorder 174; and emotional regulation 175; and early abuse 185; and parental withdrawal 176, 178; and shame 189–90; and abandonment 191

Bowlby, J. 5, 10, 40

Brady, I. 217

brain, adolescent reorganisation 221; as anticipation machine 62; and early trauma 171; and Einstein 61; and myelination 21; and plasticity 55, 229; and pruning synapses 62; and right hemisphere 53, 54, 97, 143; and scanning 4; and triune brain 51; as toolshed 51; incomplete at birth 27

breastfeeding 139, 141, 249; and PUFAs 119, 233; and stress response 138

Brown, G. and Harris, T. 151

Bulger, James (and Thompson and Venables) 205–7, 211

Burrows, G. 239

Cadoret, R. 197

cancer personality 115, 120

cancer and stress 124

Cardinal, M 174, 181

Carroll, R. 43, 121

Carver, R. 134

Caspi, A. 201

Chida, Y. 124

child maltreatment, see abuse

Chopra, D. 122

Clyman, R. 40

Coleridge, S. T. 28

Connolly, B. 212

corpus callosum 21

cortisol 76, 77, 80, 83, 159; and anorexia 131; crossing placenta 20; and loss of control 143; and nursery school 65, 99; and inequality 89; and inflammatory response 150; and secure attachment 90; and sleeping patterns 83; and prenatal depression 26; high cortisol 97, 150; high cortisol and disorganised attachment 171; high cortisol and hippocampus 172; high cortisol and negative feelings 153; low cortisol 98–9; low cortisol and aggression 100; low cortisol and autoimmune conditions 98, 101,120 ; low cortisol and immune system 98, 116, 123, 163; low cortisol and PTSD 163, 101

Curtiss, S. 71

Cusk, R. 38, 94, 238

cytokines 10, 117, 119; trigger depression 150

Damasio, A. 4, 6

dandelions and orchids 35 see serotonin-short allele

dependency 111

depressed fathers 155

depressed mothers 36, 156, 145; in pregnancy 25; postnatal depression 74

depressed mother relationship with own mother 148; see also baby of depressed mother

depression 134, 143, 144; and genetic predisposition 135–6; and left prefrontal cortex 149, 144, 145; and enlarged amygdala 145 ; and poverty 147; and rejection and loss 136; and serotonin 127, 135; on the rise 245; rate of depression 138; and hippocampus 164,165; and high cortisol 149, 151

Dettling, A. 65, 92, 99, 153

Di Pietro, J. 19

disorganised attachment, see attachment

disruption and repair cycle 133, 153, 236

dissociation 188

DJ Goldie 214

Donald 210

dopamine 35, 60, 83, 122, 187; in prefrontal cortex 140; and deprivation 140; and low serotonin 199; dopamine genes 199, 201

dorsolateral prefrontal cortex 68–70, 149

eating disorder 128

Einstein, A. 9, 61

emotional regulation 45, 93, 120, 121, 226, 227, 246; and psychopathology 244; and verbalising 67–9, 71–3; and suppression of emotion 121; and depression 153

empathy 53, 110, 207

embryo 16

Enlightenment 6, 226

enmeshed family 130

epigenetics 196; and early adversity 159; and inheritance 162; and PTSD 159; and intergenerational transmission of stress 96; and anti-social behaviour 196, 197; reversibility 229

Essex, M. 95

faces 49, 59; and eye contact 60; negative faces 65, 67

Fairbairn, R. 154

Fanny and Alexander 169

fat storage 17, 18

fathers 238, 239; and baby's emotional regulation 202; depressed fathers 155

Fearless 157, 162

Fellows, S. 158

Field, T. 44, 232

fight or flight 76, 122, 159; and depression 153

Fonagy, P. 30, 114, 135, 189, 193

Frankl, V. 161

Freud, S. 7, 29, 30, 45, 86–7, 226,227

Friedan, B. 245
frontal cortex *see* pre-frontal
   cortex and orbitofrontal
   cortex

Garber, J. 153
Gendlin, E. 72–3
genes 10, 35,82; and criminality
   195, 218; and PTSD 166;
   dopamine genes 199, 201; *see
   also* dandelions and orchids,
   epigenetics, MAOA-L gene.
Genie 57, 71–2
glutamates 172
Goleman, D. 53, 125
government 2, 222, 240
Gunnar, M. 4, 153

Harlow, H. 56
Heckman, J. 223
Heisenberg, W. 9
Hippocampus (diagram 52), xi,
   20, 21, 22, 26, 61; and chronic
   stress 163, 165; and cortisol
   84, 172; development of 166;
   and depression 164, 165; and
   high cortisol 150; and
   memory 69–70; and PTSD
   166; and stress 80; and
   parenting 85; postnatal
   recovery 27; and touch 84;
   and exercise 231; and
   neurogenesis 231
Holmes, J. 170
Holzel, B. 222, 231
HPA axis (diagram 78), *see*
   stress response
hypothalamus 20, 75,76,79, 159

immune system 122, 123;
   'body's brain' 123; and ACE
   study 118–19; and blood
   122; and cortisol 116, 123;
   and emotion 116,117; and
   early stress 118; and touch
   119

inflammatory response 116;
   and neurogenesis 154; and
   depression 150; and early life
   151
insula 49

Katzenbach, J. 235
Kleinian theory, 147
Kochanska, G. 210
Krystal, H., 107, 131

Lawler, S. 241
LeDoux, J. 50, 54, 243
LeShan, L. 115
Ligocka, R. 161–2
Linehan, M. 180, 185
low birth weight 19
lymphocytes 80, 116
Lyons-Ruth, K. 147

MacLean, P. 51
Main, M. 70–1
MAOA-L gene xi, 199, 200, 201
massage 232
McCarthy, M. 74
meditation 222, 231, 232, 234
mentalising 114, 189
Minegawa-Kawai, Y. 54
mirror neurons 49
Mollon, P. 182
Montague, A. 58
Morrison, R. 51

narcissistic personality
   disorder 181, 183; and shame
   183
narrative self 70
neurotransmitters 77, 83, 141,
   233
norepinephrine 81,83,140, 141,
   204
nursery school 65, 92–3; and
   low cortisol 99

obesity 18
Odent, M. 242

Olds, D. 223
omega-3 fatty acids 21, 141; and depression 141, 142; anti-inflammatory effect 232; and serotonin 232
orbitofrontal cortex (diagram 52), 53, 149; and control of amygdala 183; and early stress 199; and smiling 54, 55; experience dependent 55; and abuse 56, 57; maturation 64, 66, 67; and cortisol 84
orchid child *see* serotonin-short allele
oxytocin 119, 139, 140; and amygdala 163; and breastfeeding 119; and touch 119; and early separation 25

Panksepp, J. 4, 49, 68
parasympathetic nervous system 43, 66
parent-infant psychotherapy 57, 178–9, 222, 223, 250
parenting, harsh 118, 211; abusive parent 36; and conduct disorder 201, 211; and emotional regulation 202; and heart disease 203; and stress 212; warm parenting 208; as emotion coach 40; qualities of good parenting 246; parenting education 250; *see also* working mothers
Patagonians 24
Pert, C. 4. 6, 77, 102, 121, 122, 133
Pinker, S. 194, 195, 205, 207' and 'abuse excuse' 204
placenta xi, 16, 20
post-natal depression *see* depressed mother
Potter, D. 125–7
poverty (or low Socio Economic Status) 19, 58, 85, 89, 94; and

stress 118; and depression 147
pre-frontal cortex (diagram 52), 20, 227, 242; development 61; and self-awareness 45; and social experience 27, and pre-natal stress 21; ventromedial 208; *see also* orbitofrontal cortex
pregnancy 15; and alcohol 16; and smoking 198 ; women working in 19, 22, 23, 24
PTSD 159; and genes 166; and inflammatory response 163; and attack on World Trade Centre 164; and Vietnam veterans 165
PUFAs (polyunsaturated fatty acids) *see* omega-3

Raine, A. 196, 200; and murderers' brains 211
Rich, A. 31–2
Rifkin-Graboi, A. 26
Romanian orphans 56, 57, 95, 149, 229, 230
rupture and repair *see* disruption and repair cycle
Rutter, M. 195–6, 229

Sapolsky, R. 89, 142, 203
Schore, A. x, 5, 53, 59, 60, 66, 176, 182, 189
self-control 45, 207, 210, 211, 227, 233; and fear 217
self-esteem 108, 109, 173
self-regulation 39, 82, 110, 121, 227; and putting feelings into words 115; and hunger 46
Seligman, M. 142
separation 65, 91, 92, 99, 118
serotonin 26,35,76,122,123, 127; and cortisol 164; and amygdala/anterior cingulate circuit 163; and depression 135, 127, 149; and post natal

stress 198, 230; and sugar 127; low serotonin; and antisocial behaviour 199; and dopamine 199; and orbitofrontal cortex 199; and recovery 230; and omega-3 levels 232, 233
serotonin, short allele 199; and secure attachment 201; and positive development 35, 230
set point 33, 83, 96
Sexton, A. 185–9
sexual abuse 185, 187, 32
shame 66, 67
Siegel, D. 62
Slavich, G. 117
smoking and antisocial behaviour 198, 199
social referencing 59
Solomon, A. 143, 149
Stephenson, P. 212, 215
Stern, D. 4, 40
Strange Situation test 5
stress 19; definition of 75, 88, 90 ; prenatal 20 ; and cytokines 117 ; and social inequality 89, 58; and secure attachment 90–1; and separation 91
stress response HPA axis (diagram 78) 75, 76, 86, 98,103; programmed in womb 164; and early critical period 95; development 20, 21, 172; fight or flight 76,122; in babyhood 95, 139; and cancer 124; and epigenetics 96; and forceps delivery 86, 88;

systemic 8, 10; and unpredictability 93, 94, 97; recovery 230–1
Suttie, I. 111, 113
Symington, N. 110
systemic paradigm 8–10

Temoshok, L. 116
temperament 35, 86, 87, 88, 197, 198
thrifty phenotype 17
toddler 59, 61, 65, 66, 209, 210
touch 58–9; and immune system 119; and hippocampus 84
trauma definition 158; and secure relationships 160
Tucker, D. 54
Turner, J. 50, 59
Type A 203, 204

Van den Boom, D. 87
Van der Kolk, B. 160

Wait and Wonder 223
Watt, D. 30
Westen, D. 131
Wiener, N. 9
Winnicott, D. 140
women's movement 32
working memory 68
working mothers 20, 22, 23, 37, 245; preference for part-time work 37, 241

Yehuda, R. 164, 196

de Zulueta, F. 185,187